Henry of Navarre

BIOGRAPHIES *by* HESKETH PEARSON

Henry of Navarre (*1553–1610*)

Henry of Navarre
The King Who Dared

by

HESKETH PEARSON

HARPER & ROW, PUBLISHERS
New York and Evanston

To GERMAINE and NORMAN HUNTER
(*with whom we shared a delightful
journey to the country of Navarre*)

The King is come to marshal us, in all his armour drest,
And he has bound a snow-white plume upon his gallant crest.
He looked upon his people, and a tear was in his eye;
He looked upon the traitors, and his glance was stern and high.
Right graciously he smiled on us, as rolled from wing to wing,
Down all our line, a deafening shout, 'God save our Lord the King.'
"An if my standard-bearer fall, as fall full well he may,
"For never saw I promise yet of such a bloody fray,
"Press where ye see my white plume shine, amidst the ranks of war,
"And be your oriflamme to-day the helmet of Navarre."

. . . .

A thousand spurs are striking deep, a thousand spears in rest,
A thousand knights are pressing close behind the snow-white crest;
And in they burst, and on they rushed, while, like a guiding star,
Amidst the thickest carnage blazed the helmet of Navarre.

. . . .

Now, God be praised, the day is ours. Mayenne hath turned his rein.
D'Aumale hath cried for quarter. The Flemish count is slain.
Their ranks are breaking like thin clouds before a Biscay gale;
The field is heaped with bleeding steeds, and flags, and cloven mail.
And then we thought on vengeance, and, all along our van,
"Remember Saint Bartholomew", was passed from man to man.
But out spake gentle Henry, "No Frenchman is my foe:
"Down, down, with every foreigner, but let your brethren go."
Oh! was there ever such a knight, in friendship or in war,
As our Sovereign Lord, King Henry, the soldier of Navarre?

. . . .

IVRY by Lord Macaulay

Contents

List of Illustrations

The publishers appreciate the courtesy of the Bibliothèque Publique et Universitaire, Geneva, in permitting the portrait of Henry of Navarre to be reproduced in this volume.

The author wishes to express his grateful thanks to Madame Annie Brierre for choosing the pictures from the Bibliothèque Nationale, Paris, to which acknowledgements are also due.

Preface

The character of Henry IV appealed to me at the age of
twelve when I came across him in the stirring pages of
Dumas and Stanley Weyman. Since then my interest in his
personality has steadily increased and I have read so many
books about him that he seems to me an old friend who
would be much more at ease in the modern world than in his
own. With the single exception of his grandson, Charles II
of England, he was the only monarch in history who had a
thoroughly civilized outlook, who would be accepted today
as an intelligent contemporary. Both he and his grandson
were far ahead of their times: they were rational, sensible,
tolerant, humane, witty and wise, infused with a keener sense
of liberty, equality and fraternity than most republicans;
though if they were living in the present age they would have
to conduct their love-affairs with greater discretion.

Perhaps the most extraordinary aspect of Henry as a
statesman was his conception of a federation of freedom-
loving countries, bound together to frustrate the designs of
an aggressive tyrannical power and to keep the peace of the
world. A few historians have questioned whether such an
idea ever entered his head and have attributed the entire
scheme to the fertile brain of his minister the Duke of Sully.
But as these sceptics have at the same time tried to prove that
Sully's excessive vanity destroyed the authenticity of much in
his record, it was scarcely feasible for them to assert that he

would have disclaimed authorship of this stupendous plan. The truth is that Henry was a highly imaginative man, while Sully was a masterly executant, and I have not the least doubt that the project, for many years a close secret between the French King and the English monarchs, Queen Elizabeth and James I, emanated from the far-seeing mind of Henry, especially as we know that at the age of thirty he proposed to the English and German Courts that a League of Protestants should be formed for the defence of their religion throughout Europe, obviously the germ of the Great Design which was later to occupy the thoughts of the King and his chief minister and to result in a vast accumulation of war material at the Paris arsenal. Henry hoped and believed that a show of force would make the dominant Hapsburgs cease their pursuit of power, and it is reasonable to suppose that he embarked on his last venture before gaining the active collaboration of all his allies either because he felt convinced that the house of Austria would climb down or because he knew that he must win a quick victory in order to gain the vigorous support of those who sympathized with his aims but feared to show their hands.

Phenomenal in his own age, Henry would be remarkable in any age, and my aim has been to disentangle the man as far as possible from the story of petty crimes, squalid intrigues, silly squabbles, childish bigotries and puerile brawls of his period, and to portray him as one who, with all his weaknesses, gave distinction to his epoch and lustre to his Crown.

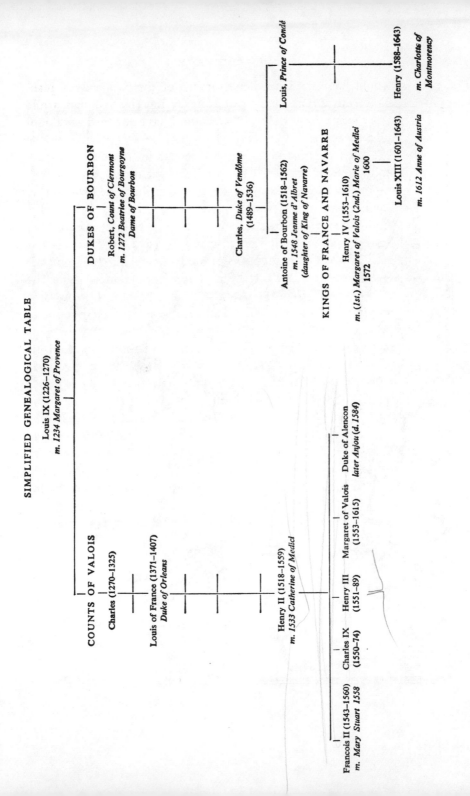

SIMPLIFIED GENEALOGICAL TABLE

Louis IX (1226–1270)
m. 1234 Margaret of Provence

COUNTS OF VALOIS

Charles (1270–1325)

Louis of France (1371–1407)
Duke of Orleans

Henry II (1518–1559)
m. 1533 Catherine of Medici

Francois II (1543–1560)
m. Mary Stuart 1558

Charles IX
(1550–74)

Henry III
(1551–89)

Margaret of Valois
(1553–1615)

Duke of Alencon
later Anjou (d. 1584)

DUKES OF BOURBON

Robert, Count of Clermont
m. 1272 Beatrice of Bourgoyne
Dame of Bourbon

Charles, Duke of Vendôme
(1489–1536)

Antoine of Bourbon (1518–1562)
m. 1548 Jeanne d'Albret
(daughter of King of Navarre)

Louis, Prince of Condé

KINGS OF FRANCE AND NAVARRE

Henry IV (1553–1610)
m. (1st.) Margaret of Valois (2nd.) Marie of Medici
1572   1600

Henry (1588–1643)
m. Charlotte of
Montmorency

Louis XIII (1601–1643)
m. 1612 Anne of Austria

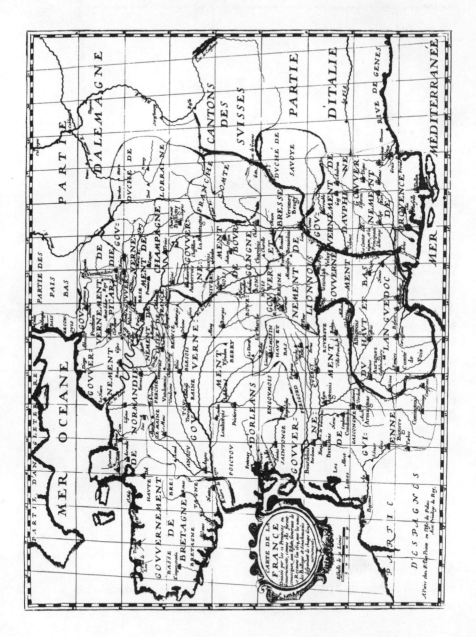

CHAPTER ONE

In the Name of God

Although such treatment would not now receive medical assent, it seems to have had the desired effect on a new-born baby in the sixteenth century. The parents had nothing to do with it, but as their first two children had not survived infancy a grandparent took the matter in hand when they were about to produce a third. Since he was Henry d'Albret, King of Navarre, and had no other issue, he wished for a healthy heir, and told his daughter Jeanne to sing a song while suffering the pangs of labour, 'in order that you may bring me a child who will neither weep nor make wry faces.' She contrived to do so, and the boy entered the world without crying. To fortify his grandson with the manliness he would be called upon to display, the King then rubbed the baby's lips with a clove of garlic and made him suck some wine from a golden cup.

The birth took place at the castle of Pau in Béarn on 14 December 1553, and the infant Henry was baptized with the rites of the Roman Catholic Church by the Cardinal of Armagnac. His parents were Jeanne d'Albret, only child of the King of Navarre, and Antony of Bourbon, Duke of Vendôme, who was directly descended from Louis IX, King of France, a derivation which placed himself and his son in succession to the French throne if the last Valois kings failed to produce male heirs. Apparently the King of Navarre had little confidence in Antony's efficiency as a father, and decided to superintend the boy's upbringing, removing him from the

1

castle of Pau and placing him in the castle of Couraze, close to the valley of Lourdes. Here, when old enough to toddle, he was encouraged to be robust. He climbed the rocks and mountains with naked feet and uncovered head; he dressed almost as a peasant and received no toys; his food consisted of brown bread, beef, cheese and garlic; and no one was allowed to flatter him or treat him as a prince. His grandfather felt convinced that many parents had lost their children by pampering them with French delicacies, and as the spartan régime to which young Henry was subjected produced a vigorous constitution and an unspoilt nature the King of Navarre's method was justified. When the old King died in 1555 and Jeanne became Queen of Navarre, her small son's mental education became as strict as his bodily exercises were sturdy, and the one fixed idea of his life was implanted in his mind: a distrust and dislike of Spain, whose ruler had stolen by force a large portion of the kingdom of Navarre.

In his sixth year he accompanied his parents to the Court of France for the marriage of Mary Queen of Scots to the Dauphin Francis. The reigning monarch, Henry II, attracted by the child's appearance, embraced him and asked 'Will you be my son?' Pointing to Antony, now King of Navarre, the boy replied 'There is my father.' 'Then will you be my son-in-law?' asked the French King. 'With pleasure,' said the youngster, or words to that effect. In time he acted on the suggestion.

For an exhibition of human nature in its least engaging manifestations the period into which he was born has few parallels in history. Following the death of Henry II, King of France, in 1559, his widow Catherine of Medici fought for the control of the country. Their eldest son, Francis II, husband of Mary Queen of Scots, died in 1560, and was succeeded by a younger son, Charles IX, with Catherine as Queen Regent. In order to maintain the authority of the Crown she had to prevent either of the chief opposing families from gaining too much power. They were the house of Lorraine, whose main representatives were the Duke of Guise and his brother the Cardinal of Lorraine, strongly supported by the Roman Catholics, and the house of Bourbon, represented by Prince Louis of Condé and his brother Antony King of Navarre, strongly supported by the Huguenots. The Lorraine family claimed descent from Charlemagne, the Bourbons were admittedly of royal blood. During the short reign of Francis II the influence of the Guise brothers was supreme, but Catherine equalized matters when she became Regent by placing Antony, King of Navarre, in the position of Lieutenant-General of the kingdom. It was a cunning move because Antony, though brave, was a cipher, with a stronger inclination to girls than to government.

Catherine was an Italian by birth and temperament, with a passion for power, a ruthless will, a subtle scheming brain, a complete lack of moral feeling, and a callous indifference to the sufferings of those who caused her inconvenience. Although a Roman Catholic, she was quite capable of siding with the Protestants if it served her turn. Indeed the edict of 1562, which permitted the Protestants to worship in many places hitherto denied them, was considered subversive and sacrilegious by the extreme Catholics. The sole object of this 'Florentine shopkeeper', as the French nobility called her, was to keep France in the family, and with this end in view she strove to maintain internal peace and friendly relations with foreign powers. In her case patriotism and selfishness went hand in hand. She was furious when Gaspard of Coligny, the great Protestant leader, agreed to hand over Calais and Havre to the English in exchange for help with men and money, because it showed that he attached more importance to his religion than to his nation. A basic insincerity made her a shameless opportunist. One of her methods of influencing and corrupting men was to keep a bevy of lovely girls in her train, known as the *escadron volant* (flying squadron), all of them coached in guile, and the man would be difficult to please if one of these beauties could not ensnare him, discover his secrets, and weaken his resistance to whatever the Queen Mother required.

Antony, King of Navarre, was an easy victim. Never a declared convert to Protestantism, he yet supported the Huguenots because they might further his ambition. But an appeal to his vanity sufficed to turn him back to Catholicism. It was intimated by the family of Guise that he could expect to be King of France, since Catherine's sons were feeble and unlikely to produce male progeny; that if he divorced Jeanne d'Albret and married Mary Stuart he could aspire to the throne of England, the Pope having excommunicated Elizabeth. Soon in the toils of Catherine's beauty chorus, he remained uncomfortably conscious that Jeanne was a devoted wife, and did his best to make her change her religion, now sternly Protestant; but his endeavours merely had the effect of changing her heart, for she lost faith in him and ceased to love him.

While Antony was gradually becoming a tool of the Guise faction his son Henry was being rigorously instructed in Protestant precepts, the best teachers being employed by his mother Jeanne. For a time he stayed with his father at the Court of France, where at the age of eight he impressed everyone with his liveliness, mental quickness and personal charm. He absorbed Latin and Greek with ease, enjoyed reading Plutarch's Lives, translated Caesar's Commentaries, and chose as a motto 'To conquer or to die', which rather disturbed Catherine, who with her sickly sons and the improbability of a Valois succession wobbled between her fear of the Guise devil and her alarm over the Bourbon deep-sea. For a year or two Henry's scholastic companions at the château of Vincennes and the college of Navarre were Henry, Duke of Anjou, brother of Charles IX, and Henry the eldest son of the Duke of Guise. No sign appeared in their youth of the future rivalry and enmity between the three Henrys. But while they were yet boys the first of those religious wars that were to lay France waste for a generation started in 1562.

We need not concern ourselves with the causes and origins, the rights and wrongs, of these civil wars. All wars are due to the ambition and avarice of the few, the dreams and discontents of the many. Hatred, revenge, cruelty and fear are soon spawned from 'the intestine shock and furious close of civil butchery', and the whole abomination is plausibly cloaked and sanctioned by such comforting euphemisms as religion or loyalty or patriotism or idealism. Enough to say that all France was desolated and her agriculture destroyed, while life was turned into a nightmare for her inhabitants. Nearly every town and village was sacked repeatedly by whatever party was momentarily victorious; the massacre of populations and the torture of individuals were matters of routine. As the Catholics were in a large majority, it appeared obvious to them that if the slaughter of Huguenots went on long enough they would soon be exterminated. But it did not work out like that. The Huguenots were hydra-headed; every defeat seemed to put new vigour into them; and it is permissible to wonder whether the whole trouble was not caused by envy and jealousy, due to the greater ability of those who had the intelligence and courage to protest against the corruption of the Roman Church. Needless to say the Huguenots did not deal kindly with their persecutors when in a position to hit back, and many Catholics were slaughtered in the name of Calvin, as at Nîmes, in 1567, when the Protestants celebrated Michaelmas day by flinging 150 people who disagreed with them into a well. The situation was made worse by the behaviour of foreign mercenaries engaged by both sides but often unpaid. They could pillage and murder and ravish with the gratifying sense that whatever they did could not be retaliated on their own families or property.

Personalities changed as the years went by, but the slaughter, the deceitful truces, the hypocritical edicts, the hideous crimes of violence, the mock alliances, the general anarchy, the pumped-up fanaticism that fought in the name of God: all these went on. Antony, King of Navarre, died from a wound at the siege of Rouen in 1562, and his son Henry soon found himself head of the Reformed religion, his adversaries being the King of France, the Council of the Realm, the Pope of Rome, the Emperor of Austria, the King of Spain, and all the Catholics of Europe. In 1563 the Duke of Guise was assassinated by a Protestant; in 1569 the Prince of Condé was assassinated by a Catholic; and their sons followed in their gory footsteps. Admiral Coligny, a dauntless figure, took Condé's place as military leader of the Protestants.

Coligny was a man of inflexible honesty and unflinching bravery, but his honesty did not prevent him from demanding large sums in payment for loyal services, and his bravery was unaccompanied by compassion. Ruthless in war, he executed prisoners, ravaged the countryside and pulled down churches. When the choice between Protestantism and patriotism had to be made, he placed his conscience before his country. Indifferent to sentiment, especially in women, he enraged Catherine by letting the English occupy Havre, and then, when it suited his purpose, he drove them out, earning the lasting enmity of the English Queen, Elizabeth. Against this man of iron the nominal leader of the Catholics was the Duke of Anjou, brother of the King, the real commander being Marshal Tavannes. The Catholics won two battles, at Jarnac and Moncontour, the second of which brought fame to Anjou, who had displayed much intelligence, though his eulogists overdid their praise in comparing him with Julius Caesar and Alexander the Great. The chief effect of both battles was to put new heart into the Protestants, and it began to dawn on their opponents that the Huguenots could not be annihilated by war. Charles IX was declared of age in 1563, but power remained in the hands of his mother Catherine, and as the years passed without much profit to the royal cause it occurred to her that a stroke of policy she had meditated in the past should now be effected.

Young Henry of Navarre had become very popular with the Huguenots. At the age of thirteen he displayed the qualities of an intelligent and agreeable young man. A magistrate of Bordeaux described him in the year 1567:

> He demeans himself towards all the world with so easy a carriage that people crowd round wherever he is . . . He enters into conversation as a highly polished man . . . he is very well informed and never says anything which ought not to be said . . . I shall hate the new religion all my life, for having carried off from us so worthy a person.

We are told further that 'he insinuates himself into all hearts with inconceivable skill', that men liked him and the 'ladies do not love him less'. His hair, which became dark in a few years, was inclined to red in those early days: 'His face is very well formed, the nose neither too large nor too small' (it became a beak in later years), 'the eyes extremely soft, his skin brown but very smooth, and the whole animated with such uncommon vivacity that if he does not make progress with the fair it will be very extraordinary.' We learn also that he

> loves play and good living. When money fails him, he has skill enough to find more, and in a manner quite new and obliging towards others. That is to say, he sends to those whom he believes his friends a promise written and signed by himself, begging them to return him the note or the sum which it bears. You may judge whether there is any house where he is refused. People regard it as a great honour to have one of these billets from the Prince, and everyone does it with joy.

Henry's popularity extended to the field of battle. Dedicated by his mother to the cause of the Protestant faith, he joined his uncle Condé in 1568, saying that he did so for the sake of

economy, because if the Princes of the Blood were killed one
at a time the cost of mourning to the family would be considerable, whereas if they were all killed together it would be
less expensive. 'I know who started this conflagration in
France, and I could put it out with one bucket of water.'
'How so?' asked a friend. 'By making the Cardinal of Lorraine
drink till he burst.' He was present at several engagements and
showed no little acuteness in criticizing the tactics of the
leaders. His language was already fairly free, though he
confined himself to a single oath – '*Ventre Saint-Gris!*' – which
had been enforced on him by his early governors, who feared
he might enrich his vocabulary by copying his neighbours.
The oath he used was derisively applied to the Franciscan
monks and referred to the colour of their clothes, St Francis
being known as Saint Gris.

It was clear to Catherine that young Navarre would prove
dangerous in the years to come unless allied to the house of
Valois and separated from the Huguenot nobles, and it was
equally clear to her that the Protestants could not be subdued
by fighting. Indeed by the middle of 1570 they were doing too
well, and to prevent them from marching on Paris she agreed
that a treaty should be signed granting them liberty of
conscience, the open exercise of their religion in two towns
of each province, the possession of La Rochelle and other
places, the restitution of their confiscated estates, and certain
further concessions. This treaty of St Germain brought what
is known in history books as 'the third religious war' to an
end, and Admiral Coligny was satisfied, saying that he would
rather die than see France again in a state of anarchy and
crime.

The King and his mother were soon making much of Coligny,
who was invited to Blois, where the Court resided in the
autumn of 1571, and embraced with enthusiasm by Charles IX.
Favours were showered upon him, and the King even agreed
with him that France could be united and all thoughts of

civil war obliterated by fighting Spain in the Netherlands. The young Duke of Guise retired from the Court, having aroused the King's ire by aspiring to the hand of Margaret, sister of Charles, and Coligny's feeling that the royal family had ceased to be anti-Protestant changed to conviction when it was proposed that Margaret should be married to Henry of Navarre. But his attitude was not shared by Henry's mother, Jeanne d'Albret, who had a rooted distrust of Catholic policy, especially when it seemed to favour the other side. The Court moved to Paris in December 1571, accompanied by Coligny, who daily became more certain that the Huguenots had nothing further to fear from Catherine and the Catholic faction and did his utmost to persuade Jeanne that all was well. What appeared to set the seal on the good intentions of the Catholics was the action of the Cardinal of Lorraine, uncle of the Duke of Guise and hitherto the implacable persecutor of the Huguenots. He now laboured to obtain a papal dispensation for the Catholic-Protestant alliance of Margaret of Valois and Henry of Navarre. We may guess at the bait proffered to his Holiness in return for the dispensation.

For six months Jeanne d'Albret held out, though begged by her courtiers, importuned by the Huguenot nobles, and repeatedly reassured by Coligny. At last, with grave misgivings, she accepted the King's invitation and left the castle of Pau early in February 1572. Her daughter Catherine, aged eleven, went with her, but her son Henry remained behind in Béarn until negotiations for the marriage were completed. They were received at Tours by Charles and the Queen Mother, luxuriously lodged at Blois, and honoured with a warmly respectful friendship that would have been flattering if Jeanne could have believed it sincere. Once after humouring a leading Protestant the King was heard to ask his mother: 'Have I not played my part well?' Catherine replied: 'Very well, my son, but you must continue to do so to the end.' Jeanne's suspicions were not lulled by his performance or

Catherine's, and she wrote to her son from Blois that the Queen Mother treated her 'with treachery and deceit'. She was clearly bemused by the Machiavellian duplicity of Catherine, and though she thought Margaret 'handsome, discreet and docile' she could not shut her eyes to the effect on Henry's future bride of 'the most execrable and corrupt society that ever existed. I meet with none who are free from its influence. Your cousin the marquise' (just married to the young Prince of Condé) 'is so much changed by it that there is no longer any appearance of religion in her, except that she does not go to mass; but, idolatry excepted, she does as the papists do'. Margaret returned the love of the Duke of Guise; but when their mutual passion evoked the rage of the King her brother, the Duke married Catherine of Cleves, which freed Margaret and himself for the pleasures of love-making.

Jeanne remained convinced of the sinister designs of the French Court and knew that there was more in the match than met the eye. 'As I write privately,' she confided in her son,

> the bearer will tell you what kind of life the King leads, putting no restraint on himself whatever. It is a great pity. I would not for all the world that you should come here to reside; for you could never escape the contagion except through the great Grace of God. My wish, should you be married, is that you and your wife should retire from this scene of corruption, which indeed I had believed to be great, but find it far worse than I had imagined. It is not the men who make love here to the women, but the women to the men.

Margaret was lovely, but like the rest of the women she patched and painted herself, spoiling her complexion and lessening her beauty. At length Jeanne's opposition was worn down by the constant pro-marital arguments of Coligny and other Huguenots, who won her reluctant consent. She then expressed a wish that the marriage should take place at Blois, not Paris, and be solemnized by the rites of the Protestant religion. But this did not at all suit Catherine, who insisted on the capital as the scene of the festivities, though she agreed to a compromise in the matter of the ceremonial, the words of which were to mix expressions of both religions, leaving the believers of each dissatisfied.

For some time Jeanne hoped that the Pope would not concede the necessary dispensation; but when she remarked to the King that she did not believe it would be granted, he gave her no encouragement: 'Not so, dear aunt, for I honour you more than the Pope, and fear him less than I love my sister. I am not a Huguenot, neither am I a blockhead; but if M. le Pape continues to be stupid I will take Margot by the hand and will publicly lead her to the Huguenot temple to marry Henry.' It happened that M. le Pape died, and his successor was more accommodating. While the subject was still being debated at the Vatican the French Court left Blois for Paris, followed thence on 4 June 1572 by the Queen of Navarre, who had a cool reception, the population of the capital being strongly pro-Guise and fanatically Catholic. Having written to her son advising him to brush his hair properly and to avoid temptation when he reached Paris, Jeanne d'Albret died suddenly on 9 June, from natural causes according to the Catholics, poisoned in the opinion of the Protestants. Although evidence can be cooked to favour any theory or belief, the view that the Queen Mother murdered Jeanne cannot be substantiated. Besides the act was not politically expedient, and Catherine was nothing if not a politician.

Henry was on his way to Paris when he received news of his mother's death. Assuming his title as King of Navarre he continued the journey, arriving in the capital to find the Court in mourning and the wedding postponed. He and his cousin the Prince of Condé were accompanied by several hundred Huguenots, and though his reception in the streets lacked

11

enthusiasm his appearance made a good impression. Not exactly handsome, he compared favourably with the nobles about him, with his sharp lively eyes, thick eyebrows, black wavy hair and aquiline nose.

In spite of warnings Coligny still trusted the King, whose fondness for the Admiral increased and who seemed keener than ever on the war with Spain, which his mother and brother so strongly opposed. Many Huguenot nobles and gentlemen visited Paris for the marriage which would, it appeared, unite the religions and give peace to France. The more suspicious ones reminded the others of what had happened at Amboise in 1560, only twelve years before, when, trusting to the King's solemn promise of safety, a large body of Protestants had entered the château and were butchered by the Guise party, the entire Court, under the benign direction of the Cardinal of Lorraine, witnessing the tortures and agonies to which the Huguenots were subjected. This sort of behaviour was not peculiar to the Catholics of that time, a certain number of whom, under the impression that they were guests at a Huguenot banquet on a certain occasion, discovered too late that they had been invited for the pleasure of having their throats cut. Despite such proceedings on both sides, Coligny felt so certain that the King was now friendly to their faith that he managed to allay the suspicions of all but the most sceptical. Reasonably honest himself, he could not believe in dissimulation on so vast a scale.

In a sense his confidence was justified. Charles IX was a weak unstable creature, as easily influenced one way as another. With his bent shoulders, his thin rickety legs, his pale complexion, shifty eyes, and a facial expression now fierce, now drained of life, the close observer might have guessed that he was subject to extreme moods, violent and frequent, which would quickly succeed each other. Fits of passion when he would listen to nothing were followed by periods of prostration when he would agree to anything. He was capable of embracing

a man with warmth at one moment and ordering his murder at
the next. He detested his brother Anjou, partly because the
Duke was his mother's favourite child and partly because of
his military reputation which was mainly due to the ability
of others; yet there were times when Charles could weep tears
of brotherly affection over Anjou. At present he was wholly
under the influence of the calm and incorruptible Coligny, and
Catherine suffered many anxious moments owing to what she
regarded as a dangerous aberration in her son.

It had been decided at the Vatican that a dispensation could
not be granted by the Pope unless Navarre professed the
Catholic faith, re-established that religion in his own kingdom,
and agreed to be married according to the rites of the Roman
Church. Charles IX, using the phrase 'in the interests of
religion', begged the Pope not to insist on these conditions;
and though the dispensation had not arrived when the
marriage took place on 18 August 1572, the King managed to
convince the officiating Cardinal of Bourbon, uncle of Navarre,
that it was 'on the way'. With much pomp and splendour the
ceremony took place on a scaffold erected before the porch
of Notre Dame. It was reported that Margaret did not answer
when asked whether she would willingly take Henry for her
husband; so Charles placed a hand on his sister's head,
compelling her to nod acquiescence. Her heart was elsewhere,
while Henry's did not palpitate. After her reluctant union the
bride entered the cathedral to hear mass, Henry and the
Huguenot nobles passing the time by promenading the nave
or conversing in groups about the porch.

The marriage was celebrated by four days of licentious
revelry, concluding with an attempt on the Admiral's life.
On 22 August Coligny had an audience with the King. Leaving
the Louvre on foot with a few friends, a shot from an arquebus
was fired at him through the window of a house, the ball hitting
the finger of his right hand and breaking his left arm. The
marksman, suborned by the Duke of Guise at the instigation

of the Queen Mother and Anjou, got away. On hearing the news, the King swore in a rage that the Admiral should be avenged. Navarre and Condé hurried to see Coligny and afterwards asked permission to leave Paris where their lives were clearly imperilled. But the King guaranteed their safety and ordered his brother to send a detachment of guards to protect Coligny. Anjou did so, but took care to have them commanded by a man who hated the Admiral. An instant enquiry into the affair was ordered by the King, whose mother was chiefly responsible for the crime. She had hoped that the Guise faction would kill Coligny, whose followers would avenge his death by killing Guise, thus restoring the complete ascendancy of the Crown. With the wounding of Coligny her plot collapsed, and she had to think rapidly of something else. Her sole ambition being to keep the throne for her children, she was appalled by the prospect of an enquiry which would inculpate herself and her favourite son Anjou, and she knew that the King would seize on the discovery to destroy his brother. She decided at once to side with the Guises, the sole alternative being an increase of Coligny's influence over the King.

Totally unaware of the doom awaiting him, the Admiral prevented his followers from rushing to the Louvre and slaying Guise in the King's presence, thus sealing his death-warrant and ensuring the forthcoming massacre. Having received the attention of a surgeon, Coligny requested the King to visit him for the purpose of discussing certain matters of importance. The Queen Mother and Anjou were much concerned over these matters and determined that Charles and Coligny must not be left alone together. They had kept the Pope and Philip of Spain fully informed of the agreed anti-Spanish policy of Coligny and the King, and felt that at such a moment the Admiral should not be in a position to play upon the weakness of Charles. So when Coligny asked for a private conversation, Catherine pretended that the Admiral's health was her main anxiety and that the exertion of talk would result in fever. The King gave way and left with his solicitous parent.

The attempt to murder Coligny aroused the fears of the Huguenots in Paris, and a general exodus was expected. Now was the time to act if the Catholics wished to rid themselves of their chief Protestant enemies; and after dinner on Saturday, 23 August, Catherine had a talk in the garden of the Tuileries with Anjou, Nevers, Tavannes and de Retz. Some seven years earlier the Spanish Duke of Alva had advised her to render the Protestant party harmless by killing their leaders, and her council of Catholic nobles now assented to this advice. At eight o'clock that evening the Queen Mother and her son Anjou went to see the King, who was paralysed by her eloquence. She expatiated at length on a great plot by the Protestants, who would avenge the attempt on their leader's life and seize power; France would be ruined, the house of Valois exiled; they must act at once to save the Crown and the country; and so on until the King's head reeled. But as he hesitated she changed her tactics, shed tears, and asked permission to leave the Court with her son Anjou, as they could not face the coming catastrophe. Stupefied, Charles still hesitated; so she begged him to hear the advice of his best counsellors. He agreed, and at eleven o'clock that night they stood before him, played on his fears, and gave further reasons for nipping the Protestant conspiracy in the bud. Half-mad already, the King now went clean off his head; and when the Queen Mother charged him with cowardice, adding that she would leave him and take his heroic brother Anjou with her, the demented monarch gave way to his naturally sadistic instincts. 'Kill them all, so that not one will be left to reproach me afterwards,' he raved, and dashed from the room yelling 'Let them all be killed! Let them all be killed!' Catherine determined that Navarre and Condé should be spared, as their disappearance would give complete power to the family of Guise.

The help of the municipal authorities was then invoked at the prompting of Guise, in order that the Catholic citizens should be armed and distinguished from their victims by white crosses in their hats and white linen cloths round their left arms. Orders were hastily despatched to the leading provincial towns authorizing the performance of similar acts, and all was prepared for the 'deed of dreadful note' early in the morning of Sunday, 24 August, the feast of St Bartholomew. The Queen Mother with her cherished son Anjou went to a room overlooking the courtyard of the Louvre to witness the beginning of the butchery, and in the silence they became aware of what they had done. They had unchained one devil to kill another, and they wondered whether Guise with the mob behind him would not be more dangerous than Coligny and the Protestants. Their sudden doubts were resolved by the sound of a pistol-shot. Terror gripped them, and they sent off a message ordering Guise to do nothing against Coligny, an injunction that annulled everything that had been determined. Their messenger soon returned with M. de Guise's apologies: the command had come too late: the Admiral was dead. Already the tocsin was sounding from the church of St Germain l'Auxerrois, and hell had been let loose in the cause of Christ.

The first act was committed by the Duke of Guise, whose hired assassins despatched Coligny and flung his body into the courtyard, where the young Duke kicked the bloodstained face. Those Huguenots who were staying at the Louvre were slain in their beds. The Catholics were incited by lies of a Protestant plot, and the mob behaved as mobs always do, the innumerable small vexations of life being vented in a carnival of blood-letting, brought about by a combination of rage, panic, revenge, resentment, greed, and the thrill of freedom from all restraint. The massacre lasted three days in Paris and longer in other towns. The number of victims is unknown, because innumerable bodies went floating down the Seine (and other rivers) and were flung into pits wherever they were washed ashore, and the registers of burial grounds only tell half the tale, but several thousands must have perished in Paris alone and many more thousands throughout France. It had not the effect intended by those who set it going. Instead of terrifying the Huguenots and forcing them to abjure their beliefs, it strengthened their conviction of the villainy of a religion that could do such things, made fiercer their struggle for religious independence, and united them in face of so diabolical a danger.

The young princes who were spared, Navarre and Condé, did not remain long in a state of suspense. Having witnessed the stabbing of their adherents, they were brought before the crazy King, who with dire imprecations gave them the choice between death, the Bastille or the Mass. Navarre seemed to favour the last, but Condé was less adaptable and might have been killed on the spot if the Queen Mother had not intervened. They were given three days to think it over, with death at the end if their thoughts did not chime with the King's. But after three days of bloodshed Charles IX, haunted by the dead faces of his erstwhile friends, began to suffer from a guilty conscience, gave orders that the massacre should cease, threw the odium for it on the Guises, and pretended that the leading Huguenots were guilty of crimes and conspiracies for which they had paid the penalty. This was the story circulated to the leading Protestant powers, but it failed to convince them. The news of the event was received with different feelings in the Catholic countries. Rome expressed joy with bells and bonfires, and the Pope attended a Mass of thanksgiving; while Philip of Spain, reported to have laughed for the first time in his life, sent a message of congratulation on the performance of so holy a deed. It was undoubtedly a great triumph for those who believed in purification by murder.

Henry's wife, Margaret, had no prior knowledge of the massacre; but she helped Catherine and Charles to keep her husband in subjection for a while, passing on the information

17

she picked up on the occasion of his first attempted flight. True she tried to help him later to get away; but there was no love lost between the newly married pair, each taking a reasonable view of the enforced union, neither resenting the other's constrained relationship, and both being indulgent to sexual caprices, Margaret having her love-affairs, Henry his, the nuptial couch remaining unoccupied, except perhaps when they wanted to sleep. Henry was for several weeks under strict guard at the Louvre. He perceived that not only would the future be made intolerable for himself but that his cause would ultimately suffer unless he fell in with the King's demands; so he renounced his faith and became a Catholic, doing the same for his sister. Under extreme pressure he also sent orders that the Protestant form of worship must be abandoned in his own dominions and the Catholic religion re-established. His fellow-Huguenots knew that such orders had been extorted from him, took no notice of them, and prepared themselves for war. Henry had every intention of repudiating his own act the moment he was in a position to do so, being firmly convinced that oaths under coercion were not worth the breath with which they were uttered.

Having failed to capture La Rochelle and other strongholds of the reformed faith, Catherine patched up a peace with the rebellious Huguenots, designing to break it when convenient, and arranged for the election of her son Anjou to the Crown of Poland, knowing that Charles was on his last legs and that her favourite would soon be called back to rule France. She was a woman of considerable ability and her present object was to keep on good terms with Philip of Spain while trying to fix up a marriage between her youngest son, the Duke of Alençon, with Queen Elizabeth of England. Her trickiness was often successful, but in the long run it failed and helped to bring about what she most feared and loathed: the emergence of the Duke of Guise as leader of the Catholics and of the King of Navarre as a great Protestant commander.

To the delight of the French monarch, his brother Anjou left the country to become King of Poland. But not for long. The weak-kneed feeble-minded Charles, terrified by the memories of what he had permitted on St Bartholomew's day, exhausted by delirium and racked by remorse, died on 30 May 1574, his end possibly hastened by a considerate mother. The King of Poland wasted no time in quitting his dominions, where his reception had not been effusive, and returned to France via Austria and Italy, since there were too many Protestants in central Germany. His mother relied on his military genius to bring the Protestants to their knees, her affection having weakened her judgment, for his victories were gained by the errors of his opponents. On his return, therefore, she hoped to greet a soldier, but what she got was a saint, or at least one who appeared to behave in a saintly manner, for at Avignon he took part in a procession of flagellants, who were under the impression that laceration of the body was good for the soul. He was crowned at Rheims as Henry III in February 1575, and two days later he married Louise of Lorraine, who might have been the happy wife of a respectable husband but who became a wretched nonentity as the queen of a depraved Valois.

The new King soon heard that Henry of Navarre had made attempts to escape from Vincennes; and when Navarre explained that his actions had been due to the rigour of his confinement, that he had been spied upon and allowed no freedom, his fellow-monarch graciously said, 'Well, now you are free.' But as Navarre's movements were thenceforth strictly watched, his freedom was that of an animal allowed out of a cage into a compound. Still forced to conceal his feelings, to pretend a religion he could not accept, to partici- pate in commands he detested, to witness acts he abhorred, his position at Court remained that of a lackey and an object of ill-concealed mirth. Catherine knew his weakness and never let him want for high-class whores, but he continued to steer clear of the monarch's male favourites and never allowed anyone to share his thoughts or influence his actions.

The Court of Henry III was a mass of corruption. The King had his pimps and minions, and did not much discriminate between male and female bedfellows, frequently following his orgies of lust with public exhibitions of repentance, when he dressed in sackcloth and scourged himself with whipcord, though his hind quarters were probably well padded. His people were heavily taxed, and the money, meant for war or other state purposes, was squandered on his favourites. When some of his male lovers were murdered by the followers of his brother, he gave them state funerals and raised marble monuments over their graves, which satisfied his aesthetic sense. His artistic tastes were further exemplified in the rich clothes and jewels which he wore and the fashions he invented. Rings, bracelets and earrings adorned his person; his body was anointed with perfumes, his face painted and powdered; and occasionally he dressed as a woman, with a pearl necklace on his open bosom, being waited on by court ladies attired as men.

The Valois brothers abominated one another, and Charles IX's hatred of Anjou was now matched by Henry III's hatred of Alençon, who fully requited the emotion. Not long after he came to the throne Henry fell ill and believed that his brother had poisoned him. Becoming worse he thought that death was near, sent for his brother-in-law Navarre, and begged him to kill Alençon, taking possession of the throne after that happy event. But Navarre had nothing of the assassin in his nature and recoiled from the proposal. It happened that both he and Alençon were at that time in the toils of one of Catherine's beauties, Charlotte de Sauves, who used her charms to enslave them, the Queen Mother being anxious that they should not get away and stir up trouble. But even the prospect of removing a rival in the lists of love did not tempt Navarre to obey the King. Soon Alençon fled from the

Court, gathered a number of discontented Catholics about him and terrified Catherine by joining forces with the Protestants.

Navarre, too, had decided that his life was in danger and once more seriously considered the possibility of freedom. 'It is the strangest Court you ever saw,' he wrote to a boyhood friend:

> We are always ready to cut each other's throats. We all carry our poniards and all wear mail shirts and frequently a breastplate under our tunics . . . You would never believe how strong I am in this court of friends. I affront everybody and only wait the opportunity for a fight. For they say they will kill me, and I wish to strike first.

Civil war was raging all over the country and the lives of individuals were of little account. Assassination was a daily occurrence, whether by poison, poniard or strangulation; justice and mercy were non-existent in high places; brothers and sisters, parents and children, eliminated one another for money, position or power; and it is probable that Navarre owed his continued existence to the fact that he played the fool so convincingly. Catherine felt, in one respect rightly, that there was little to be feared from him if he were entangled with a pretty woman; but had she suspected for a moment that his lustful nature was equally balanced by mental shrewdness, he would not have remained long in the world to exercise the second quality. Even so she took no risks. His guard of honour consisted of papist spies upon his behaviour. These, with her squadron of belles, were considered sufficient to secure him, though she added to such attractions the promise that he should be given the post of Lieutenant-General, like his father before him. He pretended to believe in her promise and actually discussed what he intended to do in that position with the Duke of Guise, who reported the conversation to the

French monarch, his recital producing roars of laughter from the courtiers. Navarre's assumed simplicity was further illustrated when, shortly before he attempted to escape, a rumour reached the Court that he had fled. He doubtless started the rumour to allay suspicion, because he quickly followed it by appearing in person and putting the Queen Mother's mind at rest with a humorous sally.

Too many people had been in the secret of his earlier endeavours to get away, and this time the number was reduced to half a dozen, chief among them Agrippa d'Aubigné, poet and historian, whose affection had kept him a prisoner with Navarre. It was arranged that they should make up a hunting party in the forest of Senlis, and to throw dust in the eyes of his captors Navarre suggested that the Duke of Guise should accompany them. But Guise was not inclined to do so, as might have been guessed, and Henry started off in the first week of February 1576, guarded by two of the French King's officers. While he slept at Senlis one of those in the secret revealed it to the King. D'Aubigné, who was to follow the next morning, divined what had happened, mounted his horse at once and managed to get through the gates of Paris a few minutes before the order arrived to guard them strictly. At Senlis in the early hours he broke the news that they had been betrayed, and Navarre instantly decided to make a dash for freedom. But what was to be done with the King's officers? Several of Navarre's attendants proposed that they should be killed, but he refused to countenance such an act. The officers, probably aware that their lives were in jeopardy, were easily persuaded by Navarre to take messages to the French King, and the fleeing party spurred their horses through the forest. They crossed the Seine at Poissy, rode for over fifty miles without drawing rein except to change horses, and arrived at Château-neuf the same night, a distance of some ninety miles. Next day they reached Alençon, where Navarre at last felt secure from pursuit. He praised God for his deliverance from Paris, where his mother had mysteriously died and where his best friends had been murdered. 'Never, unless I am dragged there, will I ever return!' he exclaimed. But fate ordained that he should often return of his own free will.

CHAPTER TWO

Civil War

People who have not understood the springs of Navarre's nature, and whose attitude to institutional religion has been punctilious, have criticized his behaviour at certain crucial moments in his life. But to appreciate his actions, above all his lack of action when everything seemed to call for energy, we must grasp the simple fact that he did not share the bigoted faiths of his day and knew instinctively that there could be no peace or prosperity for himself or France while the country was ravaged by fanaticism. The unity and welfare of the nation were only possible, in his opinion, if hatred could be exorcized from dogma and people allowed to worship God in the manner suitable to their temperaments. Like Guise, like all men of action, he was ambitious; but his ambition was guided by benevolence to his species, while that of Guise was fostered by malevolence to all who did not hold his opinions. Henry was constitutionally incapable of believing that any faith could contain the final and absolute truth, and in that respect, as in many others, he was far in advance of his age. Happy in himself, and with every intention to enjoy life, he wished others to be happy and to enjoy life, a state that could not be achieved under any form of fanatical rule with its attendant ferocity and inhumanity. Comfortable in his own mind, he could not bear cruelty, revenge and discontent; and the greater part of his life was spent in assuagement.

His followers were impatient with him for not abjuring the Roman Catholic religion the moment he was at liberty to do so; but while raising an army he wished to conciliate the more moderate Catholics who showed a disposition to join him, and it was not until he entered the Protestant stronghold of La Rochelle some months later that he felt it prudent to renounce the Catholic faith, declaring that he had been forced to adopt it under duress. At that time the situation had become very serious for the Valois monarchy. The King's brother, Alençon, with a growing army, had formed an alliance with the Protestants; the Prince of Condé, who had escaped from the Court before his cousin, was in command of German mercenaries; and the King of Navarre was already making his power felt on the Loire. While the French King was busy inventing new fashions and collecting canine pets and putting rouge on his face, Catherine determined to separate her younger son from the Protestants and agreed to a treaty in which all Alençon's demands were met while those of Condé and Navarre were approved, though in their case the Queen Mother 'reserved to herself the pleasure of breaking her word', as a chronicler of the time phrased it. Alençon became the Duke of Anjou, received vast possessions and returned to his allegiance. The other parts of the treaty in which the Huguenots were granted freedom of worship throughout the country and legal equality with Catholics, were broken as soon as convenient, and another war of religion, or rather irreligion, was soon on the way.

The treaty annoyed the Duke of Guise, who longed to annihilate the heretics, and as it displeased the Catholic faction he took advantage of the circumstance by forming the Holy League, originally designed by his uncle the Cardinal of Lorraine (since dead), the true objects of which were in effect to exterminate the Huguenots, to confine the King in a monastery, and to place Guise on the throne. Since the destruction of heresy appealed to all except the most moderate Catholics, membership of the League increased by leaps and bounds. It was authorized by the Pope and backed by Philip of Spain, who sent men and money to forward the holy work. The instant he perceived what was happening, Henry III did his best to put a spoke in Guise's wheel by announcing that as Catholic King of France he naturally assumed leadership of the League, there being nothing in the articles drawn up for his approval that hinted at his deposition in favour of Guise. On 1 January 1577 he proclaimed that he had signed and authorized the Holy Catholic League. But Guise was too clever for him, the form signed by the monarch being quite different from the one to which his subjects had subscribed. Anyhow the recent treaty with the Protestants was quickly scrapped and a new war commenced, or the old war continued, the Duke of Anjou now fighting for the Crown against his late confederates.

The dreary wretched business went on for the better part of a year when a new treaty was patched up by Navarre at Bergerac, but it was scarcely worth the parchment it was written on, the country still being subjected to sporadic bursts of godly murder and sacred crime.

In the hope of establishing order, and with the object of seeing how the land lay, Catherine started on a long tour of the south in August 1578, taking with her Margaret, Queen of Navarre, who had not seen her husband since his escape from the Court more than two years before. They stayed for some time at Nérac, which was Henry of Navarre's favourite residence and where his sister Catherine presided over the Court. The Protestant leaders gathered together either at Nérac or at Pau, to which the Court occasionally moved, and such names as Duplessis-Mornay, a stern Calvinist, the Viscount of Turenne, a convert from Catholicism, and Maximilien of Béthune, Baron of Rosny, a youth of seventeen, graced the Court of Princess Catherine, who at different times was offered marriage by the Duke of Anjou and Philip of Spain; but the extraordinary girl felt that she would like to marry for love. The platoon of beauties in Catherine's train made something of a sensation in the south, but the arrival of his wife annoyed Navarre, who refused at first to see her, at last consenting on the advice of his friends. She remained at Nérac for two or three years, a *modus vivendi* being established between herself and her husband, she taking no notice of his amorosities, he merely requiring that hers should be conducted with discretion. While busy attacking various towns that refused to acknowledge his suzerainty, he was equally occupied in laying siege to the daughter of his sister's governess, whose surrender was more easily obtained.

The haphazard manner in which hostilities were conducted may be illustrated by a single incident. The inhabitants of Villefranche in Périgord decided to seize the neighbouring town of Montpasier; but it happened that the citizens of Montpasier had also decided to seize Villefranche, and by an odd coincidence on the same night. The parties took different routes and did not meet each other. Since both towns were left undefended, they were easily taken and the men of Villefranche pillaged Montpasier while the men of Montpasier pillaged Villefranche. On discovering what had happened the following morning, they 'came to a composition', related the Baron of Rosny; 'everything was restored to its right owner, and they returned to their respective habitations'.

Navarre seemed to enjoy the excitement of action and was usually seen in the hottest place during an engagement. 'It was not in our power, by the most earnest entreaties, to make him take more care of his life', said Rosny. There were not a few Roman Catholics among his followers, and the animosities displayed between the two religions made leadership a tricky business, Navarre finding it almost as difficult to keep peace among his partisans as to win skirmishes against his opponents. Exhibitions of personal courage were therefore vital to his purpose, and if he had not been naturally brave he could not have maintained his position.

His courage was put to a severe test when, just before another official war broke out, he determined in May 1580 to capture the town of Cahors, which, though part of his wife's dowry, had not been handed over to him by the French King. Cahors, protected on three sides by water, was strongly fortified and well garrisoned; but with the help of the petards, which had just been invented and were now used for the first time, Navarre managed to get into the town, and the fight began. His small force was fiercely opposed and a fresh effort was called for in almost every street, the storm of shot from the garrison being augmented by the showers of stones, tiles and logs from the housetops. The combat continued for five days and nights, reinforcements arriving at intervals for both sides, and throughout that time the attacking party could scarcely rest. Navarre was in the thick of it, bloody and weary, leading a few soldiers to storm a house here, forcing others to relieve a hotly-pressed group there, and continually engaged in hand-to-hand fighting. His officers begged him again and again to retreat, but he told them that death was the only alternative to victory and that the sole possible retreat would be his life from his body. By dint of his 'matchless fortitude' the town was captured, his reputation as a soldier was securely founded, and he could relax in the arms of his latest inamorata.

He managed to combine, with equal facility, gallantry in the field and gallantry in the bed. The Catholics disliked the first, the Huguenots disapproved of the second, and even the Court drew the line at some of his sports. During the Queen Mother's sojourn in the south her own and Princess Catherine's Courts were for a while at Foix, and it occurred to Navarre that the ladies would be amused by a bear-hunt. But some of the bears tore the horses to pieces, others mauled a number of soldiers, and one bear, badly wounded, mounted on a rock, threw himself down headlong with several of his tormentors held in his paws, and crushed them to death. The ladies did not seem amused, though they had witnessed far more horrible incidents with men and women as the victims of human savagery. Possibly it amused Navarre to note the Queen Mother's distaste for this kind of sport, though he would never have staged such an exhibition if he had known what the result would be.

His high spirits infected both Courts, and not a few extreme Catholics liked and admired him. The things that vexed ordinary men seemed not to touch him. His wife's sexual promiscuity, the fact that for a while she raised a small army and carried on a local war against him, the papist poisoners awaiting their opportunity to rid the world of a dangerous heretic, the intention of the Guise party to use his Catholic uncle as a puppet, placing him on the throne if the French King died: Navarre took it all in his stride and laughed away his anxieties. This uncle, the Cardinal of Bourbon, accompanied the Queen Mother on her southern tour and tried to argue Navarre out of his Protestant opinions. But the latter pulled the Cardinal's leg: 'They tell me, dear uncle, that some people wish to make you King. Bid them make you Pope. It would suit you much better, and then you would be greater than all the kings put together.' Navarre could not even depend on the man who next to himself was regarded as the chief Protestant leader, for the Prince of Condé frequently acted solely in his own interests. In the midst of treachery, intrigue, murderous conspiracy, broken treaties, and frequent warfare, which kept him on horseback for days and nights together, Navarre maintained an even temper, a constant gaiety, a never-failing toleration, a light-hearted courage, an honesty of purpose and a thoroughly unfashionable humanity, that made him unique in his time and hardly to be matched as a ruler at any time. His capacity to love women tenderly and passionately, and never to revenge his shortcomings on them, illustrated a nature in which affection, loyalty, kindliness and protectiveness were the outstanding features.

Early in the fifteen-eighties he fell deeply in love with the Countess of Gramont and Guiche, known as 'La Belle Corisande', whose husband the Count of Gramont had been killed at the siege of La Fère in 1580. A widow at the age of twenty-six, she had fair hair, blue eyes and plump rosy cheeks, and Navarre found so much pleasure in her company that every minute he could snatch from the strenuous efforts of fighting and organizing was spent with her at Pau. Although a Catholic she pawned her jewels and mortgaged her estates for money to pay his troops, and he wrote to her at moments when, utterly exhausted, he could scarcely keep his eyes open. 'I read your letter every evening,' ran one message; 'if I love it, how much must I love her from whom it comes?' And another: 'My soul, hold me in your good graces; believe my fidelity to be pure and unspotted; it never had its like . . . Your slave adores you to distraction.' In spite of his assurance that he would be faithful to her till death, she could not feel complete confidence in the singleness of his devotion, calling him changeable. 'What action of mine have you known to be variable – I mean in what relates to you?' he asked; 'I have always remained fixed in the love and service I vowed to you, God is my witness.' But the evidence of the Deity was not sufficiently audible to Corisande, and he begged for her sympathy:

How grievous are domestic evils! All the troubles that can afflict a mind are continually exercised upon mine. I say everything at once. Pity me, my life, and do not add your kind of torment; it is what I dread most . . . Love me, my all. Your favour is the consolation of my soul in the midst of afflictions; do not refuse me this support. Good-night, my life.

The phrase 'I say everything at once' no doubt referred to the promises forced from him by other mistresses. But his love for Corisande remained pure and unspotted, in the sense that he never allowed his love for one woman to infringe upon his love for another. 'My heart! I am a better man than you reckon me,' he cried, and he reassured her with: 'Ah, my life! thou art made for me . . . I kiss thy beauteous eyes a thousand times.' Always he longed to be with her: 'Goodnight, my life. I wish I were in the corner of your chimney, warming your pottage.'

In June 1584 the Duke of Anjou expired from the same disease that had been fatal to his elder brother Charles, commonly called 'the sweat', probably a combination of consumption and haemophilia. Navarre now became heir to the French throne and 'the mark against which is directed all the perfidy of the Mass', as he told Corisande. Henry III urged him to go to the French Court and attend Mass, so that he could be acknowledged as legitimate heir. Philip of Spain tried to bribe him into making war against the French King, who had recently helped the Netherlands in their fight against Spain. Navarre declined to visit the French Court and thanked Philip for his offer, loyally sending full details of it to Henry III. Meanwhile his Calvinist mentor, Duplessis-Mornay, took occasion to read him a lecture: 'Those amours to which you give so much time, and which have hitherto been so public, are no longer suitable or possible. It is now time, sire, that you should make love to the whole of Christendom, and especially to France.' Navarre paid as much attention to the Huguenot's advice as to the French King's request and the Spanish monarch's proposal.

A month after Anjou's death the Prince of Orange was murdered at the instigation of Philip of Spain, upon which Navarre was generally recognized as head of the Protestant movement in Europe and the attempts to kill him were too numerous to mention, though one may be recorded to illustrate his own attitude. A man named Gabaret joined a small party attending the King, who had cause for suspicion, strengthened by the sight of the fine horse on which the fellow was mounted to facilitate flight. Pretending to admire the animal, the King said he would like a gallop, asked the other to dismount, leapt into the saddle, seized the loaded pistols at the saddle-bow, and addressed the would-be assassin: 'I am told that you seek to kill me. I could now, if I pleased, kill you instead.' He then discharged the weapons into the air, leaving the man free to try again, which he did several times. By nature merciful, Henry was wily enough to perceive that reports of such actions were quickly circulated and increased his popularity when they were compared with the ruthless cruelties of the other two Henrys, the King of France and the Duke of Guise.

As heir to the French throne he became the focus of Catholic hatred, and the Guise faction concentrated on him all the sectarian animosity in the country. The power of the League increased; lies were fulminated by priests in churches; and printed libels appeared on church walls in every district. Henry's incompetent uncle, the Cardinal of Bourbon, was proclaimed heir to the throne, though Guise, the putative descendant of Charlemagne, had every intention of transferring the Crown to himself at the first opportune moment. The French King feared and hated Guise so much that he took precautions for his personal safety, instituting a private bodyguard of forty-five gentlemen who lived at Court on handsome pay; furthermore, he began to show friendship with Navarre, the only possible alternative to Guise. But Navarre had learnt to put no trust in Catholic princes, and had already proposed to the English and German Courts the formation of a League of Protestants for the defence of their religion throughout Europe. The seed was thus sown in 1583 for the grand scheme which towards the end of his life he hoped to realize.

In 1585 the Holy League brought pressure to bear on the feeble effeminate King of France. It became clear to Navarre that the country would again be wasted by war, and he issued a manifesto replying to the lies of the League, wherein he stated that he was no enemy of the Roman Catholics, that he had never disturbed the public peace, that such actions as he had been compelled to take were in defence of his people and his faith. He begged the King to prevent the shedding of Christian blood and allow him to decide the quarrel convulsing France in personal combat with the Duke of Guise, man to man, two to two, or ten to ten, so that the populace might no longer suffer from these contentions. But neither the King nor Guise was concerned over the shedding of Christian blood; nor were they disposed to settle the future by a tournament; and Navarre's appeal was soon answered by the League in a manner that ensured war.

Considering his natural impetuosity Navarre's behaviour during the period preceding 'the war of the Henrys' was remarkable. In spite of an agreed truce parties of the League took possession of towns and places of strategic importance; but with the French King's promise of amity, and his clear assurance that the latest edict of toleration to Protestants was irrevocable, Navarre held his hand and kept the peace. 'Our patience lasts as long as it may; God grant that it may continue', he wrote. But he knew that sooner or later he would have to sustain a serious attack and he never for a moment relaxed his vigilance. 'Excuse me if I do not write with my own hand, for I have so much business that I have not leisure to blow my nose.' Such was the message received by one of his principal adherents.

In the middle of 1585 the League forced the pace, practically ordering the King to issue an edict compelling his subjects to become Catholics, forbidding the exercise of Protestantism under pain of death, and in effect authorizing the annihilation of the Huguenots. As usual the King wobbled, the Queen Mother and the fanatical Duke of Joyeuse advising him to yield to the demands, his other favourite the Duke of Épernon counselling him to fight the League. But at last the backbone-less monarch gave way, and in July he directed the parliament of Paris to proclaim the revocation of all the edicts of toleration granted to the Huguenots, and to condemn all non-Catholics to death or exile. When Navarre heard of the King's shameful surrender to Guise, he told someone that his moustache had turned white on that side of his face supported by his hand. But whatever the effect on his moustache, his head remained cool. He sent letters to Elizabeth of England, the princes of Germany and other Protestant states, asking for money and armed assistance, and he declared war against the League in the name of France. Henry III then sent a Cardinal and various theologians to persuade Navarre to embrace the Catholic faith, with promises of security if he agreed. But Navarre now knew the worth of the French King's promises, disregarded the threat that a furious war was about to be made on him, and said that he could not abandon from fear a religion which he had adopted from conviction.

Not content with the monarch's collaboration the Leaguers sought that of the Pope, and in September 1585 a Bull of excommunication against Navarre and Condé was issued from the Vatican, in which they were described as 'Henry de Bourbon, pretended King of Navarre, and Henry de Bourbon, pretended Prince of Condé.' The Pope, Sixtus V, claiming 'the authority, surpassing that of all terrestrial kings and princes, given by God to St Peter and his successors', then declared that the sword of vengeance was unsheathed against those 'two children of wrath, a bastard and detestable generation of the House of Bourbon', those two 'relapsed heretics . . . guilty of treason towards God'. All their lands, offices and possessions were henceforth to be forfeit, their succession to any sovereignty void, while their subjects were absolved from their oaths of fidelity and commanded to 'render them neither service nor obedience, under pain of being included in the anathema pronounced on the princes'. This lively document concluded with an exhortation to Henry III that he must act in accordance with the oath taken at his coronation to exterminate heretics. The king sent the Bull to parliament for affirmation; but the Guise faction had not yet complete control over Paris, and the French national spirit was aroused by what was regarded as a piece of Italian insolence, parliament asserting that the Pope's communication 'merited only to be thrown into the fire in the presence of the whole Gallican Church'. Parliament even went so far as to threaten that they would rather resign in a body than register such an arrogant Bull.

Navarre promptly replied to the papal denunciation with a *tu quoque*, which must have delighted most of his fellow-countrymen, whether Catholic or Protestant, though it cannot have produced much mirth in the holy city. In view of what eventually happened to the writer, there is a pleasing irony in some of the phrases:

Henry by the Grace of God, King of Navarre, Sovereign of Béarn, first Peer and Prince of France, opposes the declaration and ex-communication of Sixtus V, calling himself Pope of Rome; maintains that it is false, and appeals against it as abusive to the Court of the Peers of France, of whom he has the honour of being the first; and, as touching the crime of heresy, of which he is accused by the said declaration, he says and sustains that Sixtus V, calling himself Pope, has, saving his Holiness, falsely and malic-iously lied, and that he himself is heretic, which he will prove in any full and free council, lawfully assembled; to which, if he do not consent and submit, as he is bound by the canons, he, the King of Navarre, holds him and declares him to be Antichrist and heretic, and in that quality declares against him a perpetual and irreconcilable war . . . and, as in times past, the Princes and Kings his predecessors have well known how to chastise the temerity of such gallants as the pretended Pope Sixtus, when they have forgotten their duty, and passed the bounds of their vocation, confounding temporal with spiritual things, the said King of Navarre, who is nothing their inferior, hopes that God will give him grace to avenge the injury done to his King, to his house, to his blood, and to all the Parliaments of France, imploring for this purpose the aid and support of all truly Christian Princes, Kings, towns and communities affected by this act. Also he prays all the allies and confederates of this crown of France, to join him in opposing the tyranny and usurpation of the Pope, and the leagued conspirators in France, enemies of God, the State, and the King, and of the general peace of all Christendom.

Condé subscribed to this protest, which was fixed to the gates of the Vatican by some enthusiastic adherent of the Bourbon princes, but failed to arouse a christian spirit in St Peter's successor.

The next move on the part of Guise was to compel the King to issue a new edict giving the Protestants fifteen days in which to become Catholics, the alternatives being death or exile, in either case with confiscation of property. Parliament again displayed a rebellious tone and registered the edict under protest. The League then determined to spike the parliamentary guns by taking control of the capital and forming a revolutionary government known as 'the Sixteen', which was supposed to represent the sixteen sections of Paris but which in reality ruled solely in the interests of the Duke of Guise and Philip of Spain. The King, now seriously perturbed, asked Navarre to despatch a trustworthy representative for discussions which might lead to an understanding between the two monarchs. Navarre sent the Baron of Rosny, already his intimate friend and most trustworthy counsellor. In the course of several interviews it appeared that the sole obstacle to collaboration was Navarre's religion. Rosny, a firm Huguenot, argued that if Navarre changed his faith he could only join the King as a single soldier, whereas if the question were waived the entire Huguenot army would support the King against the League. But Rosny quickly perceived that no good thing could be expected from the man who received him. Henry III seemed more concerned over a game of cup-

and-ball with his favourites than with the dangers to his throne. A Spanish hood hung down over his shoulders, a little cap such as collegians wore graced his head, and a basket containing two or three small dogs was suspended by a ribbon from his neck. Birds flitted and monkeys gambolled about the apartment, several hideous dwarfs gibbered in corners, and amidst the screeching, warbling and babbling the King stood in a fixed attitude as if paralysed, staring at his visitor without a motion of head, hands or feet. Altogether the atmosphere was not favourable for the discussion of highly confidential state matters, being more suitable for the diffusion of scandal, the King writing to tell Navarre that his wife Margaret had given birth to a bastard, but feeling that he had gone too far qualified the accusation in a second communication with the statement that Navarre's own mother had not been free from scandal. On reading this Navarre laughed and said to his companions: 'The King, by both letters, does me much honour. In the first he calls me a cuckold, and in this the son of a whore. I am very grateful to him.'

Navarre, wisely, did not hope for a reconciliation with the King and worked as never before to fight the League. He enlisted armed men from every quarter, fortified and provisioned the places held by the Huguenots, furnished the defensible towns with all the ammunition and artillery he could collect, obtained money from all possible sources, persuaded many nobles to forward his endeavours, disciplined his soldiers, kept an eye on everything and seemed to be everywhere, scarcely resting body or mind, indefatigable and cheerful. Condé and other noblemen were detailed to hold Poitou, while Navarre himself remained in Guienne, where he conducted 'the war of the Henrys' with all the skill of a born guerrilla. Working with a small body of highly-trained lightly-armed veterans who were accustomed to incessant fatigue and travelled without baggage, he scoured the country with such rapidity that the slow-moving Duke of Mayenne, brother of Guise and commander of the main League forces, never knew his whereabouts, except intermittently when Navarre intercepted supplies or cut off stragglers or stayed long enough at one spot to save a hard-pressed garrison. Nevertheless, Mayenne felt sure that Navarre could not escape the net that was slowly enclosing him, and even the latter's followers advised his withdrawal to England. But he was unimpressed, saying 'The Duke of Mayenne is not so terrible a person as to stop one from walking about Guienne for some time to come.' He knew that Mayenne would exhaust his troops by attacking all the strongly fortified places. 'They have surrounded me like a beast of the chase,' wrote Navarre at one crucial moment, 'and think that they will take me by the net. For my part I intend to pass through them or over them', and he amused himself with hunting when not engaged in warlike measures.

Condé failed in his campaign and had to retire for a short while to England. To save the situation Navarre dashed north into Poitou and captured several towns. La Rochelle was endangered by League troops under the command of Marshal Biron, the most notable artillery officer in France, who intended to take Marans, one of the keys to La Rochelle. Although opposed by the military leaders in the great Protestant city, Navarre, recognizing its importance, put Marans in a condition to withstand a siege so skilfully that Biron battered it in vain. At this point the Queen Mother made another attempt to win over Navarre to the King's side, and there were meetings between them; but all Catherine's promises failed to seduce 'the Béarnais', as the Catholics called him, and their conferences were concluded with Catherine's bitter complaint that her son-in-law's obstinacy over religion stood in the way of peace and that all she required was tranquillity. To which her son-in-law answered: 'Madam, I am not to blame in this war. It is not I who prevent you from sleeping in your bed; it is you who prevent me from sleeping in mine. The trouble that you take nourishes and pleases you; tranquillity you look upon as the greatest enemy in life.'

Yet another attempt was made on Navarre's integrity by a man he highly esteemed, the Duke of Nevers. But though the Duke said that he personally would never serve under a Protestant sovereign, Navarre continued to insist on liberty of conscience for all his followers and himself, together with the maintenance of the edicts which had been granted in their favour and then revoked, assuring Nevers that he desired nothing so much as to die fighting against the Spaniards and the League. Nevers reported to the French King that Navarre was the same man they had always known:

Neither years nor troubles change him in the least. He is still agreeable, still joyous, still, as he vowed to me a thousand times, devoted to peace and your Majesty's service. He told me in the fullness of his heart that he only wished he had forces enough to deliver you in a single day from all the authors of the League without even obliging you to give your consent.

What all the efforts of the Catholics failed to perform was nearly accomplished by a few pigs. While the conference with Catherine was still undetermined Navarre backed his horse in a race against two fine animals belonging to one of the King's ministers. He was winning easily when some swine rushed across the road under the feet of his horse, which fell and rolled over him. Picked up senseless, with blood flowing from mouth and nose, he was carried into the château of St-Brie, where he soon regained consciousness and asked what had happened. The surgeons wanted to know the exact spot where he felt most pain. He replied that he was in no pain at all, a rational reply in those days when suffering from surgeons, and though they said that he must rest for some time he was soon in the saddle again, attacking and taking various towns in the hands of the League. One of them, Fontenoy, surrendered the moment it became known that he was present in person, and we hear that no formal capitulation was drawn up, 'the security of his word being so well known that the garrison did not require any writing'. His promises, as always in war, were kept, and the Catholic soldiers marched out with all the honours.

As Navarre had anticipated, Mayenne frittered away his forces by attacking well-prepared strongholds, and soon returned to Paris. But another commander now took the field, and a large army went south under the Duke of Joyeuse, whose object was to beat Navarre before reinforcements from Germany could join the Protestant troops; and he assured Henry III that he would bring back the heads of Navarre and Condé as trophies of victory, Condé having returned from England and joined the army. It was necessary for Navarre that the town and castle of Coutras should be occupied, as it secured the passage of his army across the river Dronne, some twenty-six miles north-east of Bordeaux. Already he had sent the artillery across the river when he found that Joyeuse was upon him with the intention of forcing a battle before he could put the stream between them. The guns and troops that had gone over were ordered at once to return, but they could not join him until the battle had begun and he prepared for action with his three remaining cannon. With an eye for strategic position and contingencies that no other commander of his time possessed, he faced an army of double his number with the calm assurance that his men would fight a great deal better than those of the League. The Catholic force was spectacular with its shining armour, brightly coloured banners and brilliant accoutrements, but the Protestants looked more serviceable with their rusty armour, stained leather coats and ragged banners. Someone remarked on the splendid appearance of the Catholic troops. 'We shall have the better aim when the fight begins', said Navarre. Before the engagement he addressed those who surrounded him, dwelling on the wickedness of war, on his own efforts to avoid it, and on the vital necessity of defending their religious freedom. 'Let them perish who are the authors of this war,' he declared, 'and may the bloodshed this day rest upon them alone.'

But the lover as well as the warrior was revealed just before the battle commenced. Duplessis-Mornay marched up to him and spoke in terms of solemn admonition, saying that Navarre had deeply injured a respectable citizen of La Rochelle by seducing his daughter, and that God would not support a man who had not repaired and repented such an offence. Navarre had an accommodating disposition, disliked hurting people's feelings, and was as ready to repent as to share a bed. He was also shrewd enough to appreciate the military value of a moral gesture. Promptly dismounting, he publicly acknowledged the act, expressed his remorse, promised reparation (which he performed), and begged forgiveness of the family he had wronged. The Protestant troops then knelt in prayer for victory, led by their ministers. 'The King of Navarre is frightened,' exclaimed Joyeuse: 'Look! he kneels.' But one of his captains knew better: 'Do not fancy such a thing, sir; these men only do so when they are resolved to conquer or die.'

It was a terrific combat on 20 October 1587. Navarre had placed his few guns in such a position that they ploughed down the Catholic infantry, while the artillery of Joyeuse could not be sufficiently elevated and merely ploughed up a sandy hill. Cavalry charges and hand-to-hand fights took place all over the field of battle, and Navarre's cavalry, formed in squadrons, each supported by a small body of arquebusiers, were more effective than their opponents formed in line. When the main charge of the Duke's greatly superior cavalry took place Navarre called to his supporters: 'On, in the name of God, for whom we draw the sword!' and prepared to lead the counter-charge. Some of his friends tried to get in front of him to break the shock of the collision, but he yelled 'To your places – to your places – do not hide me – I would be seen!' and led his squadrons forward at a brisk trot. Wherever the fight was hottest Navarre's white plumes waved and he seemed to be enjoying the thrust and parry of the encounter. Again and again his personal valour was put to the test, and a follower noticed that his sword was dripping with blood. After the main League forces had been routed a compact body of armed and mounted men were seen advancing, and an officer suggested to Navarre that it must be the head of another Catholic army, receiving an unexpected answer: 'Well, my friends, this will be what was never seen before: two battles in the same day.' But the general rout discouraged the oncoming troops, who joined it.

The action lasted from nine to ten in the morning and resulted in a complete victory for Navarre. The Catholic general, Joyeuse, was slain and scarcely a fourth of his army escaped, the remainder being killed or captured. It was the first triumph for the Huguenots in a pitched battle, and it was secured by the sagacious leadership and personal bravery of Navarre against an army twice the size of his own. At a blow he was recognized as the greatest general in France.

The booty was immense, and the Huguenot troops were not godly enough to overlook it. But success did not turn Navarre's head. He displayed no exultation when the standards of the enemy were brought to him, treated his noble prisoners with courtesy, restored the arms of some, dismissed others without ransom, and even freed a man who had proved a bitter enemy for some years. The condition of the wounded received his immediate attention, and altogether he behaved more like a considerate and affable host than a conquering monarch. Asked what terms of peace he would now demand, he replied, 'The same as before,' namely the permitted right of Protestants to exercise their religion, and he despatched an officer to supplicate peace from Henry III.

The victory of Coutras disclosed an aspect of Navarre that puzzled his followers and has worried some historians, but it need not perplex us unduly. He felt sure that in time he would become King of France, since Henry III was too fond of boys to beget any, and he wished to rule a country purged of religious dissension, which would only be possible if he loyally supported the Valois monarchy and convinced the Catholics who formed the greater part of the nation that they had nothing to fear from him. Had he followed up his present victory, he was bound to come into collision with the King, whose army was on the Loire, and he was optimistic enough to think that the recent action would prove his value to Henry III, who would ultimately side with him against the League. He perceived that some of his noble followers wished to enjoy the spoils of battle and pursue their own courses; so he raised no objection to their retirement, knowing that they would answer future calls upon them the more readily if allowed to do as they pleased at the present moment. He also wished to follow his own inclination, and his critics have explained his failure to take advantage of Coutras on the ground that he longed for the immediate admiration and embraces of the Countess of Guiche. They have even gone so far as to assert that he lost no time in joining his mistress at Pau, but the manuscript accounts of his household expenses prove that he stayed at several places well off the direct route, presumably with the purpose of transacting important business. He reached Pau seventeen days after his great victory and laid the captured banners at the feet of his beloved Corisande, no doubt earning a satisfactory recompense.

CHAPTER THREE

Murder

Meanwhile the third Henry of the war, Guise, had not been idle. Although the French King had managed to head-off the German mercenaries who were coming to the help of Navarre and had given them permission to leave the country without molestation, the Duke of Guise decided to have a victory of his own and attacked the retreating troops, cutting them to pieces, after which his popularity with the Catholics increased. Already the mob had hailed him with cries of *À Reims! À Reims!* and would have liked to see him crowned there, but now he felt that he had the King at his mercy and following a short visit to the Pope he issued the League's orders to Henry III: that he should order the publication of the decrees of the Council of Trent, which in effect made disagreement with the dogmas of the Church a crime; that he should at once establish the Inquisition in France; that he should issue an edict authorizing the confiscation of all property held by the Protestants; and that he should surrender to the League the cities they needed. Such demands ought to have been regarded as treasonable, but the King as usual vacillated. The intention of Guise was to enter Paris and seize the King, if his well-bribed Council of Sixteen, aided by Guise's sister the Duchess of Montpensier, had not done so before his arrival. From what we know of the monarch's habits, the extreme hatred felt for him by the Duchess must have been due to his failure to be captivated by her charms.

On hearing of his danger, for he had a good spy in the League's confidence, the King ordered 4,000 Swiss soldiers to occupy the *faubourgs* of Paris, and when the Queen of the League, as the Duchess was called, made an attempt to entrap him on the way from Vincennes he upset her plan by returning with an escort of cavalry. Although he made it known to Guise that he was well guarded, the Duke stated his intention of visiting Paris to talk matters over, upon which the King sent a message begging him 'to suspend his journey'. When this request failed of effect, the King sent several verbal orders to stop the Duke. But nothing could now stop the Duke, who arrived in Paris early in May 1588 and received a frantic welcome from the populace, such as the King had never been able to inspire, a welcome that would have been excessive if Guise had been a great soldier as well as a consecrated saint. When the King learnt that his orders had been disobeyed he screamed with rage, exclaiming 'He shall die for it!' but when one of his officers suggested the instant decapitation of the Duke his rage abated, his courage ebbed, and caution prevailed.

Guise first called on the Queen Mother, and together they made their way to the Louvre, the crowd yelling *À Reims!* The sight of the Duke again roused the King to anger, and he spoke abruptly: 'I warned you not to come.' Guise replied that his enemies had calumniated him and he wished to justify himself, adding that he would not have come if he had been explicitly forbidden. There followed a brief argument as to the exact terms of the royal messages, interrupted by the King's dismissal of Guise in a sentence: 'It is by your conduct that you will justify yourself, and I shall judge of your intentions by the effect of your presence in Paris', or something to that effect. It is possible that the Duke's next visit to the Louvre would have been his last, because the King talked of having him killed; but Guise took the precaution to arrive with four hundred armed men, and the King's forty-five guardsmen were not adequate to deal with them.

A regiment of French guards was ordered into the city together with the 4,000 Swiss from the suburbs, and it seemed that the King would soon bring the Duke to his knees. But the people decided otherwise and began feverishly to raise barricades with the object of isolating the troops, preventing their movements and cutting off communications between the various detachments. Many of the citizens were armed, and the barricades quickly became fortresses. The King dared not order the soldiers to fire on the people, who took advantage of his weakness by pushing their barricades nearly up to the Louvre; and at last the soldiers, prevented from retaliation, hindered in their actions, fired on by the arquebusiers of the League, made no attempt to resist the populace and sued for their lives. The monarch's final humiliation occurred when Guise, requested to quell the tumult, rode through the city with a cane in his hand, issued commands which were at once obeyed, saved the lives of the unfortunate soldiers, and restored tranquillity to the French capital. So ended the famous Day of the Barricades, 12 May 1588.

The King spent the night imprisoned in the Louvre, while the Queen Mother set out to negotiate with Guise, who was in no mood to compromise. His commands were simple and direct: that he should be made Lieutenant-Governor of the kingdom, that Navarre and the princes of the house of Condé should be excluded from the succession, that the King's favourites should be exiled, the forty-five guardsmen disbanded, and the principal government posts given to leaders of the League. Catherine tried hard to make him moderate his demands, but failed. She tried again the following morning, and failed again; but while they were still in conference the King, acting on a warning she had sent him, walked unobtrusively from the Louvre to the royal stables, mounted a strong horse, and with a few attendants rode away, swearing he would never re-enter his rebellious capital except by the breach. He kept his word, but there would be no breach.

Excessively annoyed at the King's escape, Guise pretended that his own actions had been misunderstood and sent message after message urging his Majesty to return. But Henry III had been thoroughly frightened and stayed first at Chartres and then at Rouen, where he did a deal of praying. Futile whenever strength of character was vital, he soon granted everything the League demanded, entered into a wholly anti-Protestant pact in July, ordered an assembly of the States-General at Blois in order to ratify these new decrees, and received the Duke of Guise at Chartres with open arms.

Although the Prince of Condé had died earlier that year, possibly poisoned by his wife, Guise was determined to prevent that branch of the Bourbon house from attending the meeting of the States-General and to deprive it of the right to succession; also to obtain a decree sanctioning confiscation of Navarre's territory and his expulsion from France as a heretic, or preferably his death at the stake. Already the Cardinal of Bourbon, the puppet of Guise, had been declared first Prince of the Blood and heir-presumptive to the throne. But matters were not progressing favourably that summer for the Catholic religion. The Invincible Armada despatched by Philip of Spain against England was made vincible by British seamanship and ultimately wrecked by the northern climate, which suggested to many godly folk that God was a Protestant; while Navarre's activities were crowned with success in Poitou, where he seized towns, armed and manned them to resist the League, fought battles, shot partridges, and made his name so alarming to the enemy that men like the Duke of Mercœur, governor of Brittany, fled expeditiously at his approach. All the same he was terribly short of money for his troops, and he wrote to ask one Protestant nobleman if he had been able to raise some thousands of pistoles by the sale of his woods: 'Should it be so, do not omit to bring me all that you can, for in my life I never was in such need. I know not when, nor how, if ever, I can repay you; but I promise you plenty of honour and glory, and money is not diet for gentlemen such as you and me.'

However hardly pressed, he still had time for Corisande, to whom he sent 'for your menagerie two young tame boars and two fawns', which had been following him about everywhere, even to church. He asked her to make him a favour 'for I will wear none save your favours in this war. I have only two hundred horse against three hundred, but I will see if the others will fight. If they do so, I will fire a pistol shot for love of you'. Such were his tribulations that he confessed to her: 'I cannot fail to become either mad or a very skilful man before long.' And again: 'If I were not a Huguenot, I would turn Turk.' But he lived so intensely in the moment that while preparing for the defence of Marans and Charron he enjoyed the scenery and tried to communicate his pleasure:

Ah, how I wished that you had been there! . . . It is an island, enclosed with bushy marshes, where at every hundred paces there are channels to enable one to go and gather wood in boats. The water is clear, with but little current, the channels are of all widths, the boats of all sizes. Among those solitudes are a thousand gardens, whither one goes by boat . . . Few are the houses from the doors of which one cannot enter one's little boat . . . There is an infinity of insular mills and farms, all sorts of birds that sing, all sorts of sea birds too. I send you some of their feathers . . . The land is covered with corn, and very fine. One can be there pleasantly in peace and safely in war. One can rejoice there with one that one loves, and lament an absence. Ah, how pleasant it is to sing there.

He had already told Corisande that a place would have to be desolate indeed for them to be bored together.

The Duke of Nevers, with whom Navarre had always been on good terms, went forth with a large army to check him,

Margaret of Valois (1553-1615), first wife of Henry

Maximilien de Béthune, Baron of Rosny,
subsequently Duke of Sully (1560-1641), by Quesnel

but the size of the force left him undismayed and in December 1588 he wrote: 'If Monsieur de Nevers amuses himself with attacking anything, I am resolved to give him battle.' The Duke even intended attacking Navarre, who reported: 'The enemy are near us. Monsieur de Nevers is resolved to be beaten.' A letter to his fair Corisande contained this sentence: 'I am going to St Jean to collect my troops, to visit M. de Nevers, and perhaps to do him a signal displeasure, not in his person, but in his command.' But they did not meet because Navarre was suddenly stricken with fever, followed by pleurisy, and for some time he hovered on the brink of death. The news reached La Rochelle in January 1589, and though it was night-time the bells of all the churches rang for prayers, the entire population emerging from their homes in consternation. Their prayers for their hero and defender went on for several days until news came of his recovery, when affliction changed to exultation. He told Corisande that 'Twice in the twenty-four hours I was so reduced that they were obliged to turn me by the help of my sheets', and 'Assuredly, my heart, I saw the heavens open, but I was not deemed good enough to enter them. God still wishes to make use of me.' Had the crisis of his illness continued for two hours, 'the worms would have made a great feast of me'. But nothing could damp his cheerfulness for long, and when capable of composition he entertained a correspondent with 'change of holy thoughts to keep him merry' in this fashion: 'I am in hourly expectation of hearing they have sent to strangle the Queen of Navarre; this, with the death of her mother, would make me sing the *Nunc Dimittis.*' His second pious wish had already been granted, as we shall shortly hear.

It is perhaps unnecessary to say that the deputies elected to the States-General, which commenced operations at Blois in October 1588, were for the most part the creatures of Guise, who daily increased his influence over them; and the various sessions soon proved to the King that he was practically powerless, since the resolutions of the deputies were passed regardless of the royal authority. It was clear, too, that in the end the King would be taken to the capital practically as a prisoner and that the country would be governed solely by Guise. All sorts of possibilities were considered and rejected by Henry III. It could easily have been shown that Guise was a traitor, for he had received large sums from foreign rulers such as Philip of Spain and was now plotting against his own monarch. But if arrested and tried his popularity was such that no tribunal in the land would dare to condemn him, no prison in Paris was strong enough to hold him, and the result would be his enthronement. If on the other hand an open attempt were made to kill him on the King's authority, the armed followers who surrounded him would quickly convert an execution into a battle. There was only one way out: simple assassination privily committed. Likely enough the King had already considered this course before going to Blois, but he was both weak and cowardly, and nothing short of grave danger to his person could rouse him to action. The haughty arrogance of Guise, and the contempt with which the States treated his Majesty's commands, were necessary to 'screw his courage to the sticking-place'.

His first choice of a man to do the deed was unfortunate. He picked on Captain Crillon, a famous soldier who laughed at shot and sword but regarded assassination with an inauspicious eye. He reminded the King that he was a soldier and a gentleman, not an executioner, but said that he would be pleased to challenge the Duke and do his best to kill him in open and fair combat. As the Duke was also a first-class swordsman, the King thought this too risky, and having taken counsel with several noblemen who advised the Duke's arrest and trial he approached the less scrupulous commander of his forty-five guardsmen. As this body had been formed for the express purpose of protecting his Majesty from the machinations of the League, he was on safe ground, and the commander at once fell in with his project. All the plans were worked out by the King, who showed much friendliness to the Duke while preparing them. To make certain that Guise would not be attended by his normally large escort, the King announced on 22 December that he intended to pass Christmas in retreat at Notre-Dame de Cléry, between Blois and Orleans, and would settle any pressing business at a council meeting early the following morning, the Duke and his brother the Cardinal being summoned to attend. To make assurance doubly sure, the captain of the King's guards informed the Duke that before the council met the royal corps wished to petition him as Grand-Master of the Household for payment of arrears. The keys of the castle were then handed over to the captain so that his men could be admitted, which meant that the Duke's guards would be excluded from their accustomed post.

Guise evidently had no suspicion of foul play, though he had been warned that his life was in danger; and on finding in his napkin at dinner that night a scrap of paper urging him to take care as the King intended his destruction, he threw it under the table with the words 'He dare not!' Some of his adherents sensed his peril and advised him to leave Blois, but he cut them short with: 'Affairs are now in such a state that if I saw death coming in at that window I would not seek to avoid it by going out of the door.' He relied on the Queen Mother, without whose approval he firmly believed the King would not commit such an act. She was at the moment in bed with gout and knew nothing of her son's plot. A final effort to persuade the Duke to leave was made by the Marchioness of Noirmoutier, who, as Charlotte de Sauves, had once enchanted Navarre and Alençon. She spent the night with Guise, but to no purpose except the usual one.

At four o'clock in the morning of 23 December 1588 two priests were praying in the royal oratory for the success of an undertaking which would be to the advantage of the realm, while the King moved about his closet in a state of agitation, already frightened by his decision and almost in a mood to forgo it. But the commander of the guard composed his terrors and provided stimulation. At seven o'clock the Duke of Guise arrived in the council chamber, where his brother the Cardinal and the Archbishop of Lyons awaited him. He asked for some sweetmeats and one of the King's valets-de-chambre brought him a box of dried plums. While eating them he was told that the King wished to speak with him in the *cabinet vieux*, which adjoined the royal bedroom. He entered the ante-room leading to the cabinet and saw several of the King's guardsmen with their commander. No one moved to raise the tapestry which hung before the door of the cabinet, so Guise crossed the floor of the ante-room and put out his hand to draw it aside. As he did so a guardsman sprang at him and stabbed him in the throat with a poniard, upon which the others rushed at him and struck him in several places, his legs being firmly held by one of them so that he could not parry their blows. The commander delivered the *coup de grâce* with a sword-thrust in the back.

When silence was restored the King came from his bedroom and looked for some time at his late enemy now still in death. '*Mon Dieu!* how tall he is! He seems taller dead than when alive,' said his Majesty, who then, according to one account, kicked the corpse in the face, just as Guise himself had kicked the bloody head of Coligny, murdered by his orders sixteen years before. The King went to break the good news to his mother, saying that, having killed the King of Paris, he was again King of France. Catherine expressed the pious wish that the death of Guise would not result in her son being king of nothing at all. She died a fortnight later in her seventieth year, and if half of what she professed to believe were true she and her sons would be destined to a not inconsiderable period of roasting in the oven of the hereafter.

Having gained strength from the action of others, the King

ordered Guise's brother the Cardinal, who had inherited the office of his dead uncle, to be killed, after which the bodies of the two men were consumed in quicklime, their bones being thrown into the Loire, so that the Leaguers could not make relics of them. Guise's eldest son, the young Prince of Joinville, now became Duke, and that no pretender to the throne should remain at large he was imprisoned, together with the Cardinal of Bourbon. An attempt was made to arrest the Duke of Mayenne, brother of the murdered Guise, but he got away to Paris and immediately placed himself at the head of the League. If the manifestations of popular feeling were anything to go by, he could have been crowned King of France, but he had not the energy and determination of his brother and let the chance slip, satisfying himself with the title of Lieutenant-General of the kingdom. The League and its myrmidons, the Council of Sixteen, were in complete control of Paris, and over half the cities of France would have acknowledged Mayenne as monarch in the excitements and execrations that followed the murder of Guise.

For indeed it looked as if Catherine's fears were justified. Her son suddenly became the most hated man in his dominions. Guise had been the people's hero and his physical appearance had fitted the part. He alone could calm the mob with a word or the lifting of a hand. Though treacherous and brutal, he was adored by the multitude, largely because he seemed so manly and single-minded compared with the King, and no one doubted his desire to eradicate the Huguenots. The news of his assassination was received throughout the country with a howl of horror, rage, sorrow and despair. The Jesuit preachers took advantage of the occasion by inciting their listeners to greater hatred of the Protestants; the parliament instituted a criminal process against Henry of Valois 'lately King of France'; that hotbed of ecclesiastical reaction, the Sorbonne, declared the deposition of Henry III, authorized his subjects to abandon their allegiance and urged them to make war against him; the Pope excommunicated him; and the citizens of Paris, when not yelling imprecations, prayed deliriously in churches hung with black.

The King, as was his custom, fluctuated. He made advances to the League; he addressed the Pope; he tried to convince everyone that Guise had intended to kill him and assume the crown; he laid the blame on anyone except himself. But his explanations and advances were ignored, and now his only hope lay with Navarre, who published a declaration, regretting that he had not been called to the assembly of the States-General at Blois, 'which perhaps France will one day reckon among its errors, there being no such good physician as one who loves his patient.' But he entreated all parties at this moment 'to seek tranquillity and abandon the unjust enormities to which they have given themselves up for so many years'. He showed how the attempt to suppress him and his cause had utterly failed, and closed with an appeal to all classes to unite with him 'as a good servant of the King, a French subject, and first Prince of the Blood' and establish peace, law and order. This declaration was signed early in March 1589, and it followed a stiff campaign during which he had captured many towns occupied by the League.

These successes of Navarre, concurrent with the approach of Mayenne at the head of a large army which threatened Tours, compelled the King to arrange an interview with the Protestant leader, whose counsellors warned him that his life would not be worth a moment's purchase if he agreed to a meeting, since the King could at a stroke make his peace with the Pope and the League by killing a heretic Prince. After carefully weighing the pros and cons, Navarre felt that the only hope of peace for France was the defeat of the League by the two kings and decided to take the risk. The King was then at the palace of Plessis-les-Tours, and Navarre journeyed thither. 'The ice is broken,' he wrote, 'not without many warnings that if I went I should be a dead man. I passed the

water, recommending myself to God.' He was received with
warmth, and the King welcomed his advice, especially his
views on the papal excommunication. There was but one
remedy for it, said Navarre: 'It is to conquer as soon as we can,
for if this happens you will get your absolution absolutely, but
if we are beaten we shall be excommunicated, aggravated and
reaggravated.' The King agreed Navarre's plan of campaign,
and having spent a night at the palace 'the Béarnais' returned
to his headquarters. Mayenne, feeling safe with the Huguenot
leader at a distance, launched an attack on Tours, which might
have been successful had not Navarre returned rapidly and
converted Mayenne's temerity to caution. The army of the
League retired, the royal armies advanced, and Navarre was
able to tell his mistress Corisande that 'many of the King's
people come over to me, but none of mine are willing to
change masters'. He also began to feel the usual effect of
constant success: 'It is God's will still to make me His
instrument.'

At the end of June 1589 the forces of the two monarchs
began their march towards Paris, seizing the towns en route.
They laid seige to Pontoise, the inhabitants of which would
have been put to the sword by order of the King if Navarre
had not interceded for them. An honourable capitulation was
granted, and a fanatical preacher even announced from his
pulpit that 'the heretic Béarnais' was a better man than the
Catholic Valois. While saving people's lives Navarre was in
the doldrums because Corisande had heard that military
affairs did not wholly absorb his thoughts. Writing from the
camp before Pontoise on 14 July, he took the tone of an
injured lover:

My life! I am sorely displeased when I find you entertain doubts
of me; through spite, I will not endeavour to remove them.
You are greatly to be blamed, for I swear to you I never loved
you more ardently than I do at this moment; and I would sooner

die than forfeit the promises I have made you. Believe this, and
live in confidence of my fidelity. Good-night, my Life! A million
kisses.

He was being perfectly honest because he never considered
that going to bed with one woman had the least effect on his
feelings for another, and it troubled him when those he loved
could not see eye to eye with him.

Reinforced by Swiss and German mercenaries, the royal
army beleaguered Paris, the French King taking up his
quarters at Saint-Cloud, Navarre at Meudon. This was in
July 1589. The people in the capital were apprehensive. Some
of the leaders, such as Mayenne and his sister the Duchess
of Montpensier, seem to have favoured a method of delivering
the city from imminent danger, and when they heard that a
young fanatical monk named Jacques Clément had been led to
believe by his superior that his dream of freeing France from
a tyrannical King would, if realized, result in his canonization,
they promised him earthly rewards should he be temporarily
deprived of a heavenly one. But such was his state of mind
that he would have preferred beatitude to a bishopric, and he
set out for Saint-Cloud with a passport, either signed by an
eminent royalist prisoner under a misapprehension as to its
use or forged in his name, and a letter from another captive in
the Bastille who favoured the King, either written by him as a
result of deception or counterfeited. Clément's credentials
were scrutinized at the King's camp and he was interrogated.
The next day, 1 August, the King heard that a monk with
important letters and intelligence from Paris desired to speak
with him. Always anxious to display his sympathy with
religion, the King instantly granted the interview. The monk
entered, handed some letters to his Majesty, and said that he
had a secret verbal message for the monarch's private ear.
At a sign from Henry his near attendants withdrew a few
paces, and Clément went within whispering distance of the

King, who leaned forward attentively to hear the message and received a knife in his belly. With a loud cry he sprang up, pulled the knife out, and struck the assassin on the forehead. Heaven was at least kind to Clément, who was quickly despatched by the King's guard instead of being taken, tortured and broken on the wheel.

At first the King's wound did not seem fatal, and Navarre, riding at full speed from Meudon, received an affectionate welcome, being acknowledged as the legitimate heir to the throne. In the event of his death the King commanded all the officers of the Crown who were present to swear obedience and fidelity to Navarre, and they did so. Navarre then returned to the castle of Meudon and was sitting down to supper when a message reached him that the King could not live. Again he galloped to Saint-Cloud, arriving at daybreak on 2 August to learn that the last of the thirteen Valois sovereigns, who had reigned over France for some 260 years, had just expired. It was the day on which the two Henrys had determined to commence the assault on Paris.

CHAPTER FOUR

For the Crown

The joy-bells rang out in Paris when the news came that the murderer of Guise had himself been murdered. The monk who had done the deed was deified, or at least sanctified, and on hearing of it the Pope compared the act as a miracle with the resurrection of Christ. The mother of Clément was suddenly discovered to be a wonderful woman who had conceived a saint. She was paraded through the streets as a sort of holy relic, receiving so many presents and so much eulogy that she found it difficult to discriminate between herself and her halo and soon went mad. At such a moment the Duke of Mayenne could easily have been recognized by the League as King, but he had the caution of a lazy man, one who preferred the pleasures of the table to the thrills of battle, and the old Cardinal of Bourbon was proclaimed King of France under the title of Charles X, though he was still in captivity at the castle of Chinon.

Meanwhile the rightful King, the Béarnais henceforth to be known as *Henri Quatre*, started his reign with grave disadvantages. His kingdom, ravaged by civil war, racked by religious dissension, rent by the hatred of political faction, would have to be conquered before it could be united. A protracted period of lawlessness and bloodshed had banished justice along with commerce, and the entire country suffered from disorganization, ferocity and anarchy; but the nobles who surrounded him showed no disposition to make his path smooth. Though they had just sworn to support Henry IV, they were more concerned with their own importance than with loyalty to a heretic, and one of them voiced the feeling of most in saying aloud that he would rather give himself up to any of their enemies than serve under a Huguenot monarch. Henry left them to argue the matter out and made his own arrangements, securing the loyalty of the French and Swiss guards, writing to the Protestant countries for aid, and finding out those of the late King's followers whose loyalty could be trusted.

At last a deputation from the Catholic nobility waited upon him, headed by the Duke of Longueville, the spokesman being Marshal d'O, who at great length explained that they could not fight for a Protestant King and exhorted him at once to become a Roman Catholic as the only way of retaining their services. Henry turned pale with anger, but soon composed himself and addressed them:

Amongst the many wonders, gentlemen, with which God has pleased to visit us within the last twenty-four hours, that which is caused by your proceeding I should never have expected. Your tears – are they already dried? The memory of your loss, and of the entreaties of your late King, not three hours ago, have they vanished together with the respect which you owe to the words of the dying? . . . Which amongst you would wish to perfect the joy of the Parisians and destroy an army of thirty thousand men by bringing confusion into it? It is impossible that all here can have agreed to take me by the throat at the first step of my accession and to force me at such a dangerous moment to do what men have been unable to compel many humble persons to do because they know how to die. And from whom can you expect such a change of faith except from a man who has none at all? Would it be more agreeable to you to have a king who is without a God? Would you trust in the faith of an atheist? and in the day of battle would you follow with confidence the will and guidance of the perjured apostate? Yes, as you say, the King of Navarre has suffered great disasters without being shaken. Can he cast off spirit and heart on the steps of the throne?

He then appealed to their riper judgment when they had given more thought to the matter, adding that those who would not pause to deliberate had his 'full leave to seek their wages under insolent masters. I shall yet have amongst the Catholics all who love France and their honour'.

As he finished speaking a Catholic, the Baron of Givri, entered the room, threw himself at Henry's feet and exclaimed: 'I have just seen the flower of your nobility, sire, who reserve their tears for their dead King till they have taken vengeance, and wait with impatience the commands of their living monarch. You are the king of the brave and none but cowards will abandon you.' The deputation withdrew to confer, the result of their deliberations being that the Catholics were divided into three sections: those who unconditionally acknowledged Henry as their leader, those who promised to serve him if he agreed to be instructed in their religion, which carried the threat of disservice if he failed to be convinced of its truth, and those who abandoned him at once to join the League. Some of the second lukewarm group were purchasable with promises, and Marshal Biron was bribed into loyalty, the others being despatched into the provinces where they exercised authority, Henry being cunning enough to perceive that they would at least defend their own property from attacks by the League. To keep them quiet on the religious question, he agreed to be instructed in the Catholic faith and to maintain it throughout the realm. He also promised that the Catholics who held offices under the late King should continue to hold them. Naturally his consent to receive schooling in the Catholic religion displeased the Protestants, many of whom deserted him as a consequence.

Indeed it soon became evident that the number of Catholic

and Protestant defections rendered the continued siege of Paris impracticable, and Henry made up his mind to march into Normandy, where he hoped to obtain supplies of men and arms from Elizabeth of England. He did not wish to be encumbered with half-hearted followers, and crossed two rivers on his way in order that those who had no stomach for the venture could easily withdraw. Mayenne with a large army followed him, having assured the Parisians that he would capture 'the Béarnais' and lodge him in the Bastille. But Henry did not think this likely and wrote to Corisande:

My health is good and my affairs are going well, compared with what many people thought. I have taken Eu. The enemy, who are now double my strength, thought that they would take *me*. After accomplishing my enterprise, I drew near to Dieppe, and am waiting for them in a camp which I am fortifying. It is tomorrow I shall see them, and I hope, with God's help, that if they attack me they will have an ill bargain of it.

Dieppe, Caen and Boulogne were handed over to him without a blow, and while Mayenne approached, with an army now increased to three times the number of troops at the King's disposal, Henry made ready to receive the leaguers, taking up his position on a stretch of tableland facing the valley through which ran the river Béthune, with the castle of Arques on his right and the town of Dieppe on his left. He laboured day and night with his whole army digging trenches, erecting redoubts and constructing ravelins. 'It is a marvel how I live with the labour I undergo', he wrote.

At first there were several sharp conflicts, each ending with the repulse of the leaguers, but Mayenne was preparing for a large-scale assault on the King's position at Arques. At one skirmish the Count of Belin was taken and brought to the King, who received him with courtesy and good humour. The

Count, having expected to see a large army, was astounded at the sight of a few scattered parties of men, but the King explained that his chief forces were invisible: 'You do not perceive all that I have with me, M. de Belin, for you do not reckon God and the right on my side.' Henry did not rest on the night before the expected attack, and on the morning of 21 September 1589 breakfast was taken to him in the trenches. He asked some of his chief officers to share it with him, but they had hardly commenced when he heard that the enemy were advancing in battle array. The morning was misty and the troops of Mayenne could scarcely be seen as they moved towards Arques. The contest started badly for Henry because some German mercenaries pretended to surrender to the royal army and having been taken within the lines suddenly attacked their captors from the rear. But they were soon dealt with. In other parts of the fog-blanketed field Henry and Marshal Biron led charges of cavalry which everywhere drove the leaguers back, the King himself, as always, being a fighter as well as a director. But the cry was still 'They come' and it looked as if Mayenne's numbers could not fail to break through when as by a miracle the mist lifted and exposed the whole force of the leaguers to the artillery which Henry had carefully placed in the castle of Arques and which commenced to tear holes in the advancing masses of cavalry and infantry. The cannon of the League could not reply and Mayenne's army retreated in disorder. A few more successful skirmishes, several reinforcements of the royal army, and the arrival of some 5,000 English and Scottish troops, gave Mayenne food for thought and he left 'the Béarnais' victorious. Henry was in high spirits and wrote to the most valiant man he knew:

Brave Crillon, hang yourself for not having been here near me last Monday, on the finest occasion that has ever been seen, and which, perhaps, will never be seen again. Believe that I greatly desired you at it . . . I hope to be next Thursday in Amiens,

where I shall make but little stay, as I mean to undertake something, for I now have one of the finest armies that one can imagine.
It lacks nothing but the brave Crillon, who will always be
welcomed and well regarded by me. *À Dieu.*

The something he meant to undertake was the capture of
Paris, whither he marched. Little encouragement arrived in
these days from Corisande, partly owing to her knowledge
that he had been openly living with Esther Imbert, the girl
at La Rochelle whose seduction had caused a painful scene
just before the battle of Coutras. Henry had made no secret of
his temporary infatuation and had actually written to Corisande on the loss of his natural son by Esther: 'I am greatly
distressed by the death of my little one . . . he was beginning
to talk.' But Henry was now paying ardent addresses to
another lady, the Marchioness of Guercheville, who refused
to become his mistress even when he wrote her a promise of
marriage as soon as he could obtain a divorce from Margaret.
Such promises were his usual method of overcoming considerable female resistance to sharing his bed, and one of them
caused him much anguish in the future. Perhaps Corisande
could understand the passionate assault that resulted in
Esther's child but resented the protracted siege of the
Marchioness, for we find Henry complaining that she sent a
letter to her son but not to him. 'If I did not render myself
worthy of one, I did at least all I could', he wrote. 'You do
not find the roads dangerous when you wish to give pleasure
to the least of your friends. But if it be a question of writing to
me to give me some contentment, then the roads are dangerous
. . . I finish certainly believing that you do not love me.'
Another of her notes is acknowledged in this fashion: 'I have
received your letter; it required very little time to read it . . .
Do you think it right to behave so oddly? I leave that for you
to judge.' On hearing that she could not rely on a man of his
fickle temperament, he again called on God to certify the

truth of his devotion. But he was about to meet another damsel for whom his affection henceforth could be attested by the Almighty with greater conviction.

His victory changed the name of the place where it was won, which became known as Arques-la-Bataille, but it was not unattended by personal mortification. His Catholic officers were enraged by the Protestant religious service which he attended in his camp; their soldiers were infected; some Huguenots were hurt in a brawl; and the King, both angry and sorry, finished his prayers in the open field. The lies spread by the League about Henry at this time followed the pattern of propaganda at all times and would have done him much harm if he had been half as bad as they painted him; but somehow the truth disseminates itself, and people were beginning to appreciate his benevolence, toleration, good humour and chieftainship. Still more extraordinary, they believed his word could be relied upon. But where there are mobs there is hysteria. If Paris had not been in the hands of the fanatical and ruthless Council of Sixteen, and if the inhabitants had not been terrified by their raving priests with the prospect of being butchered by a diabolical heretic, Henry would have entered his capital after routing Mayenne at Arques. As it was, Paris gave him so much trouble that he had to transform himself from soldier to politician before he could win it.

Having paid his soldiers with the money sent by England's Queen, he reached the environs of Paris with an army of 20,000 men, thrice the number with which he had opposed Mayenne at Arques, and on November 1 he surprised and took possession of the *faubourgs* on the left bank of the Seine. Much bloodshed ensued which Henry could not prevent, and it was almost certainly the knowledge that his soldiers would wreak a terrible vengeance on the Parisian populace that made him decide to withdraw his army and give battle to Mayenne, who was near the city with Spanish reinforcements.

Before leaving he climbed to the top of the belfry of St Germain-des-Prés, from which he could see into the city and judge the state of the inhabitants. His guide was a monk, and he suddenly remembered the man who had plunged a knife into the last King of France. Thereafter, he decided, no monk should accompany him anywhere until the man of God had been carefully searched for lethal weapons.

Mayenne duly arrived in Paris and steadfastly declined to leave it for the field of battle merely to oblige Henry, knowing himself to be no match for the wily Béarnais. Mayenne ate and drank profusely, rested for long periods and was slow in all his movements, while Henry seldom spent more than fifteen minutes at the table, rarely slept for more than three hours at a time, and was heard to say that he could win a battle while Mayenne was putting on his boots. Henry's chief trouble at this period was the discontent of his Protestant followers, many of whom left him at the most critical moments. They were jealous of his friendship with the Catholic nobles, and their envy was as troublesome to him as the bigotry of the Catholics. Nevertheless he did not lose heart, and since Mayenne would not come into the open and fight him like a warrior he occupied himself by taking such places as Étampes, Vendôme, Le Mans and Alençon, sweeping the whole country between Paris and the Loire in eighteen days and exercising his invariable clemency by preventing his men from acting with the barbarity of their opponents.

Considering the temperamental differences between two of the greatest and most successful soldiers in history, it is curious that in a letter to Corisande early in 1590 Henry indicated a viewpoint that half a century later was echoed by Oliver Cromwell in the phrase: 'No man goes further than he who knows not whither he is going.' In the opening sentences of the letter from Henry to Corisande we have his version of the same thought:

Certainly I make good progress, and go as God conducts me, for I never know what I shall do in the end; nevertheless my actions do miracles, so are they guided by the supreme Master. [At which point Cromwell drops out.] I love nothing but you, and in this resolution I will die, if you give me no cause for the contrary . . . Farewell, my heart – a thousand kisses. As I finished this letter the inhabitants of Bayeux brought me the keys – it is a fine town.

After a short stay at Tours, the King spent the early months of 1590 in a whirlwind campaign over northern France, accomplishing more than all the Roman Catholic commanders had done in the last two reigns. No one thought he could take the nearly impregnable town of Falaise, least of all the Count of Brissac, governor thereof, who replied to Henry's call to surrender: 'I have made a vow not to listen to the word "surrender" for at least six months to come.' On which Henry commented: 'The Count has made a rash vow, but I will undertake to absolve him from it and convert the six months into six days', which he did. The fall of Falaise was followed by that of Honfleur, and then Henry learnt that a considerable Spanish army had been sent by Philip from the Netherlands to support Mayenne. Having waited to collect more troops than he had with him, Henry hurried up the left bank of the Seine to relieve Meulan, which was being battered by the League forces on the right bank. He wished to survey the enemy's position and with a few attendants crossed the river, entered the town, and accompanied by Rosny ascended the tower of St Nicaise. Mayenne's guns were pointing directly at the church and as the King mounted the stairs a cannon ball passed between his legs. The stairs were so much damaged by the shot that to leave the steeple he had to slide down a rope. As Mayenne would not cross the river to give him battle, Henry laid siege to Dreux. But Mayenne now received the large reinforcements of Spanish troops and crossed the river to relieve Dreux. At once Henry marched back to meet him, taking up a position on the plain of Ivry, which with his keen eye for favourable ground he had already chosen. The League force was vastly superior in numbers, while the Spanish force was highly disciplined, their equipment extremely efficient, their commander Count Egmont a zealous and brilliant leader, whose father, beheaded by the Spaniards in 1568, was later to be immortalized by Goethe and Beethoven.

During the night before the battle Henry rested for two hours, and at daybreak on 14 March 1590 he was on horseback in complete armour, his head bare as he fervently prayed before his troops:

> O God, Thou knowest my thoughts and seest my heart. If it is to my people's advantage that I should possess the crown, then favour my cause and protect my arms. But should I be one of those kings whom Thou givest in Thy wrath, take from me both life and crown, and grant that my death may deliver France from the calamities of war, and that my blood be the last that be shed in this quarrel.

Turning to his own squadron, he held up his casque, decorated with a large plume of white feathers, and spoke again: 'Companions, God is with us. There stand His enemies and ours. Here is your King. Upon them! and if you lose your colours rally to my white plume. You will find it in the road to victory and honour.' One of his officers mentioned that he had named no place for a retreat if necessary. He replied: 'There is no other retreat than the field of battle.' An incident occurred that revealed both the fighter and the diplomat. The commander of the German mercenaries had asked that his troops should be paid what had long been owed them. 'No brave man ever asked for money on the eve of a battle', Henry sharply rejoined. But he relented and just before the engagement he went up to the disgruntled officer, saying: 'Monsieur de Schomberg, I have injured you. This day may be the last of my life, and I would not take away the honour of any gentleman. I know your valour and your merit, and I beseech you to pardon and embrace me.' The German was overcome: 'Sire, you wounded me yesterday, it is true, but today you kill me; for the honour you do me will force me to die in your service.'

Though leading a much larger force, Mayenne yet displayed caution, and Henry had to advance his line in order to compel the leaguers to fight. Even then it was necessary to open fire with his artillery before Mayenne would engage. After that it was charge and counter-charge. The King at the head of his squadron plunged into a forest of lances, and for a quarter of an hour they were hidden from sight by the dense mass of the enemy's cavalry. Henry led a charmed life. In the thickest of the battle he was unscathed. His prodigious feats inspired his followers, and soon the leaguers were seen to waver. A scene of confusion was followed by rout, and Mayenne's cavalry fled from the field. When at last Henry emerged from the conflict covered in dust and blood, a shout of *Vive le Roi!* greeted him. Collecting all the horsemen he could rally he galloped after the enemy to the gates of Mantes. Securing his own safety, Mayenne, having crossed the Eure, ordered the bridge to be broken and left many of his followers to be slain by the royalists. Count Egmont was killed, and about three-quarters of the League forces were slain or drowned or captured. Only twenty of the nobles who fought for the King were killed, among them Schomberg, but many were wounded, including Rosny, whose account of his hair's-breadth escapes from death and almost mortal injuries supplied a vivid page or two in his memoirs. All the cannon, luggage and standards of the enemy fell to the victors.

The battle of Ivry crowned Henry's career as a soldier, but as with the victories of Coutras and Arques he did not follow it up. Had he marched straight to Paris the dismay of the citizens would have compelled its surrender. At first that was clearly his intention, and we do not know for certain why he changed his mind; but our knowledge of his character explains his inaction. The Huguenots still longed to revenge the massacre of St Bartholomew, and he knew that in the heat and hatred generated by the storm of Paris he would be unable to prevent terrible reprisals. He wished to enter the capital as a harbinger of peace, not as a hero of war, and to start his effective reign with a wholesale butchery of those who belonged to the religion of the great majority of his people would have been an appalling political error, quite apart from his naturally humane instincts. Of course his severe critics have accounted for his dilatory behaviour by dwelling on a love-affair, and he obliged them by having one, but his failure to make good his victory was due to prudence and benevolence, of which he gave a singular manifestation when two regiments of Swiss Catholics, abandoned by Mayenne, surrendered after the battle. Henry sent them back to their native country, supplied them with money and provisions, allowed them to keep their ensigns and merely asked the cantons to reprimand them for violating the treaties between Switzerland and the Crown of France.

After his great triumph over Mayenne his correspondence with Corisande and his appeals to Antoinette Guercheville form a sort of fugal movement:

To Corisande (5 April 1590): '*Mon Âme*, we have won a victory . . . May God give me as great a victory over your heart! That will be everlastingly more precious to me.'

(May 14): 'I kiss your hands, your mouth, your eyes, a million times.'

To Antoinette (18 May): 'After having hovered so long about the desired pot, the point must be coming near when Antoinette will confess her love for Henry. Lady mine, my body begins to enjoy health, but my soul must suffer affliction until you have taken this leap. Since you have the warrant of my words, what difficulty prevents you from making up your mind, what hinders it from making me happy? My fidelity deserves to have you push aside all obstacles. Do so then, my Heart, and let us make a wager as to which will show the truest, the most faithful love . . . Love me, my All, for I shall adore you to the grave. On this truth I kiss your white hands a million times.'

To Corisande (15 July): '*Mon Âme*, I love nothing in the world as I love you; I am sure you will never doubt that. I kiss a million times those lovely eyes that shall be dearer to me all my life than anything in all the world.'

To Antoinette (13 August): 'If I lose it' [a battle] 'you will never see me again, for I am not the man to run away or give ground. I can assure you that if I die my next to last thought will be of you, and my last of God, to whom I commend us both.'

He spent the night after Ivry at the castle of Rosny, where he was seated at supper when one of his marshals unexpectedly appeared. Henry got up, embraced him and asked him to join them: 'It is reasonable that you should take part in the feast, since you have served so well at the marriage.' With the surrender of the town of Mantes, Henry had control of the river Seine between Rouen and Paris, but for a fortnight he remained in the neighbourhood of Mantes, where he tried to make his fraudulent superintendent of finance, François Marquis d'O, disgorge money for the army which was now gathering, and where in the words of a censorious historian his free hours 'were devoted to the chase, or to amusements less pardonable'. The less pardonable amusements consisted of his attempts to soften the heart of the Marchioness of Guercheville, at whose feet he placed the colours taken at Ivry; but the sight of them failed to overcome her resistance to his amorous appeals. In her stimulating company he forgot another lady whose assistance at a crucial moment had been invaluable the previous autumn, and the Queen of England did not hear from him about Ivry for some weeks after the battle had been won. His sorrow for the slaughter even of his enemies found vent in a phrase: 'I cannot rejoice to see my subjects lying dead upon the field. I am a loser at the very moment when I win.' On hearing that among the slain was one of his officers whose widow was pregnant, he said: 'I give to the babe in the womb the same pension which this officer enjoyed.'

On 28 March Henry started for Paris, but the fortnight's delay had enabled the leaguers to collect stores, to arm themselves against a siege, to send appeals for help to the Pope, the King of Spain and other Catholic potentates. It did not take Henry long to gain complete command of the Seine above and below Paris, as well as the outskirts of that city, and by 8 May his artillery on Montmartre began to worry the inhabitants. It was a curious situation. An army of about 15,000 men blockaded Paris and St-Denis, in which were forces some six times the number of the besiegers. The monks and priests of Paris were armed, Capuchins with cuirasses over their frocks, Dominicans with pikes and arquebuses in their hands, curés with plumes and swords, prelates with helmets and lances, few of them expert in the use of weapons and some of them more dangerous to friends than to enemies. When the King's forces first passed close to the city early in the morning, the sound of the reveille by their drums, trumpets, clarions and hautbois caused a panic within the walls, on hearing which Henry said: 'My Mistress,' as he usually called his capital, 'is very cruel to me, being displeased when I bid her good-morning or send soft music to enliven her.' Such was his mood at the moment, but with the prolongation of the siege he grew sad.

Within a few weeks the famine inside the city became terrible. The poor were soon reduced to eating bran; but when stores of grain and other food were discovered in the monasteries and the houses of the ecclesiastics, the priests and friars were compelled to feed the needy. That being exhausted, all the dogs and cats, the horses, rats and mice were killed and boiled, and sometimes dead or dying children were added to the pot. St-Denis capitulated, the garrison receiving favourable terms from Henry, but though half the population of Paris was dead or dying the city continued to hold out in the belief that it would be succoured either by a new League army or by Our Lady of Loretto, who received the daily lamentations and prayers of the populace. The novel suggestion of making paste from the powdered bones of disinterred bodies was acted upon, but the effect was innutritious.

After darkness had fallen on 23 July a quantity of starving people managed to leave the city by dropping from the walls. They implored the King for bread, with permission to quit the pest-holes in which they had been living. He could not resist such an appeal, gave them food and allowed several thousands of them to pass his lines; on hearing which Elizabeth of England wrote to him:

> If so many of the besieged had not left the city by your permission, famine would of necessity have forced them to yield. I am astonished that you should have allowed yourself to be persuaded to this imminent risk after so many delays and postponements. But you are only too tardy in doing good for yourself, loving rather to hazard all than to make an end.

But Elizabeth's heart was stonier than Henry's.

The puppet-king Charles X having recently died in captivity, the real King felt that the time had come when the poor inhabitants of Paris should be delivered from their evil leaders and given the chance to acknowledge their rightful monarch. With this purpose Henry chose 24 July for a night assault, which he witnessed from the top of Montmartre. Following two hours of terrific combat, when it seemed to the onlookers that the whole city was ablaze, all the *faubourgs* were taken, and Henry would have ordered the mining of the gates if he had not still hoped to enter Paris without unnecessary bloodshed, his humanity preventing him from gaining the capital. Again and again he was urged by his officers to seize the city and not to relieve the situation within the walls by conniving at the escape of famished wretches whose hunger drove them frantic, but his reply never varied in essence: 'I am not surprised that the Spaniards and the chiefs of the League have no compassion upon the poor people: they are only tyrants. But for me, who am their father and their King, I cannot bear the recital of their calamities without being pierced to my inmost soul and ardently desiring to afford them relief.' He even allowed representatives of the League to travel to Meaux and see the Duke of Mayenne, on condition that the city should be delivered up to him if the Duke did not compel him to raise the siege by battle. He was heard to say that for a battle with the enemy he would give one of his fingers, for a general peace two.

His good nature temporarily caused his undoing. News came that the famous Spanish general, the Duke of Parma, advancing from the Netherlands with an army to relieve Paris, would shortly join Mayenne. Taking the advice of Marshal Biron, which no doubt suited his love of action, Henry marched to Chelles in the hope that the Duke of Parma would fight. But the Spanish commander evaded him, and many of his own followers, disappointed by his refusal to let them pillage Paris, deserted him. 'God grant me peace that I may enjoy a few years of rest!' he wrote to Corisande: 'Indeed I watch without ceasing. It is scarcely credible how many persons are employed about me to kill me, but God will defend me.' And again: 'You would pity me if you saw me, for I am so burdened with business that I absolutely sink under the weight of it.' He had said before the battle of Arques that he was a King without a kingdom, a husband without a wife, and a warrior without money. He still lacked all three, and his situation had deteriorated owing to his clemency. But he made up for the lack of a wife by seducing two attractive nuns in the convents he used as headquarters during the siege of Paris, repaying them for their complaisance with the Abbeys of Vernon and Montmartre, and possibly a third who received the Abbey of Maubuisson. He had in a sense already begun to flirt with the Church.

Having obeyed the orders of his master Philip of Spain by relieving, garrisoning and provisioning Paris, the Duke of Parma began his slow return to Belgium. All the way he was harried by the King, once again a guerrilla leader, who cut off detachments of Spaniards, captured much baggage, attacked the army at every halt, and spent nearly the whole of November in daily skirmishes with the retreating enemy, varying the toil of these exploits by wooing a new object of desire, which, wrote a virtuous biographer, 'occupied more of his thoughts and time than was consistent with his duties as a King and a general.'

She was the lovely Gabrielle d'Estrées, descended on her mother's side from a family of which some thirty females were notorious for their love-affairs, one of them being able to boast that she had been the mistress of the French King Francis I, of the Emperor Charles V, and of Pope Clement VII. The lady who received Henry's attentions, known in history and song as 'La Belle Gabrielle', had five sisters and a brother, the family being known in Paris as the Seven Deadly Sins. She had been brought up at the castle of Cœuvres, the residence in Picardy of her father Antoine d'Estrées, and was about twenty years old when she caught the fancy of Henry. Like Corisande, she had fair hair, blue eyes and pink cheeks, but she was not plump like Henry's earlier mistress, and her hair had a golden sheen. Her features and limbs were described as perfectly proportioned, and certainly her admirers found them so. One of her two lovers, M. de Bellegarde, spoke so highly of her beauty that Henry wished to see her. He went to Cœuvres, saw her, and agreed with Bellegarde. To prove the extent of his passion he later dodged the forces of the League in the disguise of a peasant, arriving at the castle with a sack of straw on his head; but his appearance on that occasion did not please Gabrielle, who continued to favour Bellegarde. Henry was not one to share favours, and when his headquarters were established at Mantes early in 1591 he made the Marquis d'Estrées a member of his council, ordering him to bring his family there. The Marquis being of an obliging nature, Gabrielle underwent a nominal marriage in 1592 with M. de Liancourt, a rich elderly widower who was advised to claim no rights as a husband and ordered to accept the annulment of the marriage some two years later. By this convenient arrangement Gabrielle became the King's official mistress.

She was present at the siege of Chartres in 1591 when Henry decided to reduce that city in reply to a series of papal Bulls, anathemas and what-not against the excommunicated heretic, which incidentally aroused the patriotic feelings of those towns like Tours that recognized Henry as King of France, their parliaments declaring the Bulls abusive, scandalous, seditious, mendacious and contrary to the liberties of the Gallican Church, and ordering them to be burnt in public by the executioner. Chartres surrendered in two months, and on Henry's entry the chief magistrate accompanied the ceremony of delivering the keys with a lengthy harangue, wherein the King was informed that the city was subject to him by divine and civil law, at which point Henry's boredom got the better of him and putting spurs to his horse remarked: 'Ay, and add also by the *cannon* law.' He then set out for Noyon with his army and Gabrielle. The garrison there put up a stiff resistance, but in August the governor asked for terms. With his invariable chivalry the King gave the garrison two days to enable Mayenne to raise the siege by a battle. But the Duke did not fancy an encounter with Henry and the town surrendered with a considerable accumulation of stores and ammunition. The gratification derived from this success was much diminished by the news of the death while besieging the castle of Lamballe of the great Protestant soldier François de la Noue, who was described by a writer of the time '*Homme sans peur et sans reproche* – the Bayard of the Huguenots.' It must be remembered that while Henry was conducting the chief campaign there were innumerable petty wars going on all over France between the partisans of the King and those of the League.

Henry had little time to spare for the indulgence of grief, and following a series of actions that would have earned a rest for most commanders he laid siege to Rouen, the last important city held by the League in the north. Elizabeth of England had just sent nearly five thousand men under the Earl of Essex, who joined forces with Marshal Biron in an endeavour to take the city. In a mood of gratitude Henry wrote to ask Elizabeth if he might cross the channel to kiss her hands and spend two hours in her company, so that for once in his life he could see the Queen to whom he was devoted body and soul, to whom he wished to consecrate his life, since he loved and revered her more than anybody or anything in the world. His letter to Gabrielle at the same time expressed precisely the same feelings for her, with the addition that he had never loved anyone else. His method of address pleased the recipients, revealed his emotional susceptibility, and harmed no one, though his mutability was liable to misinterpretation. Patient in war and politics, he was impatient in love. 'If you are a day late, I shall die', he wrote when expecting a visit from Gabrielle; and when she did not turn up at the promised time he dashed off a message: 'I swear I hate you and I will not kiss your lovely mouth, even if you beg me.'

Biron, whose loyalty was questionable, did not press the siege of Rouen with much vigour, and Essex sent the governor, Admiral Villars, a defiance which must have amused that tough fighter. The governor was challenged to meet the Earl on horseback or on foot, in armour or in his doublet, man to man or twenty to twenty or sixty to sixty, the object of Essex being to maintain that the cause of the King was better than that of the League, Essex himself a braver man than Villars, and Essex's mistress more beautiful than that of his opponent. The governor replied that duty prevented him from accepting the challenge, but he gave Essex the lie on all three points, adding that he did not much trouble himself about the last of them.

The arrival of Henry brought some energy and common sense into these proceedings, and the soldiers of the attacking forces again witnessed a King working in the trenches, constantly exposing himself to danger, leading storming parties, and risking his life in what his officers regarded as foolhardy excursions. A Dutch fleet brought reinforcements to the attackers, but at last the Duke of Parma promised succour to the besieged, and Henry went off to meet him. During the operation that ensued the King behaved in such a manner that neither his followers nor Parma could believe their eyes. He wished to find out the exact strength and disposition of the Duke's army; so having occupied the small town of Aumale he ordered 500 arquebusiers to defend the walls, 300 horsemen to keep along the edge of a hill ready to help if needed, and with 100 men he advanced to meet an army of 30,000. Rosny described the sensation of the watchers:

We looked at each other astonished to the last degree at a plan in which we saw nothing but rashness, that seemed destined to consign the King to certain death. No one daring to speak, and not being able to hold my tongue, I was in the end deputed in the name of all to represent to the King the danger to which he exposed himself, and to endeavour to make him change his resolution, which I executed, softening the terms as much as possible.

Henry simply replied that they were afraid. Rosny still protested, begging him to retire. 'Believe me,' said Henry, 'I am not so rash as you may imagine. I am as careful of my skin as another, and I will retire at the proper moment, so that no evil shall occur.' The Duke of Parma naturally assumed that the small body of horse confronting him was being used as a stratagem to lure him on, the whole royal army being concealed. But at length it dawned on him that no army lay in wait for him, and he ordered the cavalry to charge. Henry was driven back to a point where his cavalry should have been ready, but they had retired, and when he gave the order to charge no one appeared in support. The Spanish rushed on again, broke up his small squadron, and Henry with a few friends fought-hand-to-hand against a host. Somehow he managed to rally the remnant of his troop and single-handed kept the enemy at bay while his forty survivors crossed the bridge of Aumale. As he followed the last man he received the ball of a carbine in his back, but succeeded in reaching the spot where the rest of his horse were waiting. The appearance of this fresh body, coupled with the news that the King was present in person, convinced Parma that the royal army was near; so he recalled his cavalry, and Henry was enabled to reach Neufchâtel where his wound received attention. Before it had healed he was again in the saddle, saying to those who begged him to be more prudent that he must postpone the healing of his wound to a more convenient season. But he recognized that he had taken an unnecessary risk and always spoke of that engagement as 'the error of Aumale', in the course of which he was seriously wounded for the first and only time.

As a rule his hazardous adventures were justified, and he explained why: 'You say that I run too much risk. I don't do it because I want to but because I am obliged to. If I don't go into danger, nobody else will. They are all volunteers; I can't force them.' His mistake at Aumale was shortly followed by a blunder on the part of that otherwise cautious Duke of Parma, who after relieving Rouen advanced against Caudebec and placed his army in a dangerous position between two rivers. It seemed as if he would be forced to surrender, but aided by a misty night he contrived to get his army across the Seine on rafts and boats; and then commenced a slow retreat towards Belgium, leaving Mayenne in charge of Rouen. Had it been a mere question of dealing with the leader of the League, Henry would have felt reasonably secure, for 'my cousin of Mayenne is a great captain, but I am an earlier riser than he.' But his chief difficulty lay in maintaining harmony among his own followers. 'No labyrinth,' remarked Rosny, 'was ever equal to that complication of interests which divided the different parts composing the army of the King.' He had been too busy to receive that instruction in the Catholic faith which he had promised, or possibly his innate shrewdness had caused the delay; but now the Catholics, tired of war, threatened to abandon him if he did not abjure the Protestant religion, while the Huguenots menaced him with desertion if he embraced Catholicism. The Swiss and Germans refused to fight unless they were regularly paid; while the English, quite the best of his alien helpers, would not go beyond the Seine, regarding the sea as their only security. With such divisions among his troops, he did what he had always done in similar circumstances, detaching a portion of his army to follow Parma, sending another into quarters at Caen, and allowing others to return to their homes. After a vigorous campaign he solaced himself for a while in the company of Gabrielle, leaving her the moment he heard that a cannon ball had decapitated Marshal Biron at the siege of Épernay, and dashing thither forced the town to surrender in August 1592.

Parma died in December and the situation in Paris became acute. A moderate section of the League formed a Third Party, which was determined that the Crown should remain in the royal house of France, the plan being to marry the Infanta of Spain to a French prince of the blood, who must be a Catholic.

But there was also a strongly anti-Spanish feeling among the moderates, and Henry felt that the time had arrived when he must either become a Catholic or give up all hope of being King of France in anything but name. He entered into negotiations with the Vatican and into conversations with theologians.

Gabrielle d'Estrées, Marchioness of Monceaux,
subsequently Duchess of Beaufort (1573–1599)

Marie of Medici (1573-1642), second wife of Henry,
by Pourbus

CHAPTER FIVE

For the Country

Henry is supposed to have said that Paris was well worth a mass. He may not have said it but he certainly meant it. Indeed he was keenly aware that the amity and prosperity of the whole country depended upon himself and that civil war would be a permanent condition in France unless he became a Catholic. The situation as he saw it was simple enough. He thought that if he remained a Protestant nearly all the princes of the blood royal, the nobility and those at the head of affairs, would join the League; whereas if he became a Catholic the majority of Protestants would unite against him and elect another leader. So he discussed these points with his chief friend and adviser Rosny, a staunch Huguenot, who assured him that if he continued to treat them with the esteem and respect due to their services the Protestants would not rebel against him, for all their intelligent leaders knew that his conversion was essential in the interests of France. Rosny went further, saying that the foundation of all religions which believed in Jesus Christ was the same: i.e. faith in the same mysteries and the same notions of the Divinity. It seemed to him that one who left Catholicism for Protestantism, or the other way about, did not change his religion, but followed for the sake of religion itself what policy suggested as the proper means to compose all differences. Although, Rosny admitted, this opinion might be erroneous, yet it was an incontestable truth that embracing the Catholic faith did not include the persecuting of all others. On the contrary, it was more than likely that God had disposed the King to make this change in order to give a new example to Europe, one more worthy of religion itself. The difference of religion, he went on, had for too long a period produced the most tragical effects in France and was a perpetual source of disorders and calamities, because of the aversion with which it inspired Catholics and Protestants alike against those of a contrary faith. The King, he believed, could remedy the evil by uniting those who professed both religions in the bonds of Christian charity and love; or, if this were impossible, by prescribing to them rules so just that both parties were contented with what was granted them. In conclusion Rosny exhorted the King to immortalize his memory by restoring harmony, plenty and security to a kingdom wasted with intestine divisions, and by the use of those abilities he had received from Heaven to merit the glory of giving happiness to France after she had begun to despair of it, thinking her wounds incurable.

Knowing that Rosny was much too astute to give advice that was not backed by knowledge and cogitation, Henry professed to be touched to his heart's core by his friend's discourse; and certainly it must have relieved his mind to know that he could still depend on the Huguenots if he joined the communion of their persecutors. He told Rosny that, though something still made him resist, he believed he would follow the counsel to which he had just listened. 'I can never use them ill, nor declare war against them, for I shall always love them', said Henry of his loyal Protestants, who after all had placed him where he was. But men are seldom grateful to those who help them to power, and few have had Henry's tenacious memory for benefits received.

It is possible that, had he relied solely on Huguenot support in France, backed by the Protestant powers of England and Holland, some German princes and a few Swiss cantons, he could have been placed securely on the throne without

Catholic assistance; but he wished to win his country with the aid of his countrymen, and he coveted the hearts of Frenchmen more than the Crown of France. Many years later, writing of Henry's conversion, Rosny declared that 'a Prince who had never deceived mankind could have no intention to deceive his God', and he believed that the King had honestly accepted the Catholic dogmas before joining the Roman Church. But there can be little doubt that Henry had made up his mind to be convinced before he received the necessary tuition; and those who think that religion should unite men instead of sundering them can perceive what was hidden from so many of his contemporaries: that, whatever his private thoughts and feelings, he was in effect more religious than any leader of his age, for he preserved the existence of his country by giving it tranquillity and abundance after a generation of savagery hardly paralleled in the world's history. In view of that fact the question of whether he subscribed to the doctrines of Rome or Geneva seems irrelevant and insignificant. He believed in God because he believed in himself, knowing that some power worked through him without conscious cerebration on his part, and that this power must be miraculous.

He had not a streak of the fanatic within him, and if it had been necessary for his benevolent purpose he would have embraced any so-called religion. But for the sake of the consciences of his countrymen, not of his own, he underwent the process of instruction and initiation. The extreme Huguenots always thought him indifferent to their doctrines and the extreme Catholics would never believe him to be a true convert; but fortunately neither extremity mattered greatly, for the people as a whole were solely concerned with food and peace, while the majority of nobles and politicians were mainly anxious that France should be ruled by a Frenchman who was not a puppet of Spain. It was fortunate for Henry that Philip II was the most stupid monarch in Europe, fortunate too that Mayenne was equally obtuse. Philip annoyed the French by announcing that he had selected the young Duke of Guise as the husband of his daughter; and Mayenne tried to convince the Spanish Ambassador that his son should marry the Infanta, at the same time swearing to the Spaniards that he would never recognize Henry as King whether he became a Catholic or not. The States-General, which met at Paris in January 1593, were clearly of opinion that, whoever married the Spanish princess, the influence of Spain would become paramount in France, a situation they declined to consider; and in April a conference took place between their deputies and the King's.

Meanwhile Henry was at Mantes attending many discussions between Catholics and Protestants. It seems likely that the leading Protestants such as Philippe Duplessis-Mornay, perceiving that Henry's conversion would benefit France, did not argue their case very cogently, for one of them admitted that 'God is not less honoured in the Roman Church than in that of the Reformation' and that salvation might be obtained in each. Since the Catholics would not make a similar avowal, Henry had a sound argument in favour of conversion. 'Prudence requires that I should be of the Catholic religion, not of yours', he told a Protestant minister, 'because in being of theirs I am saved, both according to them and according to you, but being of yours I am only saved according to you, not according to them.' The Archbishop of Bourges, Renaud de Beaune, a man of piety and persuasive talent, brought all his eloquence to bear on Henry, quoting the fathers of the Church and the works of many wise and godly men to convince the King, who had never had time to read them. He then repaired to St-Denis for further instruction, and summoned a number of the clergy in Paris, some of them fanatical preachers of the League. The Spaniards in control of the city as well as the Papal Legate were furious, and the latter threatened those who complied with the King's request with the loss of their benefices, not to speak of the Pope's censure. The curé of

St Eustacia expressed the view of the more Christian element, boldly declaring that his conscience and the canons of the Church did not permit him to refuse help to a heretic willing to be converted, adding that the Legate, if he did his duty, would also join in the good work. While the Legate paused to think that out, the curé and his 'even Christians' went to St-Denis, where they laboured with the Archbishop of Bourges and other bishops to bring the willing convert into the fold.

One Cardinal did his utmost to prevent the King from receiving absolution except by the Pope, and the Legate publicly forbade the prelates and other ecclesiastics of France to receive Henry into the Church; but people were getting tired of papal, Spanish and League fulminations; they wanted a French monarch who would know how to deal with foreign influences; and when Henry decided to abjure, the country as a whole welcomed the news with relief.

The ceremony of abjuration took place on 25 July 1593. 'On Sunday I shall take the perilous leap', he wrote to Gabrielle, who had also persuaded him to take it. 'While I am writing to you I have a hundred troublesome people about me.' At eight o'clock in the morning of that day, his black cloak and hat covering a dress of white satin, Henry went to the church of St-Denis accompanied by the princes of the royal house, many noblemen and the Crown officers, preceded by the French, Scotch and Swiss guards. The streets, strewn with flowers, were filled with a vast crowd that had ignored the prohibition to witness the ceremony issued by the authorities in Paris, and the cry of *Vive le Roi!* went up from countless throats. He was received at the entrance of the church by the Archbishop of Bourges, other church dignitaries, and the monks of St-Denis carrying cross and holy water. The Archbishop asked his name. 'I am the King.' The Archbishop asked what he sought. 'I seek to be received into the bosom of the Apostolical and Roman Catholic Church.' The Archbishop wished to know whether he really desired it. 'I do.'

Henry then knelt and read his profession of faith, the form of which was perhaps diluted to suit his position. Having received absolution and benediction, he made oath of his profession of faith at the altar, confessed to the Archbishop, and witnessed the celebration of High Mass. He heard vespers the same evening at St-Denis and gave thanks in the church of Montmartre.

An incident during the formalities at St-Denis gave him a little light relief, and he wrote to Gabrielle: 'A pleasant adventure happened to me at church; an old woman of eighty years of age seized me by the head and kissed me. I was not the first who laughed at it. Tomorrow you shall sweeten my mouth.'

Although he remained a sound Roman Catholic for the rest of his life and did his best to convert others, he attached little importance to ritual and dogma, and never changed in his fundamental feeling that goodness of heart, not doctrinal belief, was all-important. 'Those who straightly follow their consciences belong to my religion,' he had written in 1577, 'and I belong to that of all who are good and brave.' On the subject of Catholics and Protestants he once remarked to Duplessis-Mornay: 'Perhaps the difference between the two religions only appears to be so great by reason of the animosity of those that preach them. By exercising my authority I shall some day try to arrange everything.' Being a true Catholic he succeeded.

Henry's conversion brought to an end 'the wars of religion'. The League continued to make trouble in the interests of Spain, and its leader Mayenne curried favour with Philip and the Pope by forcing the States-General to accept the decrees of the Council of Trent, which meant the establishment of the Inquisition in France, a course that had been rejected by previous monarchs and parliaments as interfering with the civil authority, the independence of the nation, and the privileges of the Gallican Church.

In order to give the governors of towns occupied by the League sufficient time to reconsider their position and acknowledge the King, a three-months truce was granted immediately after the abjuration. The feeling in the country was now running so warmly in favour of Henry that most of the leading cities became royalist on terms favourable to the governors: that is, Henry had to pay heavily for their loyalty by leaving them in their positions and bribing them with promises of money. As time went on quite a number of Protestant noblemen and gentlemen followed their King into the Roman Church, but without waiting for the effects of his impressive example he despatched the Duke of Nevers to Rome with a message of spiritual submission to the Holy See and a promise to live and die in the Catholic communion. Difficulties were placed in the way of Nevers by interested parties, and Pope Clement VIII announced that he 'would never believe in the conversion of "the Béarnais" unless an angel was sent from heaven to assure him of it'. Apparently heaven, after thinking the matter over, obliged him with an angel; but at the time Nevers was so much annoyed by the indignities to which he was subjected that he left Rome in dudgeon. Henry was too crafty to depend for success on the display of regal splendour afforded by Nevers, and private agents were already at work to obtain the papal absolution. The shifty Clement was sitting on a fence, supporting the League with promises until he felt quite certain of Henry's supremacy in France.

That supremacy was being bought with promises of rewards and pensions to the nobles who saw the way the wind was blowing and handed in their allegiance at a price; and when the three-months truce was over Henry refused to continue it, feeling that his authority now extended to most parts of the country. He wished to sheathe the sword of internecine strife and substitute bargaining for blood-letting. His method was successful, though it took him a long time to redeem his pledges. Knowing that the people would never regard him as their anointed King until he had been crowned, he determined that the coronation should take place at Chartres, since Rheims was still in the hands of the League. The moment his decision was announced, the Papal Legate, the Jesuits and all the anti-royalist clergy sent up jackal-howls about the excommunicated heretic, the counterfeit convertite, and threatened the pontiff's anathema on all, whether clergy or laity, who took part in or witnessed this unholy act of 'the Béarnais'. But Henry had no time to waste on anathemas, even when accompanied by maranathas, being perfectly well aware that curses and benedictions had their market-price; and on 27 February 1594 he was crowned at Chartres. The old crown had been melted down for coin by a party of leaguers, so a new one was made on credit for the present purpose, and Henry was anointed with the miraculous holy oil sent from heaven to St Martin and preserved in the Abbey at Tours. This was supposed to be equally efficacious with the holy oil from St-Rémy used for the many kings who had been anointed at Rheims.

There was still the question of Paris, for a king must be in possession of his capital. Henry had always longed to gain it without bloodshed, and several times his ambition had been sacrificed to his humanity. Now that the royalist feeling in that city had begun to manifest itself, he felt that the time had come to bribe the governor into acquiescence. The Duke of Mayenne had appointed the Count of Brissac as governor, and the Spanish general, the Duke of Feria, trusted the man, who had been treated well by Henry after the capture of Falaise. The promise of a marshal's baton, a handsome sum of money immediately it became available, a generous pension and the governorship of two towns, helped Brissac to see the light, and he agreed to let Henry into the city early in the morning of 22 March 1594. At the last moment the Papal Legate and the Spanish Duke became suspicious, and

when Brissac went the round of the walls on the night of
21 March he was accompanied by a party of Spanish soldiers
who had orders to kill him if they heard the least sound of an
enemy approaching the gates. But all was quiet at midnight,
and by two in the morning suspicion slept. At three o'clock
Brissac and his companions went to the Porte Neuve, which
they opened, and then let down the drawbridge. Rainy weather
made the King late, and the conspirators at the gate spent a
nervous period waiting for him. When the troops arrived
they marched through the gate and quietly took possession
of bridges, squares and ramparts, pointing their cannon down
the main streets. By the time Henry entered the city his
soldiers were in possession of it, and the mob were already
aware of the fact. To shouts of *Vive le Roi!* the first of the
Bourbon kings went to Notre Dame, where he heard Mass
and whence he proceeded to the Louvre, trumpets sounding,
bells ringing, people yelling with joy. 'I plainly perceive
that these poor people have been tyrannized over,' said he.

One of the first things he did was to send a message to Feria,
saying that he made the Spanish troops a present of their lives
and property on condition that they evacuated the city without
loss of time. Feria, unaccustomed to such generosity, muttered
'A great King! A great King!' and instantly made arrangements
to depart. When they left by the gate of St-Denis the King
saluted them by removing his hat. They acknowledged his
magnanimity. He replied with the utmost courtesy: 'Adieu,
gentlemen, adieu! Commend me to your master, and go in
peace, but do not come back again.' He next proclaimed a
general pardon to all who had been in arms against him, and
every leaguer was given the choice of taking the oath of
allegiance or receiving a passport to join Mayenne. Within
a few hours perfect tranquillity reigned throughout the city.
There was no butchery, no pillage. Henry had bought, not
fought, his way into Paris, and he tried to calm the anger of
those Huguenots who found his clemency unbearable: 'If you

and all who speak thus repeated every day your Pater Noster from your heart, you would not say what you have said . . . As God has pardoned me, so will I pardon others . . .'

When the Duchess of Montpensier heard that 'the Béarnais' had arrived, she screamed 'Is there no one who will stab him to the heart with a poniard?' Henry retaliated by assuring her of his esteem and of her own safety, inviting her to a game of cards that night, an invitation she accepted. By that time she had calmed down and was so much impressed by Henry's chivalrous attitude that she wished her brother Mayenne had lowered the drawbridge for his Majesty to enter his capital. '*Ventre Saint-Gris!*' cried Henry gaily, 'I should probably have had a long time to wait there, and should not have entered at so early an hour.' He was in a cheerful mood, and at dinner he rallied an ardent leaguer on the side he had espoused in the late troubles.

'Of a truth, sire,' said the man, 'I left the sun to follow the moon.'

'But what do you say now, seeing me installed in my good city of Paris?'

'I say, sire, that there is rendered unto Caesar the things that are Caesar's as there must be rendered unto God the things that are God's.'

'*Ventre Saint-Gris!* I have not been treated as Caesar, for nothing has been rendered to me but everything sold.' ('*On ne m'a rien rendu, mais tout vendu*'.)

He spoke in the presence of Brissac and others, who had done well out of the deal. They all enjoyed the joke.

CHAPTER SIX

Warrior and Lover

'You have played the part of Alexander long enough; it is now time that you should adopt that of Augustus. It is for us to die for you, and that is our glory; it is for you to live for France, and that is your duty.' So wrote Philippe Duplessis-Mornay to Henry, and the warning was needed. He was a born soldier and a great deal happier in a camp than in a Court. His popularity with his soldiers was due to his sharing their hardships and fighting more stubbornly than anyone in his army. They admired his good humour, comradeship, heroism and amorosity, and a favourite song among them ran:

> Vive Henri Quatre, vive ce roy vaillant!
> Ce diable à quatre a le triple talent
> De boire et de battre et d'être un vert galant.

We have seen that he risked his life again and again, knowing that it was the only way in which he could keep his heterogeneous followers together. His officers and men were always ready for mutiny, and he led a weary life between recalcitrant Catholics and suspicious Protestants. Rosny constantly reproved him for reckless self-exposure, once receiving this answer: 'I cannot do otherwise, my friend, for since it is for my glory and my crown that I fight, my life and everything else ought to be of no consideration with me; this is my fixed resolution.' And he would not face the alternative: 'It is much better that I should die with arms in my hands than live to see my kingdom ruined and myself forced to seek assistance from a foreign country.' There can be no doubt too that he enjoyed the thrill of action. 'If they make war on us like foxes, we will make it on them like lions', was his characteristic remark on hearing of some treacherous attempt to stir up trouble. He had an extremely adventurous disposition, often preferring hazard to caution; and though his attendants could not help admiring his coolness in the face of imminent peril, they sometimes showed reluctance when called upon to take part in actions they considered foolhardy. Though it was an honour to be picked for his bodyguard, the danger made it undesirable. He has been criticized as a strategist and tactician, but in the world of action success is the sole criterion and he was almost invariably successful, achieving ultimate triumph with unexampled fortitude and wariness.

Apart from his qualities as a professional soldier, he was a great leader of men, matched by few in history; but the distinguishing difference between him and all the other great leaders on record was his unfailing humanity and good nature. He had all the qualities that inspired fear but employed only those that engendered confidence. Even his enemies were impelled to acknowledge 'the natural sweetness of his disposition', and so kindly was he that he never proceeded to extremities until he had tried every other method. By nature passionate, experience and strength of character gave him self-control, compelling his reason to master his resentment. In an age of delirious intolerance he remained rational. 'Nothing is so easy as to discover faults in the actions of others,' he once said, and in a period when most men were blinded by prejudice he remarked: 'I never suffer my mind to be so wedded to any opinions as to refuse to listen to better ones when they are suggested to me.' His innate benevolence made him sympathize with his enemies. 'All the forests in my kingdom,' he declared, 'would not be sufficient to furnish timber for gallows if all those who have written or preached against me were to be hanged', but when asked to punish a man who had written a satire on his administration he refused: 'It would offend my conscience to give any man trouble for only speaking the truth'. Even his would-be assassins were treated with lenience. 'He is a wicked wretch whom God will punish without my interfering,' he said of one, and a madman who tried to poniard him on the Pont Neuf was let off with the excuse that he was sufficiently punished by his madness. The Jesuits continually preached against 'the Béarnais' and instigated their half-witted disciples to murder him, saying that such an act would be both lawful and meritorious; but he left them in peace until one of their misguided adherents made the attempt, when he took the advice of his prudent counsellors and banished the order – for a time.

Nothing enraged him more than to hear that his troops had pillaged a district, and on learning that the peasants in Champagne had suffered from their depredations he ordered the officers to see that all complaints were promptly satisfied, giving a typical reason for his humanity: 'Set off with all diligence. Give orders about this affair. You shall be answerable to me for it. What! if they ruin my people, who will feed me? Who will support the expenses of the state? Who will pay you your pensions, gentlemen? As God's alive, to take from my people is taking from myself.' It was his firm belief that 'the satisfaction derived from revenge endures but for a moment, but that which is the offspring of clemency is eternal.' On being told that his unprecedented generosity to his enemies might prove prejudicial to himself, he said: 'More flies are taken with one spoonful of honey than with ten vats of vinegar.'

Himself of a liberal and gregarious nature, he disliked meanness and exclusiveness in others, and one of the few severe actions recorded of him would be approved by most people of goodwill. He was hunting one day at Grosbois, and on an impulse fairly common with him, since he disliked any form of ceremony, he quitted his company and rode alone to Créteil, a league on the other side of the bridge of Charenton. By midday he felt ravenously hungry and entering an inn asked the landlady for something to eat. Taking him for an ordinary traveller, she answered that he had come too late. 'For whom is this roast meat I see at the fire?' he asked. 'For some gentlemen in the room above – solicitors, I think,' she replied. He sent them a civil message asking if he could have a piece of their roast meat, or have leave to sit at one end of their table on paying for it. They refused both requests. So Henry despatched someone to find his attendants, who were ordered to seize the solicitors, take them to Grosbois and have them soundly whipped to teach them more complaisance to gentlemen in future. The lawyers raised objections, no doubt sound legal ones, but they were duly whipped.

Henry liked escaping from the formalities of his entourage and being treated as an equal by innkeepers, peasants and modest citizens. Many stories of his adventures among them were told, one of which may find a place here since it derived from himself. Hunting in the Vendômois and temporarily separated from his suite, he saw a countryman sitting at the foot of a tree, asked what he was doing, and learnt that he was waiting to see the King pass by. 'If thou wilt mount upon the crupper of my horse, I will conduct thee to a place where thou shalt see him at thy ease,' said Henry. The peasant mounted and as they rode forward asked how he would be able to distinguish the King from his nobles, being told: 'Thou needst only look at him who shall have his hat on, while all the rest are bare-headed.' Soon they came up with the chase and all the nobles saluted. 'Well, which is the King?' asked Henry. '*Ma finte*, sir, it must be either you or me, for only us two have our hats on.'

Considering his quite exceptional amiability of temperament, coupled with his chivalry to women, and in this case his

tender affection, it is strange that he should have treated his
sister Catherine so badly. He wished her, for political reasons,
to marry the son of the Duke of Montpensier, and when he
heard that she was in love with the Count of Soissons, and
that they had exchanged written promises of marriage, he
was angry, partly because he disliked the secrecy of the act
and partly because he distrusted the motives of the Count.
Learning that the pair were together at Pau in January 1592,
he wrote to the Princess's chief adviser: 'I have heard with
extreme displeasure of the object with which the journey of
my cousin the Count of Soissons to Pau has been undertaken.
I will only observe to you that if anything passed to which,
contrary to my orders, you have consented, or at which you
have assisted, your head shall answer for it.' Catherine
entreated her brother to forgive the Count, which he did,
but ordered her to leave Pau, which she did. But she could not
be made to love the young man who, on his father's death
in 1592, became Duke of Montpensier, and Henry was not
too busy fighting to give his mind to that signed promise of
marriage between his sister and Soissons. He charged Rosny
to obtain it by ruse if possible, by force if necessary. Rosny
hated the job and tried to get out of it, but Henry insisted and
eventually Rosny had to visit Catherine, whose desire to
marry Soissons was encouraged by Henry's one-time mistress
Corisande, who perhaps still felt a little resentful towards
her former lover. The method adopted by Rosny to obtain
possession of the document was so shabby that for the rest
of his life he suffered uncomfortable sensations whenever he
thought of it. He more or less implied that, when the King
heard of the document's surrender, he would sanction their
marriage. It was promptly given up, but instead of consenting
to their union Henry continued to use his sister as a pawn in
the political game. It is true that the same kind of thing went
on in all the reigning families of Europe, and continued to do
so for as long as they lasted; but compared with any other

great ruler on record Henry was so compassionate and civilized, so Christian and humane, that such an act of his seems incomprehensible.

Apart from his treatment of his sister, Henry carried consideration for others as far as a human being in his position could and much further than anyone else in his time and place. At a period of bigotry and prejudice, he was open-minded and reasonable; when cruelty and hatred were too common to be noticed, he was gentle, merciful and friendly; encompassed by mendacity and trickery, he was honest and sincere. His character showed in his face. A frank cheerful countenance, bright widely-spaced eyes, broad forehead, finely shaped head, a nose that some called aquiline, others hawklike, a winning vivacious expression which became so lively in conversation that he often looked, if not handsome, extremely attractive; the whole complemented by easy, animated, insinuating, obliging manners, and an agreeable if sometimes ironic mode of speech. He was above middle height, carried himself with a martial air, and had an athletic body which enabled him to play games with exceptional dexterity, to tire out his companions when hunting, and to fight or work for days and nights without taking more than a few hours' rest at irregular intervals. He could sleep in any place and wake at any hour he pleased. In spite of his simple and candid air he was so vital and observant that nothing escaped his notice, and he could form a good judgment of a man's words and actions merely from look and manner, though his own rectitude made it difficult for him to believe others to be as corrupt as they were. He had remarkably quick hearing and piercing eyesight, enjoyed overhearing himself criticized, begged his friends to conceal nothing said to his disadvantage, and gave a ready ear to advice or censure.

Although he could act with amazing promptitude and presence of mind at moments of military or political crisis, he suffered from irresolution when worried, especially in his dealings with women, when he was at the mercy of his sensuality. He loved every kind of pleasure, from gaming to hunting, but the pleasure he found in the company of women outran all reason, and his natural gentleness made him weak where they were concerned. He did not allow them to influence his choice of ministers or servants; nor did he permit them to affect the deliberations and decisions of his Council; but they disturbed him, confused his judgment, forced him to spend large sums of money he could ill afford, and because of his obsession made him frequently act in a manner at variance with the promptings of his normal intelligence. Like all strong characteristics, sensuality is inborn and nearly always a sign of a generous nature. With Henry it was stronger than ambition, though perhaps it may be said that his desire to do good was stronger than anything else in his nature. Unfortunately, when lust was in the ascendant, all other desires were suspended and his native common sense did not operate. He was well aware of this and in later life spoke earnestly on the subject: 'I every day pray to God for three things: first that He would be pleased to pardon my enemies; secondly to grant me victory over my passions, and especially sensuality; thirdly that I may make a right use of the authority He has given me and never abuse it.' It is permissible to wonder whether he was much agitated over the grant of divine pardon to his enemies, though no doubt he wished it when he prayed for it.

He indulged in many minor love-affairs, some sixty of which have been traced by careful historians, which resulted in eleven natural children whose paternity was acknowledged and no doubt many others who were supported but not recognized. Only three of these illicit unions were of importance in his life, and each lasted about nine years. The first, with Corisande Countess of Guiche, we have already described. She helped Henry in countless ways during his early years of struggle as a Huguenot leader. The second, with Gabrielle d'Estrées, now engages our attention. The third, with a very different sort of woman, we shall deal with on a later page.

Henry was thirty-eight years old when his *liaison* with Gabrielle began. She may have had two lovers already, the Dukes of Longueville and Bellegarde, and in the early days of Henry's passion he was extremely jealous of Bellegarde, who visited her when the King was busy campaigning. 'You know how offended I was on arriving in your presence, on account of my competitor's journey', wrote Henry to Gabrielle, having discovered that Bellegarde had been to see her. 'The power which your eyes had over me saved you from half of my complaints. You satisfied me in regard to speech, though not in heart; but if I had known what I have since learnt about the said journey . . . I would not have gone to see you, but would have broken off everything at once.' She had promised never to see Bellegarde again, but 'What can you promise me save what you have already done?' Henry broke out. 'What faith can you pledge me save that which you have twice failed to keep? You must give effect to your promises; you must no longer say *I will do*, you must say *I do*. Make up your mind then, my mistress, to have but one *serviteur* . . . My love can be altered by nothing in the world – except a rival.' Bellegarde was duly dismissed, and in the autumn of 1593 Gabrielle became pregnant. The first of the King's sons by her, born in June 1594, received the Christian name of César. Henry was proud of the occurrence and celebrated this confirmation of their union by making a triumphal torchlight entry into Paris on 15 September. She preceded the King in a gorgeous litter, her jewellery sparkling in the flickering lights, her black satin gown 'tufted all over with white'. He followed on horseback across the Pont Notre Dame, his dress of grey velvet, adorned with gold, his grey hat with white plumes, being matched by a dapple-grey horse. Surrounded by nobles and a bodyguard of cavalry, he acknowledged the loud cries of *Vive le Roi!* with a laughing face, and saluted the women at the windows by waving his hat.

In January 1595 Gabrielle's marriage to M. de Liancourt was annulled. She received the title of Marchioness of Monceaux; negotiations were speeded up for a divorce from Margaret, who had been living for many years at the castle of Usson in the Auvergne; and Henry legitimized Gabrielle's son in formal manner, duly registered by the parliament of Paris; a curious document containing these phrases:

> Whereas We have desired to have issue and to leave it, after Us, to this kingdom, and whereas God has not yet allowed Us to have any in lawful wedlock, since the Queen, Our spouse, has been for ten years separated from Us, it has been Our desire, pending the time when He may graciously give Us heirs, who may legitimately succeed to this crown, to endeavour to have children elsewhere . . . on this account, then, having recognized the many great graces and perfections, as much of mind as of body, that abide in the person of Our very dear and well-beloved Gabrielle d'Estrées, We, for some years past, have sought her to that effect, as being the subject whom We judged to be the most worthy of Our friendship; which We held We might do with all the less scruple and burdening of conscience, as We know that the marriage which she had previously contracted with the Sieur de Liancourt was null, and had never had effect, as is testified by the judgment of separation and annulment of the said marriage, which has since ensued. And whereas, the said Lady, after Our long suit and by the exercise of such authority as We brought to bear, did condescend to obey Us and do Our pleasure, and whereas it has pleased God that she should not long since give Us a son . . . etc., etc.

Disliking fibs and formalities, Henry must have cast a whimsical eye over the foregoing and wondered why legitimization should be a more solemn affair than procreation.

Without confiding in anyone Henry soon made up his mind to marry Gabrielle and urged forward his emissaries at Rome

to obtain the papal absolution as a preliminary to divorcing
Margaret, who offered no opposition but demanded too much
money for her compliance; and as Henry's counsellors were
strongly advising him to marry a foreign princess, the haggling
of Margaret and the hesitation of the monarch delayed the
divorce for some years. Gabrielle appealed to him both as
companion and bedfellow. He could confide all his secrets
and anxieties to her, receiving consolation and profiting from
her sensible opinions. She was popular at Court because she
had a gentle nature and tried to reconcile conflicting interests.
A Catholic herself, she did not take sides in the perpetual
quarrels between the two religions, but helped Henry to
compose them and supported his desire to give the Protestants
freedom of worship and political equality. She was partly
responsible for the submission of certain leaders of the League,
and it was she who advised the King to appoint Rosny as his
minister of finance, though this must have occurred in time
without her advice.

Henry could not be sexually faithful to anyone for a protracted period, but he was more so to her than to any other
woman because her mind attracted him as much as her body.
We have glimpses of them together on all sorts of occasions.
Attending the baptism of her aunt's son in November 1594:
'From the moment when the King, who was dressed in grey,
entered the church until he left it he did not cease laughing
with the Lady of Liancourt and caressing her, sometimes in
one way sometimes in another.' On 17 March 1595 'there
was great thunder in Paris, with lightning and tempest, while
the King was hunting in the country round Paris with his
Gabrielle, the newly-created Marchioness of Monceaux,
she by the King's side and he holding her hand. She was on
horseback, riding like a man, dressed entirely in green; and
she returned with him to Paris in that attire'. At another
christening it is related, 'the King amused himself in keeping
her *coiffure* in order, and told her that she had not enough

diamonds in her hair; for she had only twelve and it was said that she ought to have had fifteen'. Of course he loaded her with presents, not to mention offices for her relations and estates for herself; but this was only to be expected. What everyone thought peculiar was the outward manifestation of his love. Even when playing tennis he suspended the games to caress her 'before everybody'. At masquerades she would unmask and kiss him, their public behaviour little resembling that of the average king and queen, though she was certainly treated as vicereine. In her peculiar position she was susceptible to slander, which always amused Henry, and we hear from several chroniclers of a typical episode. The pair were being ferried across the river, neither of them recognized by the ferryman, who complained of the taxes. 'But doesn't the King intend to amend all those taxes?' asked Henry. 'Oh, the King is a fairly good fellow,' answered the other, 'but he has a mistress who requires so many fine gowns and so many gewgaws that there is no end to it all, and we have to pay for it. It might be allowable if she belonged only to him, but it's said that she lets many another caress her.' This was more than Gabrielle could bear and she said in a rage that the man ought to be hanged. But Henry took the thing lightly: 'You are silly. This is only a poor devil soured by poverty. I have decided that he shall pay no more dues for his ferryboat, and I am sure he will sing every night *Vive Henri et Vive Gabrielle!*'

Whenever apart Gabrielle received constant letters and messages from Henry, and it is clear that she occupied his thoughts, however trying the circumstances:

I am sending you a company of fairly good violin-players to divert both yourself and your subject, who will cherish you extremely.

I write to you, *mes chères amours*, from the feet of your portrait, which I worship only because it was done for you, not that it resembles you. I can be no competent judge of it, for I have painted you all perfection to my soul, my heart and my eyes.

My beautiful angel . . . I wear only black, and indeed I am a widower of all that can give me any joy and contentment.

I do not know what charm you have used, but I did not bear previous absences so impatiently as I do this one. It seems to me that a century has passed since I left you . . . I have neither artery nor muscle that does not at every moment bring the thought of seeing you before me and make me feel distressed at your absence. Believe me, my dear sovereign, never did love do me such violence as it does now.

Not a single day have I failed to send you a messenger. My love makes me as exacting in my duty as in demanding your favour, which is my only treasure. Believe me, my lovely angel, that I esteem the possession of it as highly as the honour of winning ten battles. Be glorious in the fact that you have vanquished me, who was never entirely vanquished except by you.

Come, come, *mes chères amours*, and honour with your presence one who, were he free, would travel a thousand leagues to cast himself at your feet, never again to stir from them.

No woman is like you, and no man equals me in knowing how to love. My passion remains the same as when I first began to love you, my desire to see you again is more violent than it was then.

You will soon see a horseman who loves you dearly and who is called King of France and Navarre, a title which is certainly very honourable but very burdensome: that of your subject is a far more delightful one. All three together are good, with whatever sauce they may be served, and I am resolved to surrender them to no one.

I make this letter very short, so that you may go to sleep again directly you have read it.

I cherish your good grace more than I do my life, and yet I am fond of myself.

To spend the month of April apart from one's mistress is not to live.

This last sentiment, usually associated with adolescence, came from a man of forty-five, Gabrielle being then twenty-seven and putting on weight to an extent that caused some contemporaries to describe her as stout. No wonder that Henry wrote to Elizabeth of England: '*L'amour est une passion à laquelle toutes les autres doivent obéissance*', though he might perhaps have addressed the remark to a more promising object. He probably considered that lady's love-life as something of an enigma. His own amorous intrigues were the theme of gossip at the English Court, and it is not unlikely that Shakespeare, whose *Love's Labour's Lost* deals with a King of Navarre and his followers Biron and Longaville, had some of Henry's exploits in mind when writing the lines

> For valour, is not Love a Hercules,
> Still climbing trees in the Hesperides?

Henry was interested in the private lives of his fellow-monarchs and asked the ambassador of Rudolph II whether the Emperor had any mistresses. 'If he has, they are kept secret', returned the cautious diplomat. 'It is true that some men have not enough great qualities to cover their failings', said Henry, who, however, showed no enthusiasm when Pierre Mathieu, selected to write the King's biography, read aloud a passage describing his partiality for women. 'What is the use of revealing that weakness?' asked Henry. 'It will be a lesson for your son,' said the historian. 'Yes, yes, the whole truth must be told,' agreed Henry after a pause. 'If you were to remain silent about my failings people would not believe you about the rest. Well, set them down so that my son may know and avoid them.'

But when weaknesses are exposed in order to be avoided they are usually copied. Mathieu would have done better to reveal the failings as an integral part of his subject's virtues and therefore necessary to an understanding of his character.

CHAPTER SEVEN

Fighting and Finance

The master of Paris could now consider himself King of France, but Henry still had to appease the Protestants who felt he had let them down and bribe the Catholics who refused to be let down. More and more towns were surrendered by their League governors at blackmail prices, such as Rouen, Rheims, Troyes, Beauvais and Amiens, and in all these dealings Henry's tact amounted to genius, though it cost him the goodwill of the Protestants, who complained bitterly that the Catholics were getting good jobs and money while they had to live on kind thoughts and promises. To raise troops he again appealed to the English Queen, explaining that his motives in changing his religion were purely political. Elizabeth, though friendly, lectured him: 'It is indeed a most perilous thing to do evil that good may come.'

One more attempt was made by Spain to animate the League and in the course of it Henry had a narrow escape. The Spanish general, Count Charles of Mansveldt, entered Picardy with an army, and it became necessary for Henry to take the well-fortified town of Laon. He laid siege to it with his usual vigour and defeated the attempts of Mansveldt and Mayenne to supply the place, capturing their large convoys of provisions. Since Mayenne was over-cautious it must have been the Spaniard's plan on being reinforced to make a surprise attack on Henry's camp and break through his lines to the beleaguered town. Marshal Biron, son of the man whose head had been blown off at another siege, treated the rumour of the meditated attack with contempt, but Henry did not feel so certain and sent the Baron of Givri with three hundred horse to reconnoitre, telling him not to come back without full knowledge of the enemy's forces and present situation. After three days Givri reported that the Spaniards appeared to be making arrangements for their retreat to Flanders and that not a single company was on the near side of the river Oise. Trusting this report Henry dined that night with thirty friends at St-Lambert, a forest-encompassed house that he had known as a youth. He had been busy all day in the trenches 'in his old grey doublet and darned trunk-hose with dogskin leggings'; his feet were bandaged and bleeding from his exertions; he was tired out; and after dinner he fell asleep. Rosny tells us what then happened:

It was extremely hot, and eight or ten of us went to seek for coolness in the thickest part of the forest of Folambray, at a little distance from the high road between La Fère and Laon. We had not proceeded more than twelve or fifteen hundred paces when a noise, which was heard from the side of La Fère, caused us to give an ear attentively. It seemed the confused mixture of human voices, smacking of whips, neighing of horses, and a dull buzz like the sound of trumpets and drums heard in the distance. We advanced as far as the high road to hear better, and we then saw distinctly, at about eight hundred paces before us, what appeared to be a column of foreign infantry, marching in good order and without noise. That which we had heard was caused by the servants and camp followers, which came after, and by the drivers of a considerable force of artillery. Carrying our view as far as it would reach, we saw defile after these waggons so great a number of troops that we no longer doubted that it was the whole army of the enemy.

We returned hastily upon our steps, and finding the King, who, just awakened, was shaking a plum tree, the fruit of which we had found delicious, 'Pardie, sire,' we said, 'we have just seen people passing who are getting ready other plums for you, and somewhat more difficult to digest.' The explanation was given in few words; time pressed; and the King had the less difficulty in believing as he told us he also had heard something for the last quarter of an hour, but that, rather than suppose Givri had so badly executed his commission, he had judged that the noise was from his own camp.

His Majesty gave orders to twelve of us who were at hand to go instantly towards the different quarters of the cavalry, of which he always carried a list in his pocket, to spread the alarm amongst them, and to press them all to hurry to headquarters; while a part of us proceeded to the infantry, to form it into battalions, and place it between headquarters and the trenches. He mounted his horse as he spoke these commands, and although he proceeded at full gallop he gave orders to all whom he met with the same precision and scope as if he had been long prepared for a battle.

Thanks to such celerity and to that admirable presence of mind which caused nothing to escape the attention of the Prince in circumstances where anyone else in his place, instead of forming a regular plan, would hardly have been capable of adopting a rational resolution, the enemy surprised no one, which perhaps saved the army from the greatest misfortunes . . . This single example would be sufficient to prove how useful it is for the General of an army, not only to possess that quality of mind which enables him to seize upon all points of a question, though they may be infinite, but to know by their names, their capacity, and their good and bad qualities, both the officers and the different corps of his army.

The capture of Laon added greatly to Henry's reputation, but he suffered two regrets. Young Biron adopted a rebellious attitude on learning that the governorship of that town had been promised to someone else, though Henry had already given him a marshal's baton and the governorship of two other towns. This upset Henry, but far more keenly he felt the death of Givri, a Catholic who had been loyal to him from the moment of the late King's death and was killed during the siege.

Something even more important than a victorious campaign in Picardy occurred in Paris. The fraudulent François d'O, who ran the finances of the country for his own profit, suddenly died. After the assassination of the last Valois circumstances had compelled Henry to maintain d'O in his posts as governor of Paris and superintendent of finances, acutely aware though he was that the man grew fat on the revenues of the state, living in great splendour, gambling heavily, denying himself nothing, and refusing the King everything. With his death Henry could begin to put the finances in order, and, as he said, 'henceforth the only Governor of Paris shall be myself'. Apart from Mayenne only two nobles of note still held out against him, one being the son of his old antagonist the Duke of Guise, the other being Mayenne's brother, the Duke of Mercœur, who held the greater part of Brittany nominally for the League. The mother of the present Duke of Guise, who had been completely won over by Henry's kindness and good humour, begged her son to yield and to make his submission in person. There was really no alternative because the province of Champagne which he governed had become royalist in sentiment. It was characteristic of Henry that instead of taking advantage of the anti-Guise feeling in the province he handsomely recompensed the Duke, gave him the government of Provence, and treated him with the utmost cordiality, embracing him, calling him nephew, and speaking of his father as 'one of the friends of my youth, though we were sometimes rivals for the smiles and good graces of the ladies'.

Leaving the Duke of Mercœur for later treatment, Henry next dealt with the *croquants*, bands of peasants who had risen in rebellion against their persecutors, the tyrannical seigniory who tortured, taxed and fined them to a state of despair, treated them like slaves, and let them starve to death with indifference. Their condition was one of the many things Henry intended to alleviate in time; but for the present he managed to terminate the revolt by remitting all their arrears of taxes and fines and by promising consideration of all their complaints and demands. This satisfied the greater number, though in a few places they continued to resist authority for a year or two.[1]

Having tried to reorganize the finances by appointing a council of eight, Henry returned to Picardy to fortify places in preparation for a war against Spain, which under Philip II had been the pest of Europe, especially France. He knew that there could be no peace so long as the Spaniards were on his northern border, and he determined to make that border invulnerable to attack. At the end of December 1594 he dashed back to Paris, where, booted, spurred and travel-stained, he received certain noblemen. The room was full of people, and at a moment when the King was stooping down to raise one of them from a deferential posture a knife aimed at his heart or throat struck him on the mouth. His courtesy had saved his life. Blood poured from his lips, and he thought for a moment that one of the noblemen had wounded him. But it quickly appeared that a youth of eighteen had done the deed, and he was seized. Henry commanded the attendants to let him go, saying 'I pardon him.' The order was disobeyed, and after some interrogation the youth confessed his crime. His his name was Jean Châtel. Having been a pupil of the Jesuits, he had got it into his head that it would be lawful and meritorious to kill a King who had not been absolved by the Pope. When it became generally known that the teaching of the Jesuits had demoralized the boy, a large crowd gathered at the College of the order and would have broken in if the King had not sent his guard to protect it. Quite recently he had stopped the parliament's proceedings against the College, and he treated the present incident with his usual light-heartedness, saying he had often heard from the mouths of trustworthy persons that the Jesuits did not like him, of the

[1] A vivid picture of them is given in one of Stanley Weyman's excellent romances, *The Abbess of Vlaye*.

truth of which he was now convinced by his own mouth.

But parliament took a more serious view of the case and condemned the wretched lad to be torn to pieces by four horses, his hand having been first struck off and torture applied. Henry was gloomy and sorrowful for several days. He detested all the ghastly things that men did to one another in a state of religious and political frenzy, things that could be described as bestial if that were not a libel on four-legged animals, and had he read them he would have echoed Shakespeare's lines:

> Timon will to the woods; where he shall find
> The unkindest beast more kinder than mankind.

Seditious writings were discovered in the Jesuit College of Clermont, the Regent of which, Guignard, having admitted his treasonable teachings, was hanged; and parliament issued a decree banishing the Jesuits from France as corrupters of youth and enemies of King and State. Among other doctrines taught by the Jesuits and sustained by Guignard was that Henry should be deposed. 'If they cannot depose him without waging war, let them wage it; if they cannot do that, let them put him to death.' It is scarcely surprising that between the years 1594 and 1610 Henry's life was attempted at least sixteen times. After one attempt he looked sad, replying to Gabrielle's sister who wanted to know why: *'Ventre Saint-Gris!* how can I be otherwise when I see a people so ungrateful towards their King, that although I have done and still do all I can for them, and though for their welfare I would sacrifice a thousand lives, if God had given me so many, yet they still try to kill me.' In spite of the danger he frequently walked the streets of Paris, and when the town council proposed that all the leaguers should be expelled therefrom he would not hear of it: 'They are all my subjects and I wish to treat and love them equally.' At balls and masquerades he took no precautions,

exposing himself as recklessly in social life or out hunting as
he did on the battlefield.

In January 1595 he adopted a course that not only endangered his life as a soldier but doubly imperilled him as a
monarch: he declared war against Spain, matching his scratch
troops against the best disciplined army in the world and
exposing himself to the daggers of well-paid and highly-
skilled assassins. Philip II would have much enjoyed watching
him being burnt alive, but failing that agreeable spectacle a
nice clean murder would have been acceptable. Henry had a
lifelong and wholly justifiable conviction that Spain was the
cause of all the miseries that had afflicted France in the last
generation, and a positive knowledge that the greater part
of his own domain of Navarre had been stolen from his family
by a Spanish monarch. He was also conscious of the wisdom
that Shakespeare put into the mouth of another Henry IV,
who advised his son how to allay civil strife:

> Be it thy course to busy giddy minds
> With foreign quarrels; that action, hence borne out,
> May waste the memory of the former days.

Philip's rage and indignation were boundless when he heard
that 'the Béarnais' had dared to defy in arms 'the King of the
Spains and the Indies', whose power in the Low Countries
had already been shaken by the unabsolved French monarch.
Spanish forces were at once ordered to advance on the north
and east of France. Assaults were delivered in Picardy and
Henry sent two or three of his best commanders to counter
them, while Biron and himself marched into Burgundy where
Mayenne would shortly be supported by Philip's troops
from La Franche-Comté.

In the course of his campaign there occurred an action
similar to that of Aumale, but not in this case due to an error
of his own. Apparently, during a reconnaissance, a body of

cavalry under Biron was attacked by much superior forces and fled in confusion. The King, with less than a hundred men, rallied the fugitives and with his small following decided to charge the enemy. He had no helmet, no armour except his gorget, and his followers were ill-equipped for such a purpose. So hazardous was his position that his friends begged him to flee on a swift Turkish horse. 'I have no need of advice but only of assistance,' he said. 'There is more peril in the flight than in the chase. Do as you see me doing.' He then cut his way through the first corps of Spaniards, threw them into a chaotic condition, hurled himself at the second, broke them up, and finished by smashing a third. After that the Spaniards desired no further engagement, and with a little clearing-up in the field Burgundy became the King's. At the head of about two hundred men he had put the fear of God (or Mars) into some two thousand, and Mayenne, who witnessed the fight, began to think that life would be more comfortable if he came to some arrangement with a monarch before whom the vaunted discipline of Spanish troops was like straw in a wind. Henry heard that Mayenne was about to leave for Spain in a panic, and with his habitual generosity, conterminous with common sense, he sent a message informing the Duke that if he would abandon his connection with Spain and retire quietly to Chalon he would be given a safe conduct, also that when certain pressing affairs had been settled they would come to some agreement. Henry was the only living ruler whose word in such a matter could be trusted, and Mayenne took him at his word. In a letter to his sister after the amazing combat just recorded, Henry said that he had fought for victory at all his previous battles but that at Fontaine-Française he had fought for life: 'Those who were not there with me must regret it much, for I had need of all my good friends, and you were very near being my heiress.'

He could easily have taken all the country up to the borders of Switzerland, but he was asked by the Swiss to restore the neutrality of La Franche-Comté and promptly did so. Also there was bad news from Picardy, where his generals had muddled everything by not acting in unison, and Henry made instant preparations for going north. On the way, at Lyons, he heard that the Pope had at last decided to grant him absolution. No doubt Henry's continued success in arms had expedited the mental process of his Holiness, and the public ceremony took place on 17 September 1595, when Clement VIII, surrounded by cardinals, sat on a throne in the portico of St Peter's. Henry's two ecclesiastical representatives kissed the pontiff's feet, and one of them read the King's confession of crime in accepting Calvin's heresy, his prayer for pardon and absolution. The supplication of the penitent was granted on certain conditions, which Henry's agents swore he would observe, though the King reserved to himself the right to unswear what did not suit him. The *Miserere* was then chanted by the choir, and at the end of each verse the holy father tapped the shoulders of the monarch's representatives with a switch. This childish charade intimated that Henry's naughtiness had received vicarious and symbolic chastisement, following which his agents were honoured and rewarded, and the title of 'Most Christian King' was bestowed on the relapsed heretic.

The situation on France's northern frontier was fairly desperate when Henry arrived there. He attributed the loss of several towns to the weakness of the Duke of Nevers and the rivalry of other generals, whose united incompetence had resulted in greater casualties than Henry had incurred at the three battles of Coutras, Arques and Ivry. Cambrai had fallen and Calais was threatened. At a meeting of the council Nevers expressed his opinion that the King should not expose himself to the danger of marching against the victorious Spanish troops with the hastily mobilized and poorly equipped army at his disposal. For once in a way Henry's natural impatience overcame his tact. 'Such advice might be very suitable for you, who would not approach within seven leagues of danger,' he snapped. The Duke felt deeply injured, and although Henry hastened to apologize for such an inconsiderate remark Nevers said that 'the balm came too late to soothe the rankling sting of those thoughtless words'. Ill at the time, he died soon afterwards, much to the relief of the King who had always found him troublesome and incompetent.

All that Henry could do on arrival in Picardy was to blockade La Fère, the advance-post of the Spaniards. He sent urgent appeals for military assistance to Elizabeth of England and the German princes, but to no avail, and while La Fère held out he fell ill. His finances were in so deplorable a condition that he could not pay his soldiers, let alone the sums with which he bribed officials into loyalty; and towards the end of 1595 he saddled himself with a further commitment. The Duke of Mayenne traded on a generosity that chiefly consisted of promises and demanded three places in Burgundy and Champagne as security for an enormous sum to pay his debts, as well as a clean bill for the past behaviour of himself and his relations, who were to be declared innocent of any complicity in the assassination of Henry III. Although Mayenne and others of the house of Guise had brought incalculable misery and bloodshed on France in the last twenty years, the King cancelled their crimes with a stroke of the pen, and henceforth Mayenne and his people were in clover. The treaty which put an end to the League was signed in January 1596. Needless to say the Protestants were resentful to the point of rebellion, and it needed all the ability of Duplessis-Mornay to prevent open insurrection. Parliament declined at first to register the treaty, but Henry exercised the power of an absolute monarch, ordered the assembly to do so, and by this far-seeing act obtained the pacification of France; for not only did he purchase the future loyalty of Mayenne, but that of the young Duke of Guise, who in a brief campaign defeated a conspiracy between the governor of Provence and Spain, capping his achievement by saving Marseilles when a fleet of Spanish galleys were just about to disembark troops to subdue it.

Soon after the treaty was signed Mayenne arrived at Gabrielle's residence, the castle of Monceaux, in order to make his personal submission to the King, who was walking in the park with Rosny. The monarch advanced to meet the Duke, who knelt down, embraced the royal thigh, made assurance of his future fidelity, and expressed gratitude for having been saved 'from the arrogance of the Spaniards and the cunning of the Italians'. Henry quickly raised him, cordially embraced him three times, changed the subject at once, and holding his hand led him through the park, pointing out the improvements that were being made. Mayenne was fat and suffered from gout as well as sciatica. Henry's usual pace was too much for him, but he could not complain. The King noticed that his companion was limping, panting and sweating, and whispered to Rosny: 'If I walk longer with this corpulent body I shall revenge myself upon him without any great difficulty for all the mischiefs he has done us.' Turning to the Duke, he asked: 'Tell me truly, cousin, do I not walk a little too fast for you?' Mayenne replied that he was almost suffocated and that if his Majesty walked but a little while longer he would kill him without designing it. 'Hold there, cousin!' said Henry, embracing him again and giving him a friendly tap on the shoulder, 'for this is all the vengeance you will ever receive from me.' The King then asked Rosny to take the Duke to the castle for rest and refreshment, adding that he should have a couple of bottles of Arbois wine, 'for I know you do not hate it'.

Mayenne's submission was followed by that of all the chief leaguers, amongst them Duke Henry of Joyeuse, commonly known as Frère Ange because when not fighting or debauching he lived as a Capuchin monk. At this time he had ceased to lead a cloistral life, seemed in no hurry to renew his religious practices, and was enjoying life at the Court, which had reverted to the licentiousness of earlier reigns. Standing on the palace balcony one day, he was chatting with Henry IV, and a crowd gathered to gaze at them. 'My cousin,' said the King, 'these people seem to be extremely well pleased with the sight of a renegade and an apostate conversing together.' Somehow the remark failed to tickle the Duke's sense of humour. He became pensive, and after arranging a marriage between his daughter and the Duke of Montpensier he went back to the Capuchins, never to re-emerge.

It seemed to the Protestants that these renegades from the League were much too well treated by the King. He always allowed the sums they demanded for the surrender of their towns and the value of their services. He told Rosny, who jibbed at the terms exacted by the governor of Rouen, that the figures should not be too closely scrutinized. These men, he said, would bring revenue to the state which would more than pay the amounts they insisted upon, and to force their surrender by arms would cost more in money, not to mention lives and time, than the purchase of their places and loyalty. He made a joke of their exorbitant conditions, and established the dangerous precedent of recompensing rebellion because he knew that, with the country as it then was, peace was worth any price. He paid the leaders of the League far more than a whole year's revenue of France at that time, and his sagacity was rewarded, for he obtained the loyalty and assistance of nearly all the men he bribed and raised his country from poverty to prosperity. At first it was essential that the Catholics should get all the good jobs, and the Protestants who had borne the heat and burden of his day were incensed by the favour shown to those who had entered the vineyard at the eleventh hour and could not accustom themselves to the notion that 'the last should be first and the first last'. But Henry was biding his time and meanwhile gave secret presents to exigent Huguenots. On one point he stood firm. Some Catholic and Protestant princes offered to sell their services in return for the creation of hereditary

governments; but though Henry was hard pressed he steadfastly refused their proposals, and so prevented the return of
feudalism and preserved the unity of France. He was in fact
a genius in the world of action and statecraft because he saw
what was immediately and ultimately important and what
despite appearances could be temporarily disregarded or
completely ignored.

Of vital consequence to France in the spring of 1596 was
the Spanish invasion of her northern frontier, and when the
town of Calais was endangered Henry quitted the siege of La
Fère and marched to Boulogne, whence he made two attempts
by sea to succour the place. But the winds drove him back and
Calais was taken by the Spaniards. This roused the Queen of
England, who had previously promised assistance if the town
were handed over to her; upon hearing which Henry had
exclaimed: 'If I am to be bit, I would rather be bitten by a
lion than a lioness!' but sent a more diplomatic refusal to
Elizabeth, who had then sulked. But the capture of the town
by Spain softened her attitude to Henry, and negotiations for
an alliance between France and England were set in train.
The loss of Calais was a shock to the French King, who
according to Rosny made use of it by encouraging his nobles
to further feats of arms: 'We must neither suffer ourselves
to be confounded nor lose courage', he told them,

> since it is in the midst of afflictions that valiant men become
> more resolute and strengthen themselves with new hopes . . .
> Let us apply ourselves to seek out the means of taking, with
> usury, our revenge upon the enemy, so that, with the favour of
> Heaven, this place may remain in the hands of the Spaniards
> only as many days as our ancestors left it years in possession of
> the English.

But the more fractious nobles seized the present moment
to press their claims to hereditary government in their

provinces, which, they assured the King, would result in large
bodies of feudal troops being always at the disposal of the
Crown. Though the royal army had begun to melt away, and
he could obtain no money to pay the soldiers, Henry did not
hesitate, and the ambitious noblemen were quickly made
aware that they had erred. The one-time Viscount of Turenne,
now Duke of Bouillon by the grace of Henry, was the prime
mover in this attempt to restore feudalism. A self-seeking
unbending Protestant, he had become the centre of conspiracy
against the King, who now sent him as ambassador to the
English Court.

In May 1596 Henry's situation was lamentable, and if he
had not obtained a loan from the Grand Duke of Tuscany he
would have failed to take La Fère. That done he wished to
besiege Arras, but on applying to his council for the necessary
sum he heard that it was unavailable. What made matters
worse was the outbreak of pestilence and famine throughout
the country that year. The weather, as so often before and
since, was unseasonable. 'We had summer in April, autumn
in May and winter in June,' reported a chronicler of the time.
The plague infected the army, which had to be disbanded.
Before his camp broke up Henry described his own condition
in a letter to Rosny:

It is now for you to make up your mind to follow my instructions
and speak to me freely; and in order that you may do so, I will
tell you to what a state I am reduced, which is that I am very near
to the enemy and yet I hardly have a horse on which I can fight
or a complete set of armour for my shoulders. My shirts are all
torn, my doublets are ragged at the elbows. My stew-pot is
often turned upside down as there is nothing to put in it, and for
two days past I have been dining and supping with one or another,
as my own purveyors declare that they can no longer supply
anything for my own table, particularly as they have been paid
no money for six months past. Well, judge if I deserve to be
treated in this manner, if I am to suffer financiers and treasurers

to let me die of starvation, whilst they keep well-served and dainty tables.

Henry's only hope of putting the finances in order lay with Rosny, who had been given a sort of advisory position on the King's council of eight which had taken over the administration on the death of d'O. But the councillors disliked Rosny's honesty as much as his manners and soon irritated him into resignation. He had seen enough to brand the conduct of financial affairs as 'organized pillage', and Henry wished to discuss the whole matter with him before calling an Assembly of Notables. The King was then at Amiens and asked Rosny to escort the Marchioness of Monceaux thither from Pontoise. Rosny disliked the job because he disapproved of his master's obsession with 'La Belle Gabrielle', but he obeyed the order. An accident on the way very nearly killed her. A league from Clermont there was a steep declivity on one side of a narrow road, at which spot the loud neighing of a mule frightened the horses that drew the coach of the Marchioness. There was a stampede, but at the moment when it seemed to Rosny that nothing could save Gabrielle the axle-trees of the coach broke and brought the lumbering vehicle to a stop. On hearing of what had happened Henry went white with fear and displayed symptoms of disquiet that Rosny had never seen in him on the battlefield or at moments of extreme personal danger. Having composed the Marchioness, and 'devoted some moments to tenderness', Henry dived into the finances, which Rosny described as 'an ocean without bottom or shore'.

The corruption, bribery and extortion that had distinguished the administration of d'O were carried on by the council of eight under the presidency of the Duke of Nevers, and the confusion, theft and irregularity had disgusted Rosny, who washed his hands of the business and retired to his country house. The moment he was safely out of the way the council felt free to purchase supplies for the army and the

King at the lowest possible prices and charge the Crown double or treble the cost, to pay foreign troops half the arrears due to them and debit the Crown with the total sum claimed. They lived in luxurious splendour while Henry often went without food and never appeared in clothes that were not torn, patched, dirty and threadbare. Much to Henry's annoyance Rosny refused to continue work with the council, knowing that it would be waste of his time, and the council raised every objection to Rosny, knowing that his presence would spoil their chances of pilfering.

The revenues of the Crown were in such an appalling state that anyone, in whatever capacity employed, could make money out of them. They were farmed out to contractors, under whom were treasurers, receivers, controllers, registrars, sub-contractors and intendants, all of them concealing their own iniquities by conniving at the frauds of others. The chief victims of this army of parasites were the Crown and the people, the treasury being empty and the community taxed beyond endurance. This vast system of moral pollution had grown up over the period of Court profligacy covered by the later Valois monarchs, and called for the labour of a Hercules to cleanse it. Eventually Henry decided that the only man in the kingdom who could be trusted to carry out such a task was Rosny, and after several 'scenes' with the inflexible Baron, who knew that without a free hand he could do nothing, he was appointed Superintendent of Finances. Rosny was surprised to hear that Gabrielle had urged the King to make the appointment. 'You will never be well served,' she told her lover, on hearing that Rosny had declined to serve under the council, 'until you have met with such a man who, purely from motives of public interest, does not fear to incur the displeasure, and even hatred, of the financiers.' But by that time Henry must have known as much.

Rosny's first act justified the appointment, though it appeared miraculous enough to arouse the King's suspicions.

Taking four districts for his personal inspection, he used his powers to break up the alliance of underlings, and having discovered innumerable overcharges and embezzlements he was able to raise a sum of five hundred thousand crowns for the King's benefit. The council, not yet disbanded, soon got to hear of it and told the King that Rosny was tyrannically imprisoning officers and clerks of the finance department and raising money by erratic means to appease his vanity. Henry was alarmed and sent for Rosny, who arrived with cartloads of money, together with the peculating receivers-general of the districts and all the registers and falsified accounts, as a clue, said he, 'to guide me further through that maze of injustice, knavery and robbery'. To his surprise the King received him coldly and asked why he had encumbered himself with money for state pensioners and suchlike people who would apply for it through the usual channels. Rosny answered that the sum was solely for his Majesty's use in the war, that no one had any claim to it, that it would normally have reached the pockets of men who had no right to it, that he had anticipated no future taxation, and that it was a mere pledge of what he hoped to raise in the future. Henry could scarcely believe his ears and requested Rosny to swear the truth of what he had said. His doubts removed by the oath, he exclaimed: '*Pardieu!* what a malicious set, and what an audacious imposture! Yet tell me, why have you put so many people in prison, and why do you drag here in chains the receivers, treasurers and other officers I hear are with you? What do you propose to do with them?' Such was the story that had reached the King from the council, and Rosny's face of blank amazement was a sufficient answer. Henry roared with laughter, embraced his honest friend, told him to go ahead with his reforms and to rely absolutely on his master's support.

Though Rosny's endeavours to bring order out of chaos were opposed at every step, from the princes of the blood downwards, by all those in fact who had previously levied money upon the farms and other revenues of the state, he revolutionized the finances of the country with an efficiency unparalleled by any other man in history. He admitted that he had 'a kind of passion for the re-establishment of the finances', and nothing less than his kind of passion, unreservedly backed by the monarch's enthusiasm, could have transformed France from a state of servitude and dependence to the position of Europe's leading power under Cardinal Richelieu in the reign of Henry's son. Let us take a glance at Maximilien of Béthune, Baron of Rosny.

He was born at Rosny, near Mantes, in December 1560, and so was seven years younger than Henry, to whose service he had been dedicated at an early age by his father. As we have seen, he had fought in the civil wars for the Huguenots, and he remained a strong Protestant to the end. His main characteristics were honesty, diligence, fidelity and prudence, though we must qualify the noun honest with the adverb relatively. In dealing with the country's finances, and as the servant of Henry IV, he was honest, but in relation to himself and to those who ruffled his vanity he was not always truthful. Jealous of certain people who possessed the King's confidence, he emphasized their faults and ignored their virtues. His temperament was stern and severe; he showed no favour to any who failed to recognize his own importance; he was too thick-skinned to feel rebuffs; and he had too high an opinion of himself to sympathize with weakness in others. People complained of his haughty demeanour, his rigid manners, his pedantic behaviour, his inability to relax. By nature a puritan, he shared none of the carnal pleasures of the other nobles, drank with moderation, ate sparingly, gambled scarcely at all, and did not seek the society of women. He rose early, seldom retired late, lived for his work, allowed little time for recreation, and made himself extremely unpopular with more fallible souls by the ceaseless exercise of vigilance, competence and assiduity. It may be said that to have a high opinion of oneself prompts one to justify it, and Rosny's probity was partly the outcome of his conceit. He prided himself on not being like other men, his opinion of his contemporaries being put in a sentence: 'When self-interested motives are strengthened by the apprehension of any danger, there are few persons who will not be induced by them to betray even their best friend.' He included himself among the few, and it did not occur to him that another of his comments had some connection with the writer's character: 'One risks nothing in depending upon the good opinion all men have of their own merit: on this head they are always their own dupes first.'

As a soldier he was brave, ready with his sword when anyone called his courage in question. 'If one were to wring your nose, milk would flow out of it,' said an officer named Frontenac, to which Rosny replied that he was strong enough to draw blood from the other's nose with his sword, and would have tried to do so if friends had not intervened. Unlike Henry, he did not enjoy fighting, but he never shirked an action and lived to be a first-class artillery officer. He hated the waste of civil war, strongly advised Henry to become a Catholic in order to put an end to internal dissension, and was clear-sighted enough to expose the cause of religious enmity: 'Compassion and tenderness are the only means that do any service to religion, and the only means that religion dictates. The zeal which is so much boasted is only rage or obstinacy, disguised under a reputable appellation.' He wanted to allow everyone 'to gain paradise as he can'.

There can be little doubt that Henry's wholly different nature was complemented by that of his friend, and that the affection between them was mutual. Henry was by turns irritated and amused by Rosny's failings and virtues. For example the Baron liked the sound of his own voice, and the King once stopped a courtier from interrupting the minister: 'We must suffer him to talk, for he is not a man of few words.'

Rosny's frugality was also not lost on the King, who said that 'he never thinks anything fine or good that costs double its real value'.

But the feature in Rosny's disposition that attracted Henry as much as it surprised him was a fixed resolution to refuse bribes in the guise of presents. Whenever gifts of money or valuable objects were sent to the Baron, they were at once forwarded to Henry on the principle that as he had received them in the capacity of the King's servant they belonged by right to his master. Sometimes Henry kept them, sometimes told Rosny to keep them; but more than anything else in an age when courtiers and officials froze on to whatever they could get, Rosny's invariable action impressed the King with his rectitude. In effect honesty was the best policy, because the King constantly sent gratuities to his faithful servant and as time went on the Baron received governorships and highly-paid posts. It would not be unfair to say that he was a snapper-up of well-considered trifles; and he was no more averse to loot than anyone else, but that was a recognized perquisite of war. 'My good fortune threw a small iron chest in my way, in which I found four thousand gold crowns,' he admitted in describing the sack of Cahors.

Such were the more prominent traits in the character of the man chosen by Henry to disentangle and clarify the bewildering chaos of corruption and chicanery that had been created by the disorders of previous reigns, by the greed and incompetence of earlier superintendents; and Rosny, having carefully studied all the obtainable information about the kingdom's revenues and the necessary expenses of raising them, entered what he called 'this labyrinth of impositions and robberies'.

CHAPTER EIGHT

Cleaning-up

The Assembly of Notables, called by Henry in a last attempt to settle the finances of the nation before they were placed wholly in the charge of Rosny, was held in the abbey of St Ouen at Rouen in October 1596. Henry's opening speech was typical of the man:

> If I were desirous for the reputation of an orator, I would treat you to more fine words than goodwill; but my ambition aims at something higher than to speak well: I aspire to the glorious titles of deliverer and restorer of France . . . You know to your cost, as I do to mine, that when called by God to the throne of this kingdom I found the country not only ruined but very near being absolutely lost to Frenchmen. But by the grace of God, by the prayers and good counsels of those of my subjects who are not of the profession of arms, by the sword of my brave and generous nobility . . . and by my own efforts and exertions, I have saved France from being lost to us. Let us now save it from ruin. Share with me, my dear subjects, in this second glory, as you shared in the first. I have not summoned you hither, as some of my predecessors have done, to compel your blind approval of my 'good will and pleasure', but have called you together to receive your counsels, to trust in them and to follow them – in a word, to place myself in tutelage in your hands, which is what kings, greybeards and conquerors have rarely shown an inclination to do. My extreme desire, however, to add those two grand titles, Liberator

and Restorer, to that of King, together with the great love I bear
my subjects, renders everything easy and honourable to me.

He then withdrew, saying, 'I will not by my presence put
any restraint on your discussions.'

The fair Gabrielle, from behind a tapestry, listened to the
King's speech and told him afterwards that she had never
heard him make a better one, though she expressed some
surprise at his remark that he placed himself in tutelage under
the assembly. '*Ventre Saint-Gris!*' he exclaimed, 'that's true,
but I mean it with my sword at my side.'

While they were deliberating he went hunting. Gabrielle
produced a daughter and much pleasantry ensued. There were
fêtes, balls, tennis-playing, running at the ring, in all of which
Henry took part, without neglecting his military, political and
financial plans. In time the notables completed their investiga-
tions and debates, having arrived at no conclusion suitable to
the state of affairs, and Henry duly dismissed them with
thanks for wasting their time. Before leaving the district he
ordered the parliament of Rouen to register the edict of 1577,
which his predecessor had been compelled to yield in favour
of the Protestants. This was a first step to the freedom
granted them in the famous edict then under consideration; and the Huguenots, believing it to be final, reviled
the King, while the Catholics inveighed against his toleration.

The leaders of both religions pestered him, repeating their
beliefs *ad nauseam*, the assumption being that the more often
they said a thing the truer it became. Henry had to act a part.
'I have been obliged to appear angry to silence those who are
solicitous to find something to blame in my conduct,' he
confided to a Huguenot after a stormy scene, and he could
not even talk for long in public with Rosny because if he did
so the Catholics became suspicious. His Protestant sister
Catherine was another source of vexation to the Catholics,

and when she was indisposed at about this time Henry tried to comfort her by playing a lute and singing a psalm in the way the Calvinists did. Gabrielle was with them and prudently put her hand over his mouth, lest his behaviour should be misconstrued by malicious tale-bearers. Fortunately for himself and for France he had a sense of humour, which did not provide him with an escape from life but with a protective shield against its harshness, stupidity and bigotry. As a civilized human being he perceived that people and their causes were inherently ridiculous as well as tragic, and that the man who could not laugh at them was only half-alive. Because of his sense of humour, which gave him a sense of proportion, he was able to enjoy existence in all its manifestations and to remain sane when the rest of the world seemed crazy. But when something had to be done, he did not think it funny to be thwarted, and another aspect of his nature was revealed. Rouen resisted his command to register the edict of 1577, and Henry, no longer pretending to be in tutelage, ordered them to cease cavilling and do as they were told. They did.

Without money Henry could not raise an army to clear his country of the Spaniards, and having reinforced the frontier towns he left Biron to watch the banks of the river Somme. Apart from his personal enjoyment of such things as ballets, masquerades, Italian farces, etc., he decided that it would be a good thing for a post-plague Paris to enjoy life or watch others doing so, and the early spring of 1597 was passed by the nobles and the Court in much dissipation and magnificence of hospitality. The King was to be seen with Gabrielle, either hunting or dancing, feasting or flirting, and occasionally he took her and their small son César to the fair of St Germain, where he bargained for trifles the child fancied. As the mere sight of him inspired the stall-keepers to raise the value of their wares, he extracted much fun out of haggling over prices, which earned him the reputation of meanness among shallow people. 'They say I am a miser,' he said, 'but I do three things very inconsistent with a miser's disposition: I make war, I make love, and I build.'

The jollifications of the Court came to an abrupt end early one March morning in 1597 with the news that Amiens had been taken by the Spaniards. At the request of the inhabitants Henry had left no garrison there, though he had advised them not to claim the privilege. As a result the city was guarded carelessly and discipline was at a premium. The Spanish commander hit on a neat trick. A cart filled with walnuts was driven by soldiers disguised as peasants into the town; but passing through the gates a sack was untied and the nuts were scattered all over the ground. The men on guard could not resist the temptation and ran about picking up the nuts. While they did so the traces of the cart were cut and the gates could not be shut. Some 3,000 Spanish soldiers concealed in the neighbourhood rushed forward and the town was occupied with little resistance. Worse still, all the supplies and munitions which Henry had ordered to be collected there in anticipation of the renewal of the war with Spain were henceforth to be used against the French. The news temporarily stunned the King, who could hardly find words to express his mortification. At last he said aloud: 'This blow is from heaven. Those poor people, from having refused a small garrison which I wanted to give them, have brought this trouble on themselves and me.' But he was not the man to receive a blow even from heaven without returning it, and after a few moments of reflection he cried: 'I have played the King of France long enough; it is time to play the King of Navarre again.' Turning to Gabrielle, he added: 'My mistress, we must now quit our arms and mount our horses and take up arms of another kind.'

Having despatched Biron with a small force, he followed with as many men as he could muster and against the advice of his council laid siege to Amiens, leaving Rosny to collect money. The Baron's arbitrary manner of raising funds aroused the hostility of parliament, which refused to register the necessary financial edict; whereupon Henry threatened to visit Paris with half a dozen more decrees up his sleeve if they did not obey his command. 'I only ask to be treated as they treat the monks, *victus et vestitus,*' he said to the man who spoke for parliament: 'Now, Mr President, I often have not enough to eat; and as for my clothing, just look at it!' and he pointed to his well-worn doublet. The edict was registered, the money supplied, the royal army reinforced, the artillery augmented, and Henry managed to frustrate the attempts of a Spanish army to relieve the city. He would dearly have liked to attack the relieving force in the field, but Mayenne dissuaded him, saying that he was there to take a town, not to fight a battle. But nothing could quell Henry's ardour. He marched on Arras and fired off cannon against the walls in the hope that the Spanish commander would emerge and give him battle. Nothing happened, and Henry observed that the Spaniards were strangely discourteous not to take a single step to meet him. Even his allies were not very helpful. The English Queen sent 3,000 troops, but expected to receive the town of Boulogne as a reasonable recognition of her aid. Henry was discourteous enough to disagree with her.

Rosny was indefatigable. He not only paid a monthly visit to the camp with enough money for the army but supplied the material for the construction of artillery and organized hospital arrangements, an almost unknown addition to the business of war. 'He may be said to have brought Paris to Amiens,' reported a contemporary, 'few of the conveniences and supplies of the capital being wanting at the camp; while the sick and wounded, from the unwonted care bestowed on them, gave to the siege of Amiens the name of "the velvet siege".' In the midst of his successful endeavours to make the war endurable to the combatants, Rosny must have pulled a long face when his master demanded money for the purchase of the Duchy of Beaufort, which the King bestowed on his 'Charmante Gabrielle' in August of that year.

Amiens still held out and Henry decided to take it by assault. Seated on his horse before the attack began, he prayed aloud to the God of battles: 'O Lord, for thy great mercy's sake, pity this poor kingdom and chastise not the flock for the errors and faults of the shepherd.' The city fell in September, and Henry, always chivalrous, permitted the Spanish garrison to march out with the honours of war. The inhabitants gave their King a terrific reception, and this time raised no objection to being properly garrisoned. Paris gave him a welcome such as no King in living memory had received, and if Gabrielle had been Queen she could scarcely have been acclaimed more warmly. The new Duchess of Beaufort entered the city on a litter just in advance of the King. Dressed in black satin, spotted with white, her jewels flashed in the torchlight, drawing exclamations of wonder from the crowd. Henry rode a dapple-grey horse and wore a doublet of grey velvet bordered with gold, the trunk-hose to match. His white-plumed grey felt hat was seldom on his head, for he continually waved it in response to the cheers of the multitude and the yells of *Vive le Roi!* The *Te Deum* was chanted on his arrival at Notre-Dame, and there was a general feeling in the air that peace would soon be proclaimed.

But Henry could not feel himself King of France until Brittany was subdued, and this was the next item on the royal programme. The Duke of Mercœur, last of the League leaders, had refused submission to his lawful sovereign and had controlled Brittany for ten years, regarding it more or less as his personal property. No sooner did he hear that Henry was about to pay him a visit in February 1598 than he sent his wife and mother to Angers to negotiate with the monarch, then on the march. It was a clever ruse by the Duke, whose suggestion was that his daughter, inheritrix of vast estates, should be affianced to César, son of Henry and

Gabrielle. This naturally appealed to Gabrielle, who accompanied Henry, and her prayers, added to the tearful entreaties of the other two ladies, soon won over the King, who had set out with the object of chastising Mercœur but remained in the province to witness the betrothal of two children, his son aged four, the Duke's daughter aged five. Mercœur resigned the governorship of Brittany in favour of his future son-in-law, who was created Duke of Vendôme by the King. As usual Henry treated the humbled governor with generosity, and having settled these personal matters in March he toured Brittany with Rosny, stamping out highway robbery and the plunder by state officers, collecting money without oppressing the poor, and regulating the affairs of the province.

The subjugation of Brittany had been easy, but Henry found it difficult to endure the bores of Brittany. He had to sit through interminable complimentary speeches and long-winded harangues. One well-meaning Breton began his eulogy with, 'Agesilaus, King of Lacedaemonia, sire,' but Henry cut him short: 'I have often heard of that Agesilaus, but I believe that before he was addressed he always dined, which I have not, so pray excuse me.' Another extolled his achievements, hailing him: 'O great King! King most benign! King most clement!—' upon which Henry chimed in, 'And why not add King most weary?'

Rosny disapproved of the pacific arrangement with Mercœur, perhaps because he still suffered vexation over the loss of a post he coveted. The Grand-Master of Artillery had been killed at Amiens, and Rosny might have been appointed in his place if Gabrielle had not interceded in favour of her father. According to Rosny 'the lady wept and declared she would retire to a convent' if the King refused her request. This is probably an exaggeration, but Henry yielded to her solicitations and her father became Grand-Master. Though Rosny was pacified with the governorship of Mantes, he remained peevish, and Gabrielle's further success in negotiations at Angers did not dispose him to regard her with more amity.

Henry had already decided to make peace with Spain if his terms were agreed, and as Philip II was about to benefit the world by leaving it the moment seemed ripe. A congress of ministers representing the powers concerned was held at Vervins under the mediation of the Papal Legate. The moment Elizabeth of England and the States of Holland got to hear of Henry's intention they despatched ambassadors with offers of money and men to support the French King if he would continue the war with Spain and recover Calais. Although he had entered into an agreement not to make peace without their consent, he recognized that he now had no alternative if he wished to consolidate France and establish order throughout the kingdom. He explained to them that many years of civil war had destroyed all subordination in his country, which would be ruined if he did not come to terms with Spain, and he pressed them to join in the treaty because a general peace would be for the welfare of Europe. The ambassadors were downcast and returned to report his unalterable decision to their respective rulers. But he refused to abandon his old allies at the instigation of the Pope, on the ground that there was 'no obligation in an oath made to a heretic', still hoped that they would join him in the peace pact, and insisted that they should be admitted to the agreement if they wished.

All this time the Huguenots were badgering him for religious equality with the Catholics, and he felt that the time had come when their wishes could be granted without danger of a renewed outbreak of civil war. He had very sensibly put it off until the country as a whole acknowledged his sovereignty, and on 5 April 1598 the famous Edict of Nantes was signed. It was the work of four men over a period of three years. It confirmed what had so often been granted and withheld: full liberty of conscience. Colleges, schools and hospitals were to be open equally to Protestants and Catholics, the former being henceforth eligible for all government offices and employments, and lawsuits in which Huguenots were interested were to be judged by an equal number of Protestants and Catholics. The Calvinistic clergy were to be paid from the royal treasury, and their religion could be openly exercised except in certain places. Full civil rights and protection were granted the Protestants, who were allowed complete control of the two hundred cities they still held, with permission to have political assemblies and religious synods and to publish their own books.

Needless to say the Catholics were horrified by this edict and the Protestants were less than grateful. The parliament of Paris raised innumerable objections, other parliaments did likewise, and the priests pronounced hell-fire from their pulpits. Henry was compelled to admonish the refractory Catholic bishops. 'You have exhorted me concerning my duty,' he told them, 'let me now exhort you concerning yours. Let us excite a mutual emulation in each other, which of us shall perform their parts the best. My predecessors gave you good words; but I, with my grey jacket on, will show you good deeds; though I am grizzled without, yet I am all gold within . . .' He also called the courts before him and dealt with parliament's remonstrances. 'There must be no more distinction between Catholics and Huguenots,' he said. 'All must be good Frenchmen, and let the Catholics convert the Huguenots by the example of a good life. I am a shepherd King, who will not shed the blood of his sheep, but seek to bring them together with kindness.' Some of his subjects had tried to intimidate him with threats, but 'I will root out all these factions and punish those who foment them. I have overleaped the town walls and I will easily overleap the barricades also.' His usual method on such occasions was to establish a homely atmosphere, a pleasant friendly background for the proclamation of his will, the handshake before the punch, as now:

> You see me in my closet, where I come to speak with you, not in my royal robes, nor with my sword and other military habiliments on, as my predecessors were wont, nor like a prince who is to receive an ambassador, but clad like the father of a family, in his plain doublet, to speak familiarly with his children. What I have to say is to entreat you to register, with the usual solemnities, the edict which I have granted to those of the Calvinist religion. What I have done is for the sake of peace, which I have concluded with the neighbouring powers around me, and would have the same observed within my own dominions . . . I made the edict and would have it observed. My will ought to be a sufficient reason, for in an obedient state they never ask their prince any other. I am King, I speak to you as such, and I will be obeyed.

The Edict of Nantes, which established the rights of the two religions, was ratified in February 1599, and saved France from unspeakable miseries until Henry's grandson, Louis XIV, revoked it in 1685, letting loose the horrors his grandfather had so wisely and so humanely curbed. Although by nature a fighter, Henry was imaginative enough to know that the people who suffered most from war were the poor, while there was always a chance that the nobles and gentry would benefit from fighting, even if they did not enjoy it. With his humane and affectionate disposition Henry's chief purpose as a ruler was to bring peace to the realm and liveable conditions for the majority of his subjects. He knew how to use his authority whenever necessary, but he had no sense of self-importance; indeed, he was more of a democrat than a sovereign. 'I have only two eyes and two feet,' he said. 'In what respect then do I differ from my subjects but that I am invested with the power of executing justice?' His most famous saying ran: 'I want no peasant in my kingdom to be so poor that he cannot eat meat on week-days and put a chicken in his pot every Sunday.' An eighteenth-century writer named Gudin de la Brenellerie wrote much that is forgotten but one line about Henry IV that is remembered : '*Le seul Roi dont le pauvre ait gardé la mémoire.*' No epitaph would have pleased its subject so much as Gudin's, and no distinction has been so well earned by a ruler.

'Kings are not born: they are made by artificial hallucination,' wrote a twentieth-century philosopher. 'When the process is interrupted by adversity at a critical age, as in the case of Charles II, the subject becomes sane and never completely recovers his kingliness.' In the case of Henry the whole of his life up to the age of forty-six was passed in adversity, from his spartan childhood to his imprisonment, from his escape to the Edict of Nantes. He never knew what it was to be coddled and deluded. He was brought up the hard way; and so when he became King the trappings of royalty meant as little to him as the trappings of religion. By that time experience had quickened his native acumen, and he never mistook the show for the reality. He had also become something of a fatalist, but instead of fettering his mind and teaching him submission the theory freed his mind and taught him defiance. The notion that everything was predetermined enabled him to accept the Christian belief in resignation to the will of God, whenever that mood was in the ascendant.

However, the will of God manifested itself to different people in dissimilar forms, and it was as clear to Henry that the Spaniards were devils as it appeared to Philip II that the French were not saints. But Philip was dying and wished to leave his son a peaceful inheritance, while Henry wanted peace for the sake of his country. He needed a little peace for his own sake too, and having settled the affairs of Brittany he retired to Chenonceaux while the congress at Vervins wrestled with the settlement between France and Spain. He was accompanied by the Duchess of Beaufort and their son César, who received the estate from the widow of Henry III in exchange for that of Moulins. Chenonceaux had been the favourite residence of Henry II's mistress, Diana of Poitiers, and on his death had passed from her to his widow Catherine of Medici. Henry of Navarre was fond of it, having spent many months there in his youth, and it pleased him as King of France to have it handed over to his son the Duke of Vendôme.

But he could not stay there for long, because the Spaniards at last agreed his terms and early in May 1598 the plenipotentiaries signed the Treaty of Vervins, whereby all the French towns that had been taken by Spain, including Calais, were restored to France, and the safety of the north-eastern frontier was secured. Cambrai and La Franche-Comté were returned to Spain, and the only part of the agreement not wholly satisfactory to Henry was that the future of the Marquisate of Saluzzo, claimed both by the King of France and the Duke of Savoy, was left to the arbitration of the Pope. The Treaty was signed by Henry in June, when he wrote to his ministers: 'I have just achieved by a stroke of my pen more exploits than would have been possible in a long war with the best swords in my kingdom.' It was in fact his main triumph as a warrior, since no general dared now to face him in the field, and about three months later his chief adversary Philip II, tortured with ulcers and eaten by vermin, passed from the scene of his diabolical deeds performed in the name of religion.

So ended the wars in which Henry had fought from his youth, wars that had ravaged France and spread barbarism throughout the realm, with the sublime object of making people change their opinions.

CHAPTER NINE

Matrimonial

A second son was born to Henry and Gabrielle in 1598, named Alexandre and duly legitimized. It would have been necessary to call a third Charlemagne, but the necessity did not arise. Having put his country in order, Henry was now concerned to found a dynasty, and since Gabrielle had been not only fruitful but helpful and affectionate, and as his love for her had in no way diminished, he determined to marry her as soon as possible. But the transformation of a mistress into a wife was not easily arranged. His chief advisers were against it, and the Church was opposed to it. Such a project would create a further obstacle to his divorce. The Pope, easy on the subject of mistresses, would be difficult if one of them were promoted to the throne. Henry had to walk warily, and he made up his mind to sound Rosny.

Taking him aside one day, the King began to talk about his desire to have a wife who should produce a successor to the Crown. He described the necessary qualifications for a future Queen: beauty, prudence, softness, wit, fruitfulness, riches and royal birth; but he frankly admitted that he could not find such a woman in any of the royal houses. He did not wish for an alliance with a German princess because 'the women of that country do not suit me; I should always fancy I had a hogshead of wine in bed with me'. He said that he would 'rather choose a wife who is a little fond of gallantry than one who wanted understanding', and he added that the woman he pictured as an ideal wife was either dead or had never been born. At this point the grave Rosny made a joke, saying that he would bring all the beauties of France together, between the ages of seventeen and twenty-five, and parade them before the King, who could talk to them personally and discover the nature of their temper and intelligence. Having signified his appreciation of the joke, Henry gradually revealed his secret thoughts in a manner recounted by Rosny:

'Since you confess that the lady I marry ought to be of an agreeable temper, beautiful in her person, and of such a kind as to give hopes of her bearing children, reflect a little and say whether you do not know a person in whom all these qualities are united.'

Rosny professed himself unable on the spur of the moment to name one, leaving it to Henry.

'And what would you say if I should name one who, I am fully convinced, possesses these qualities?'

'I should say, sire, that you are much better acquainted with her than I am, and that she must necessarily be a widow, otherwise you can have no certainty with regard to her fruitfulness.'

'So that is all you would desire. But if you cannot guess who she is, I will name her to you.'

'Name her, then, for I own I have not wit enough to find out who she is.'

'Ah, how dull you are! But I am persuaded you could guess who I mean if you would, and only affect this ignorance in order to oblige me to name her myself. Confess, then, that these three qualities meet in my mistress.' The expression on Rosny's face made Henry add quickly: 'Not that I have any intention to marry her, but I want to know what you would say if, not being able to meet with any other of whom I could approve, I should one day take it into my head to make her my wife.'

Not for the first time Rosny was placed in a quandary,

which he tried to elude by pretending to think that Henry was jesting. But the latter instantly perceived that Rosny was concealing his thoughts and said with some sternness: 'I command you to speak freely. You have acquired the right of telling me plain truths. Do not fear that I shall be offended with you for doing so, provided it be private. Such a liberty in public would greatly offend me.'

Rosny then spoke out. He said that such an alliance would be scandalous and would draw adverse opinions from all over the world; further that his Majesty would mentally suffer on that account when the ardour of his passion had abated and he could judge impartially of his own conduct. Apparently Rosny did not know that Henry's ardour had already sufficiently abated to make him the father of two children by a lady named Charlotte des Essarts, and that other affairs had occurred. Henry's love of Gabrielle was based on something more durable than physical passion. But Rosny's real objection to such a marriage was political; and he explained that as Gabrielle's first child had been born in a double adultery, Liancourt being her husband at the time and Margaret the wife of Henry, the boy's right to succession would be inferior to that of the second child, born in a single adultery, while both of them must yield to those born after the lawful marriage to Henry. Such a situation would lead to endless wars of succession.

Henry seemed to be greatly impressed by Rosny's reasoning, and closed the subject, but almost immediately reopened it by asking whether the French would rebel against him during his lifetime if he married his mistress. Rosny then treated the King to a lengthy discourse, explaining the difficulties that would arise from such an alliance. They talked together for three hours, in the course of which Henry blurted out that Gabrielle's chief complaint of Rosny was that he thought more of the glory of the King and his kingdom than of the man himself. Rosny replied that he could not defend himself from the charge, because the kingdom and the sovereign were to be looked upon with the same eyes: 'Remember, sire, that your virtue is the soul which animates this great body, which must by its splendour and prosperity repay you the glory and happiness it derives from you, and that you are not to seek happiness by any other means.'

Rosny's advice fell on deaf ears, or rather on a made-up mind. It was clear from all outward evidence that Henry designed to marry Gabrielle, who was present at every state function and treated as if she were Queen. We have a snapshot of her in the summer of 1598 at a big banquet:

> The collation there was magnificent. Madame de Guise served the Duchess of Beaufort, who was seated in a chair, and to whom with many curtsies Madame de Guise presented the dishes. She, with one hand, took what she found most to her taste, while the other hand she gave the King to kiss, he being near her.

Queen Elizabeth's ambassador, Robert Cecil, found her 'stout but really·pleasant and gracious . . . she expressed herself well and courteously . . . she spoke to me of the Queen [Elizabeth] with much respect, and expressed her desire to receive her commands'.

It may seem strange that the widow of the great Duke of Guise, hero of Paris and 'King of the Barricades', should have been prevailed upon to wait on a court-mistress, but the Duchess had been completely won over by Henry. Some time previously she had behaved in a manner that filled her with contrition, and a generous act of the King had resulted in a confession, which she followed by saying that she deserved the penalty of death. But Henry could not oblige her: 'I have never killed any ladies and I don't know how to set about it.' It is quite possible that the Duchess of Guise had also succumbed to the charm of Gabrielle, who was liked by nearly everyone except Rosny, whose vanity caused him to be jealous of those beloved by Henry, male or female. When, for instance, Rosny discovered that the bill of expenses incurred during the baptism of Gabrielle's second son, Alexandre, included such items as heralds, trumpeters, hautboys, etc., he declined to pass it; and on being told that the amounts payable at baptisms of Children of France had long been regulated, he retorted: 'What is that to me? Go, go, I shall do nothing. There are no Children of France.' The accuracy of Rosny's account of what then happened may be doubted. Knowing that Gabrielle would soon hear the words he had spoken, he complained to the King about these scandalous and reckless expenses, being told to place the facts before the Duchess of Beaufort. But Gabrielle gave him a hostile reception, and again he complained to the King, who got into a coach, called on his mistress, and gave her a dressing-down in the presence of Rosny, who reported Henry as saying to her: 'If I were reduced to the necessity of choosing whether I would lose one or the other, I would rather part with ten mistresses like you than one such servant as he is.' Gabrielle instantly changed her tactics and burst into tears. The King weakened, but recovered sufficiently to bid her make peace with his minister. She did so, and 'we separated very good friends', recorded Rosny. Some scene between the three on the subject of expenses did no doubt take place, but Henry would never have used such language to the woman he loved and wished to marry in the hearing of anyone else, least of all Rosny, a highly prejudiced party. We cannot help feeling that on this occasion Rosny's vanity affected his honesty.

Although popular at Court and tactful in her dealings with both Catholics and Protestants, Gabrielle knew that certain priests referred to her in their sermons as a lewd woman who caused much evil, and she resorted to astrologers, palmists, crystal-gazers and suchlike sorcerers for information about her future. Not all of them were optimistic, and we have it on the authority of her maid that she often wept in the night. Yet nothing seemed to stand in the way of her marriage to Henry, whose wife Margaret was enjoying herself with other lovers at the castle of Usson in Auvergne and was wholly in favour of divorce on a sound cash basis, most of the arrangements being made by Duplessis-Mornay, though Rosny asserted that himself was the chief intermediary. Gabrielle and Margaret were on good terms with one another, the latter soliciting favours which were granted, the former obtaining property belonging to Margaret, who agreed to its transference. It is true that, perhaps prompted by Rosny, Margaret wrote a letter admitting that she had put difficulties in the way of a divorce, her reason being that she did not wish to see in her place 'that disreputable slut' Gabrielle. But this was merely a trick to obtain more favourable financial terms, and the bargaining for payment of her debts plus a large pension went on without the least reference to her successor, were she slut or princess. From the higher regions of harlotry Margaret could look down on a woman who was faithful to a faithless lover.

In October 1598 Henry fell seriously ill at Monceaux with a high fever, and the affection he had inspired in his people showed in the alarm displayed throughout the country. The prospect of death did not dismay him, though he had one regret, telling Rosny: 'I am grieved to die before I have raised this kingdom to that splendour I intended for it, or convinced my people, by discharging them of part of their taxes and governing them mildly, that I love them as my children.' The moment he recovered he settled down at St-Germain to work with the Superintendent of Finances, displaying so much keenness, common sense and knowledge that, according to Rosny, the politicians and financiers were astounded. The Pope was also astounded when, tired of waiting, Henry ordered his representatives at Rome to threaten that if his marriage with Margaret were not quickly annulled he would act independently of the Holy See, just as Henry VIII of England had done. Faced with another schism from such a source, the pontiff's attitude relaxed, and Henry could feel that blackmail was more profitable than supplication. At the end of October he was in high spirits, writing to Gabrielle about their children:

> I caught the stag in an hour with the greatest possible enjoyment, and I arrived here at four o'clock and alighted at my little lodging ... My children came to meet me there, or, to be accurate, they were brought. My daughter is greatly improving and becoming a beauty, but my son [Alexandre] will be handsomer than his elder brother. You entreat me, *mes chères amours*, to carry away with me as much love as I left with you. Ah! how that has pleased me, for I feel so much love that I thought I must have carried all away with me, and feared that none might have remained with you. I am now about to hold communion with Morpheus; but if he shows me anyone but yourself in my dreams, I will forever forsake his company. Good-night to myself, good-morrow to you, my dear mistress. I kiss your beautiful eyes a million times.

While Henry could pour out words like these to the woman he loved more than all the others he loved, he was exercising despotic power over the affection of his sister Catherine. His behaviour to her shows him in the worst light and was quite unlike him; for though he was autocratic when necessary in social, political and economic spheres, his treatment of friends and relations was almost invariably generous and kindly. The only possible explanation is that the secrecy with which she had carried on her love-affair with the Count of Soissons had flouted Henry's authority, put his back up and deprived her of his sympathy. That he should be thwarted in his own household was the last straw. It was bad enough to have Catholics and Protestants plotting against him merely because he was doing his best to be fair to both, but that his sister should attempt a privy espousal with a man he suspected of ulterior designs hardened his heart. His alternative proposals were rejected by her, one of them being James VI of Scotland, afterwards James I of England, who had offered to help him in the wars with 6,000 men.

'Prepare my sister to wish him well,' wrote Henry to Corisande at that time; 'point out to her the position in which we are, and the greatness of that prince, together with his virtue. I am not writing to her about it myself. Do but speak of it to her by way of discoursing that it is time for her to marry, and that there is no hope of any other match for her than this one.' He said that the King of Scots would 'infallibly become King of England,' which made such a match vitally important to France. But all this occurred in 1588, and Catherine remained faithful to Soissons.

Now, ten years later, Henry found another husband for her, the Duke of Bar, eldest son of Charles III, the reigning Duke of Lorraine. The marriage would lay the ghost of still-remembered quarrels between the houses of Guise and Bourbon, and if only Catherine would become a Catholic, like her brother and prospective husband, nothing would suit Henry's reconciliatory purpose so nicely. Catherine fought against the marriage, absolutely declined to be converted, and the moment it became known that negotiations were in progress the priests of one religion and the ministers of the other preached violently against the union, the first because she was a heretic, the second because she would be made to worship idols. Catherine's refusal to accept the Catholic faith made it necessary for Henry to apply for a papal dispensation. It was refused, and Henry promptly resolved to do without it.

Towards the close of 1598 the marriage contract was drawn up and read to Catherine. The King signed it and handed the pen to his sister, saying that she was not being compelled to marry. But she was ill, tired of his pertinacity, sick of the whole business, and resigned herself to what seemed inevitable. The Duke of Bar arrived at the Louvre with a large retinue and was received by Catherine 'with as much graciousness as agitated feelings allowed her to assume'. She was thirty-eight, the Duke some six years younger. A big effort was then made to turn her into a Catholic and she received instruction from a number of bishops and theological experts. Rosny and Duplessis-Mornay were present to see fair play. The prelates distressed her with references to the punishment inflicted on the souls of those who did not die in the faith, and she announced positively that she neither understood nor believed a word they said. Henry, who had already been instructed and did not wish to hear it all again, absented himself while the godly men were struggling for the salvation of his sister's soul, but happened to enter the room when she made this announcement. Having a hasty temper, he accused her angrily of thoughtlessly opposing everything he was doing for her good, to which she returned: 'These Catholic prelates would have me believe in the damnation of our dear mother!' This upset the King so much that he wept and said no more.

Yet he still insisted on the marriage, though neither the Duke nor Catherine wished for it and both were acting under compulsion. For a moment it looked as if their wishes would prevail, because without the papal dispensation no bishop would marry them. But Henry refused to accept defeat and sent for the Archbishop of Rouen, an incompetent, dissipated and thoroughly unscrupulous person, who had been given the see partly because he was a natural son of Antony of Navarre and his mistress, and so Henry's half-brother. However, the Archbishop did not wish to incur the displeasure of the Pope and refused to celebrate the unhallowed union. Henry, enraged, accused the Archbishop of ingratitude and made it clear through an intermediary that he would be deprived of his job if he did not come to heel. The threat settled the prelate's conscience, and the marriage took place in the King's private room at the end of January 1599. At the last moment, in a final effort to assert the spirituality of his office, the Archbishop said that the customary rites of a chapel should be performed. The King replied that his presence was above all other solemnities and his apartment no less sacred than a chapel. The Archbishop raised no further objections, and the pair were joined in holy matrimony; but they did not live happily ever after.

For his part Henry had every intention of living happily for the rest of his life with Gabrielle, and when Margaret signed a fresh proxy for the divorce settlement in February 1599 it was sent on to Rome, whence reports hinted that Clement VIII, perceiving that if Henry could ignore the papal authority in the case of a sister he might do something equally rash in the case of a wife, was softening. There was no longer any doubt of the King's future arrangements. Early in March he gave Gabrielle his coronation ring and many other presents. She was again pregnant but active enough to start refurnishing the Queen's bedchamber which she occupied at the Louvre whenever the King resided there. She bought a majestic bed with velvet hangings of crimson and gold, and a velvet bridal robe of carnation hue, richly embroidered with gold. To strengthen her position as Queen Consort and that of her son as Heir Apparent, marriages were arranged between certain notable people and the family of Estrées, some of whom occupied important posts in northern France. To the disgust of Rosny, Duplessis-Mornay and other grave advisers, Henry put as much energy into these domestic plans as he did into a plan of battle, and they were not displeased when Nature appeared to join their frowns.

People do not pay much attention to the behaviour of the climate when nothing happens to give it significance; but if something of general import in human affairs chances to occur afterwards, they recall the elemental oddities in order to prove that God is taking a personal interest in the government of the world. So now. While Henry and Gabrielle were spending the season of Lent 1599 at Fontainebleau, queer things were in motion, such as these described in Shakespeare's *Macbeth*:

> Lamentings heard i' the air; strange screams of death,
> And prophesying with accents terrible
> Of dire combustion and confus'd events
> New hatch'd to the woeful time. The obscure bird
> Clamour'd the livelong night: some say the earth
> Was feverous and did shake.

In the minds of many these sights and sounds were linked up with the tragedy about to take place, and in a play staged in London at about that time, Shakespeare's *Julius Caesar*, one of the characters spoke for the great majority:

> When these prodigies
> Do so conjointly meet, let not men say
> 'These are their reasons, they are natural;'
> For, I believe, they are portentous things
> Unto the climate that they point upon.

Henry could sleep 'in spite of thunder', but Gabrielle was affected by unseasonable weather and the King attended to her with assiduity, taking her for long rides in the forest and putting her comfort before everything else. It is possible that she had not properly recovered from her previous accouchement, and the prospect of another depressed her. Beyond question she was ill and despondent.

The King's confessor insisted that his Majesty shouid pass Holy Week in a becoming frame of mind before partaking of the Sacrament, and for this purpose Gabrielle left him, since their union was sinful in the eyes of the Church. She went to Paris, but Henry escorted her as far as Savigny, where they spent the night of April 5th. Some of his courtiers had great difficulty in separating them when the moment of parting came. They seemed to suffer from a similar premonition, and when she begged him to take care of their children and to look after her domestics he could not speak for tears. Again and again he returned to take leave of her, and at length he was almost forced into his coach.

Gabrielle proceeded by barge to Paris. It had been arranged that she should dine on the night of her arrival at the house of Sebastien Zamet, a wealthy Italian banker from whom Henry had often borrowed money and in whose house he had frequently gambled and fornicated. Zamet had left Italy as a youth, and starting as shoemaker to Catherine of Medici had become valet of the wardrobe to Henry III. He lent money to the latter's *mignons*, and did so well for himself that he was rich at the age of thirty-six. He sided with the League when that was uppermost and with Navarre when he was in the ascendant. Zamet was on terms of friendship with Gabrielle; and although his house had a shady reputation as a centre for assignations and high play, he was a generous host and a pleasant companion.

It is more than likely that Gabrielle ate something unsuitable to her physical condition while at Zamet's. In those days that was quite sufficient to start a rumour that she had been poisoned. Some said that she had eaten an orange, others a lemon, others a salad, but as she was in a state of pregnancy and ill-health anything might have disagreed with her and upset her. Whatever the cause, she felt indisposed on leaving Zamet's for the house of an aunt near the Louvre. The following morning, Wednesday, 7 April, she still felt ill, but later in the day she was well enough to attend a service in the chapel of St Antoine. The heat there made her worse and she returned to her aunt's instead of Zamet's, where she had been invited to supper. She went to bed complaining of a bad head-ache. Next morning, 8 April, she had recovered sufficiently to attend Mass and partake of the Sacrament at the church of St Germain l'Auxerrois. At two o'clock that afternoon she again felt unwell, saying she was extremely thirsty. At four o'clock she went to bed, and labour pains were followed by convulsions, repeated for some hours. On Good Friday she was worse and too much exhausted to bear her child, but its delivery was essential. After a deal of haemorrhage the operation of embryotomy was performed, and the infant was taken away piecemeal. Cupping, clistering and all the other methods of medical extermination were applied. At that period there was no need to poison anyone in the hands of physicians, and Gabrielle would have had to be in bounding good health to survive the various fashionable cures. The pain she underwent distorted her features and limbs. In the evening she lost the powers of speech, hearing, sight and motion, remaining so until the early morning of Saturday, 10 April, when death released her.

The instant that Henry heard of her illness on Thursday the 8th he set off for Paris on horseback. But next day at Juvisy messengers met him with the news that she was in the final death agony. Half-mad with grief he was about to proceed when certain courtiers prevailed on him to return. Stricken by the news his actions were beyond his control, and they managed to get him into a carriage. Back at Fontainebleau he abandoned himself to sorrow for a while, refusing to see anyone and pacing the galleries and gardens in solitude. Rosny arrived and tried to administer solace by quoting passages from the Bible, but Henry showed no sign of response until the Baron began to dwell on the virtues of the late Duchess.

The King ordered the Court to go into mourning, black for the first week, violet for three months. Gabrielle was given the funeral of a Queen. A requiem Mass at St Germain l'Auxerrois was followed by a procession of princes, princesses and nobles to St-Denis, where a second requiem

Mass was celebrated, and later to Maubuisson, near Pontoise, where Gabrielle was interred at Notre Dame la Royale, of which her sister was abbess. Many of the royal house and the nobility were glad in their hearts, for the King would now be compelled to marry someone chosen by his sober advisers, who would not be influenced by such transient attributes as physical beauty or bodily allurement. Gabrielle's friends and relations were also pleased because they commenced to steal her belongings, her father being particularly anxious to appropriate her furniture and jewels. But the King got to hear of these avaricious designs and put a stop to their pilfering in its early stages.

For himself Henry felt that all personal pleasure in life was at an end. His sister Catherine, recently constrained by him to become Duchess of Bar, was full of sympathy. 'I know that words cannot afford a remedy to your extreme sorrow,' she wrote,

> That is why I will only employ them to assure you that I feel it as keenly myself, for both the extreme affection I bear to you and the loss I have suffered of so perfect a friend compel me to do so . . . Would to God that I might alleviate your grief by sacrificing a few years of my own. I wish with all my affection that I could do so, and with those true words I kiss you, my dear brave King, a thousand times.

Henry's reply was dated from Fontainebleau, 15 April 1599:

> My dear Sister,
>   I received your letter with much consolation. I have great need of it, for my affliction is as incomparable as was she to whom it is due; regrets and lamentation will attend me to the grave. Nevertheless, as God brought me into the world for this Kingdom and not for myself, all my understanding and care will be devoted henceforth solely to its advancement and preservation.

The root of my love is destroyed; it will not sprout again; but that of my friendship will remain ever green for you, my dear sister, whom I kiss a million times.

He signed this letter like all his others, 'Henry', not 'Henri', and many Frenchmen of that time spelt his name in the same way.

The expressions he used to his sister were undoubtedly from the heart. He was overwhelmed with sorrow. And though his natural resilience and easily-aroused passion soon cured his melancholy, there can be little doubt that his love for Gabrielle was the deepest emotion of his life.

CHAPTER TEN

Laying-up Trouble

Solemn historians who feel that because a man enjoys himself he cannot be serious, or because he is amusing he cannot be sincere, have gravely reprimanded Henry for his extravagances, his love-affairs and his quick changes of mood. He certainly treated his mistresses and friends with exceptional generosity, and he soon recovered from tragic strokes of fate. He could not remain long in one frame of mind, and it seemed to less imaginative people that his nature was too volatile to be dependable. What they failed to see was that if he had been the steady and temperate person they wished him to be, he would never have become the saviour of France. What they called his failings co-existed inseparably with the qualities that brought about his successes; for they were the recreation that enabled him to create, the weakness which balanced the strength and maintained his equipoise. As we have seen, he did not look far ahead and disliked having to make resolutions, perhaps feeling instinctively that the man who makes no plans goes further than the man with a definite purpose in view. Besides, it was so boring to conduct life according to rules; and unlike his solemn advisers, not to mention the solemn historians, he was not a bore. Nevertheless, he may have been fortunate in having a few dull people as counsellors to offset his own vivacity.

Above all he was lucky to have Rosny, whose loyalty and affection more than made up for his tedium. Henry thought him harsh, impatient, obstinate, self-opinionative and self-gratulatory, ambitious for honours and riches; but he knew that Rosny loved him and cared for his honour as well as for the glory and grandeur of his kingdom. In spite of the Baron's little fits of temper and moral lectures, Henry found no one so capable of consoling him when upset or uneasy, and he never allowed his anger with the minister to last more than a few hours; but that was easy because resentment was not in his nature and he could not endure living on distant terms with anyone. Rosny, however, was about to try Henry's patience to the limit.

Six months after the death of Gabrielle we find Henry writing to Henriette d'Entragues, daughter of the governor of Orleans. Anxious to keep his mind from brooding over Gabrielle, a few of his courtiers advised the King to visit Blois. He stayed there some time, and on his way back to Fontainebleau he stopped at Bois-Malesherbes, the residence of the Entragues family, where he met the twenty-years-old Henriette and enjoyed her conversation so much that another kind of enjoyment suggested itself. Henriette's mother, Marie Touchet, had been the mistress of Charles IX before marrying François d'Entragues. One of Marie's sons by that King, Count d'Auvergne, was therefore the natural half-brother of Henriette, and we shall hear more of him. From all accounts Henriette was dark and slim, with a feline grace and seductive body, but her thin lips, sharp eyes and short straight nose hinted at less attractive qualities. She could be very amusing, her gaiety and wit appealing to Henry, but she could also be very biting and sarcastic. She has been likened to a cat because she knew how to purr and how to scratch; but cats are repeatedly libelled. She had as much cunning as allurement, and far more guile than passion, her sole ambition being to win riches and position; but she was too clever to let this appear obvious. As hard as nails in her will to succeed, she was as soft as butter in her methods of attainment.

When a girl aroused Henry's sexual desire he did not pause to consider her character, and soon he was dancing attendance on Henriette, who was taken to Paris by her mother. He presented her with a necklace of pearls. She cautiously refused it. He sent her a box of apricots. She prettily accepted it. He asked her to go with him to St. Germain and see his children, baiting the request with a present of valuable tapestry. She returned to Bois-Malesherbes. He followed her. But making no progress in her affection, he went on to Chenonceaux, where a maid of honour engaged his attention. Likely enough that the rumour reached her by one of his emissaries, for she became more pliable. But the business had to be conducted on a solid financial basis, and her father agreed to sell her on certain terms: a formal promise of marriage with Henriette, the payment of a hundred thousand crowns down, and the appointment of Henriette's father as a marshal of France. Henry agreed to the first two conditions but jibbed at the third, feeling, rightly or wrongly, that a man who had never been near a battle should not be raised to the top rank of the fighting forces.

Rosny was shocked when asked for the stipulated sum, revenging himself by sending it all in silver pieces. But he was horrified when, one day at Fontainebleau, Henry showed him the letter promising marriage to Henriette. Every word of it, he reported, 'was like the stab of a poniard', and he returned it to Henry in frigid silence. 'Come, come, speak freely and do not assume all this reserve,' said the King. But Rosny was bewildered and remained silent. The King assured him that he could say and do what he pleased without offence. Rosny asked for that assurance to be repeated several times and to be sealed with an oath. Henry having obliged, Rosny took the paper out of his hands and tore it in pieces without saying a word. *'Morbleu!'* cried the astounded monarch: 'what are you doing? You must be mad!' Rosny agreed, adding: 'Would to God I were the only madman in

France!' Henry, in a rage, snatched the torn pieces from Rosny, who was not deterred from reading his master a lesson, to the effect that the family of Entragues was a scandalous one and that the letter just destroyed would hold up the projected divorce, for both Margaret and the Pope would oppose it if they knew who would be Queen. The King listened, then left the gallery in which they had been talking, went to his closet, rewrote the letter, and left to go hunting, passing Rosny at the foot of the staircase without noticing him.

His hunting expedition took him to Bois-Malesherbes, where the money and the letter were handed over, though he inserted a passage that Henriette should supply him with a son before the marriage took place. The document is curious enough to quote, as showing the length to which Henry would go in order to gratify his sexual appetite:

We, Henry fourth, by the grace of God, King of France and Navarre, promise and swear before God on our faith and word as a King, to Messire François de Balzac, Lord of Entragues, a Knight of our Orders, that giving us as companion Demoiselle Henriette Catherine de Balzac, his daughter, in case in six months, beginning from the first day of this present one, she should become *enceinte*, and should give birth to a son, then and instantly we will take her to be our wife and legitimate spouse, whose marriage we will solemnize publicly and in face of our Holy Church according to the rites required and customary in such a case. For greater confirmation of the present promise, we promise and swear as herein stated to ratify and renew it under our seals, immediately after we have obtained from our Holy Father the Pope the dissolution of our marriage with Dame Marguerite of France, with the permission to marry again as may seem fit to us. In witness whereof we have written and signed these presents. At the Wood of Malesherbes, this day the first of October, 1599.

Henry.

But François d'Entragues wanted that marshalship and negotiations were suspended. On 10 October the King wrote to Henriette:

Mes chères amours . . . You order me to surmount, if I love you, all the difficulties . . . By the proposals I have made I have sufficiently shown the strength of my love for those on your side to raise no further difficulties. What I said before you I will not fail in, but nothing more [meaning her father's demand to be made a marshal]. I will willingly see Monsieur d'Entragues, and will leave him but little rest until our affair is arranged or falls through . . . Good-night, heart of mine, I kiss you a million times.

But Entragues proved himself a fighter, if not a fully qualified marshal, removed his daughter to the well-fortified castle of Marcoussis, and informed his Majesty that she was no longer to be seen at Bois-Malesherbes. This did not suit Henriette, who knew of Henry's penchant for certain other ladies and felt that her father was taking too great a risk. She wrote to the King suggesting that he should invent some duty that would take her father elsewhere. He did so, and the moment Entragues was out of the way Henry arrived at the castle and transported Henriette to a charming house in Paris that had been prepared for her. 'A pretty bird should have a pretty cage,' he said. Soon he presented her with the marquisate and estate of Verneuil; within the specified time the Marchioness of Verneuil became *enceinte*; and she felt sure of a queenly crown.

But the politicians had been busy and a scheme was maturing whereby a queen would bring money to France instead of having French money spent on her. In December 1599 Henry's marriage to Margaret was annulled, and in April 1600 the contract of marriage between himself and Marie of Medici was signed by his representatives, his future wife bringing him six hundred thousand gold crowns.

It was a marriage of necessity. Henry owed Ferdinand of
Medici, Grand Duke of Tuscany, the equivalent of thirty
million pounds sterling, which had been lent to himself and
his two predecessors. In order to clear this off it had been
hinted that he should marry the Grand Duke's niece Marie.
His financial situation having become more acute in 1597,
the matter was again raised, and though he had no wish to
make the alliance he permitted negotiations in the hope of
getting another loan. Whatever his advisers may have
thought, he objected to the prospect of again letting loose
the house of Medici in the French Court, with its inevitable
gang of traitors, spies, poisoners and blackguardly fortune-
seekers. He had suffered under Catherine of Medici, and knew
the brood. All the same he was aware that Rosny and the rest
were still bargaining with the Grand Duke, though he preferred not to think about it.

Then came the need to procure a substantial sum of money
in order to send an army against the Duke of Savoy, and
Henry knew that he could not get it by taxation, nor did he
want to do so. Again he must apply to the Grand Duke of
Tuscany, the chief money-lender of Europe, and his agents
were free to make what arrangements they liked to obtain a
loan. An envoy arrived from Florence, and while Henry was
occupied with Henriette the articles of the marriage settlement were drawn up and signed. The only person who dared
face his Majesty with the *fait accompli* was Rosny, who duly
appeared before him. 'Where have you come from?'
demanded the King. 'We come, sire, from marrying you,'
calmly replied Rosny. Though Henry must have guessed it,
the shock stupefied him, and for a quarter of an hour he scarcely
moved. Then he walked up and down for some time. At last
he came to a resolution, rubbed his hands together and
exclaimed: 'Well, *de pardieu!* be it so; there is no remedy.
If for the good of my kingdom I must marry, I must.' He
acknowledged that the fear of succeeding no better in a

159

second marriage than in his first had caused his irresolution, while Rosny reflected on the strange fact that a prince who had extricated himself with glory and success from a thousand cruel dissensions occasioned by war and policy should yet tremble at the thought of domestic quarrels, which caused him more agitation than the repeated attempts to murder him.

But the prospect of private discomfort was momentarily forgotten in the need to ensure the safety of the eastern frontier, imperilled by the intransigent Duke of Savoy. Taking advantage of the French civil wars, Charles Emanuel, the humpbacked and ambitious Duke of Savoy, had conquered portions of French territory, most of which he had been forced to restore by the Treaty of Vervins; but he still held the Marquisate of Saluzzo on the Italian side of the Alps, and the Pope had been asked to arbitrate on the claims to its possession by France and Savoy. Charles Emanuel proved obdurate and the Pope abandoned his efforts to reach an agreement. Scenting the possibilities of bribery the Duke visited the French King at Fontainebleau towards the close of 1599 with the object of discussing the question, though in reality he intended, as he said, 'not to reap but to sow'. He scattered some seed in Burgundy on the way, where the governor, Marshal Biron, restless and troublesome like his father, was quite willing to garner it. At Fontainebleau he found Henriette, Marchioness of Verneuil, whose annoyance over the projected marriage of the King to the Tuscan princess made her favourably inclined to the arguments of a man with so much money to spend and so many costly gifts to distribute. Her half-brother, the Count of Auvergne, was another who did not refuse presents from Savoy, and in short the visit of Charles Emanuel endeared him to all who liked being tipped.

But Henry was not so easy to manage. He proposed that, as an alternative to giving up Saluzzo, the Duke should cede Bresse and the banks of the Rhone from Geneva to Lyons.

The Duke asked for time to consider the proposal. Henry wanted to know how much time he required. Eighteen months, said the Duke. Monstrous, said the King. At last it was agreed that Henry should have an answer in three months; and after a succession of balls, banquets, ballets and so on the Duke returned in March 1600 to Chambéry, where he set to work strengthening the fortifications of his cities, a necessary procedure because Rosny had recently become Grand-Master of the Artillery and was making cannon of such range and destructive power that the old fortresses would scarcely withstand them.

It may have come to the King's knowledge that Charles Emanuel had not only given presents to Henriette but had assured her of help in preventing the Medici marriage and forcing Henry to keep his promise to marry his mistress; because in the month following the Duke's departure Henry wrote this note to her:

Mademoiselle
The love, honour and benefits you have received from me would have checked the most frivolous of souls had it not been accompanied by such a bad nature as yours. I will not scold you further, although I could and ought to do so, as you know. I beg you to send me back the promise you know of, and not to give me the trouble of recovering it by other means. Send me back also the ring which I returned you the other day. Such is the subject of this letter, to which I require an answer by tonight.
Friday morning, 21 April 1600, at Fontainebleau.

Henry.

Clearly he had already discovered that Henriette was not the girl he had supposed her to be, and since he guessed that she would keep him on tenterhooks he sent a letter on the same day to her father:

Monsieur d'Entragues,

I send you the bearer to bring me back the promise which I gave you at Malesherbes. Do not fail, I beg you, to send it back to me, and if you wish to bring it me yourself I will tell you what reasons induce me to this, which are domestic and not state ones. On hearing them you will say that I am right and recognize that you have been deceived and that I have rather too good a nature than otherwise. Feeling sure that you will obey my command, I finish by assuring you that I am your good master.

Henry.

Neither letter had the least effect, because the father and daughter knew that the written promise of marriage would be useful for purposes of blackmail at some future date. But their refusal to obey Henry's request did not lessen the intimacy between the King and his mistress; indeed some time later he wished to take her with him in the early stages of his campaign against the Duke of Savoy, but she was advanced in pregnancy and stayed at Fontainebleau.

The three months given the Duke to make up his mind had elapsed, and Henry demanded an immediate decision. Charles Emanuel shilly-shallied to gain time, promised to restore Saluzzo, failed to implement the promise, and continued his preparations for war. He had corrupted Biron by offering him the Duchy of Burgundy, to be guaranteed by the King of Spain, and one of his daughters in marriage with a large dowry. A man named La Fin carried on the negotiations between them. Unaware that a noble on whom he had heaped honours was conspiring against him, Henry gave Biron the command of a corps, and declared war on the Duke of Savoy in August 1600.

Meanwhile tragedy had overtaken Henriette. Early in July a tremendous thunderstorm burst over Fontainebleau and the palace was struck by lightning. The shock was too much for a woman in her condition and she suffered a miscarriage, a still-born boy. All her hopes of becoming a queen were finally shattered, and in a mood of utter dejection she wrote a long letter of self-pity to Henry. 'I here speak to you in sighs, O my King, my lover, my all!' Such was the refrain of her appeal, wherein she spoke of 'the change which has now precipitated me from the heaven to which you had raised me down to the earth where I was found by you'. She told him that 'your nuptials will be the funeral of my life, and subject me to the power of a cruel discretion which will banish me from your royal presence, even as from your heart'. As she could not bear to be a person of no consequence in a Court where she had queened it, she had decided to suffer in loneliness, and her letter struck a note which cleverly blended affectionate adulation with devoted submission:

> In my inevitable exile there remains to me but the sole glory of having been loved by the greatest monarch of the earth, by a King who was willing to lower himself to such a degree as to give the title of mistress to his servant and subject; by a King of France, I say, who only recognizes the King of Heaven, and who, here below, has none equal to himself.

The close of her invocation was masterly and ensured her continued reign as mistress:

> If it be a practice for Kings to retain a recollection of that which they have loved, keep in remembrance, Sire, a demoiselle who was yours, and (save what she allowed on your sole promise) has had as much command over her honour as your Royal Majesty has over her life. Sire, from your humble servant, subject creature, and (shall I say?) forgotten lover.

Knowing Henry we may guess his answer, full of protestations and promises. Reasons of state forced him to marry a Medici, said he, but to maintain her high social position he would arrange a union between Henriette and a prince of the royal

blood, and so on and so forth. Her letter had done the trick
because it made clear that she was willing to continue their
relationship on the basis of King and mistress.

He was then in the south engaged in warlike doings and
begged her to join him when she felt well enough. The war
was being settled by Rosny's cannon. Citadels once invincible
were smashed by the new artillery. Chambéry fell, and
Henry wrote oddly-phrased instructions therefrom to one
of his servants: 'You are to accompany Madame the Marchioness of Verneuil and come with her, sending me every day
word of the place where she will sleep and news of her.'
Henriette travelled to Lyons, receiving on her way the gift
of standards taken by the King's army, as Corisande had done
after the battle of Coutras and another lady after that of Ivry.
The Marchioness had a warm reception at Lyons, and her
meeting with Henry at La Côte St André on the road to
Grenoble would have been wholly agreeable if she had not
suspected that another Court lady had recently been his
companion. They quarrelled, but a diplomatic friend did the
necessary lying and they arrived at Chambéry on amicable
terms. Here she heard from an agent of the Duke of Savoy,
whose only hope was to cause dissension in France, that if she
would allow a Capuchin, Father Hilaire, to take Henry's
written promise of marriage to the Pope, the union with Marie
of Medici would be prevented. The Duke was willing to pay
her a large sum of money for her compliance. She probably
took as much money as she could get, and certainly encouraged
the Capuchin to make the journey, though her father retained
possession of Henry's original letter, without which the Pope
could only give vague answers, and the Duke's scheme bore
no fruit.

The war went badly for Charles Emanuel from the start.
Bourg in Bresse (now Ain) and Montimélian in Savoy were
assaulted and captured. Rosny's guns could destroy ramparts
that had withstood the sieges of centuries. The fort of Ste

Catherine, a perpetual menace to the safety of Geneva, was levelled to the ground. The King took little part in these operations, being more concerned at the moment with the presence of a mistress and the prospect of a wife. But he wanted to witness the storming of the citadel of Montimélian, reputedly impregnable, and made known his intention. Rosny tried hard to persuade his master not to enter the danger zone and not to attract the attention of the besieged garrison by being present with a large train of followers. Henry seemed to assent; but when Rosny gave him a particular warning not to cross an open stone-covered field which was well within musket-shot of the battery, he promptly crossed it. Action is an escape from thought, physical danger an antidote to mental worry, and Henry, shortly to be under the cross-fire of two women, may have regarded the stony field as a haven of peace. The moment he and his party were observed the marksmen in the citadel got busy and the ground all round them was ripped up. After several showers of earth and rock, Henry said 'Let us leave, it is not pleasant here', and did so. The war was soon over and Henry won what he really needed. Savoy had to defray the expenses of the campaign, and as Henry had no designs on Italy he allowed the Duke to retain Saluzzo, contenting himself with the country to the east of the Rhone up to Lake Geneva, which adequately formed his frontier in those parts and completed his territorial designs for France; after which peace reigned throughout the realm for the rest of his life.

But peace was the last thing to be expected in his domestic circle, his habits not being of a kind to ensure it. While making love to Henriette he was writing love-letters to his future wife, who was described as 'a light brown beauty' with thick lips, black eyes, a spacious forehead, a gentle expression, 'and plenty of *embonpoint*', her age being twenty-seven. He told her that his envoy Frontenac had pictured her in such a manner that I don't merely love you as a husband ought to love his wife, but as a passionate *serviteur* should love his mistress. That is the title I shall give you until you reach Marseilles, where you will change it for a more honourable one. I shall not allow any opportunity to pass without writing to you, and assuring you that my keenest desire is to see you and have you near me. Believe it, mistress mine, and believe that every month will seem to me a century. I received a letter in French from you this morning; if you wrote it without help, you are already a great mistress of the language.

He had been taking the waters at Pougues and felt much better for them, reporting his condition: 'As you desire the preservation of my health, I recommend you to see to yours, so that on your arrival we may make a goodly child who shall delight our friends and be the despair of our enemies.'

He sent her dolls clothed in Parisian fashions, promised her a first-class dressmaker, asked for a favour which he could wear throughout the war, and wrote when he received it:

I thank you, my beautiful mistress, for the present you have sent me. I shall fix it to my headgear if we have a fight, and give a few sword-thrusts for love of you. I think you would willingly exempt me from giving you that proof of my affection, but as for what pertains to the acts of soldiers I do not ask the advice of women.

Henriette would have made some caustic comments if she had read one of her lover's notes to Marie: 'Hasten your journey as much as you can. If it were fitting for one to say that one is in love with one's wife, I would tell you that I am extremely in love with you.' His love was all-embracing, because a few weeks after writing that he was assuring Henriette that 'Since I could not kiss you, I have kissed your letter a thousand times . . . Good-night, heart, heart of mine; I kiss and kiss thee again a million times.'

In October 1600 Henry was married by proxy to Marie of Medici in Florence, his substitute being the Duke of Bellegarde, whose love of Gabrielle had caused the King so much jealousy and who had been an admirer of Henriette before Henry bought her. Bellegarde was considered the handsomest man at the French Court, while many thought Henry the ugliest; so the King was doing his best to make a favourable impression. Marie sailed from Leghorn, escorted by seventeen galleys, her own being laden with jewels. She landed at Toulon, where she received an alarming salute from Rosny's latest artillery. In her suite were two people who were to cause Henry much anxiety and to have considerable influence on his Queen. One was Concino Concini, an Italian of uncertain extraction; the other was Leonora Galigaï, of questionable origin. Passing through Marseilles and Avignon, the Medici procession arrived at Lyons on 8 December 1600.

The moment he heard of their arrival Henry left his mistress hurriedly and reached Lyons late on the night of the 9th. The gates of the city were closed, the King having wished to arrive in secrecy and see his wife before his presence was announced. He waited for an hour in the rain before he could gain an entry. Drenched to the skin he went at once to Marie's residence and hiding behind Bellegarde watched her having supper, a ritual attended by many spectators. When she had retired to her chamber, he knocked at the door, entered, introduced himself, caressed her fervently, and kissed her attendant Leonora Galigaï *à la française*. 'All that was polite, passionate and respectful, passed on both sides,' wrote the chronicler of the meeting, and they talked by the fireplace for about half an hour. He then had supper in another room, having eaten which he sent her a message that he had not provided himself with a bed, but expected she would give him part of hers, which thenceforth would be occupied by them in common. She returned word that she had come thither solely to obey his Majesty as the humblest of his servants. He undressed and joined her in bed. Their marriage was solemnized *in propria persona* the following day.

During the month's honeymoon at Lyons the Savoy business was settled, and the King learnt in the course of the negotiations that Marshal Biron had been in communication with the enemy throughout the war and would have committed treason if circumstances had been favourable. Biron, frightened by the prospect of betrayal by those whose interests he had tried to promote, confessed to the King that he had been tempted by ambition but now saw how wrong he had been, swore he would be loyal for the future, and entreated forgiveness. Henry knew a great deal more about Biron's treacherous behaviour than the Marshal confessed, but believed in his repentance and pardoned him, afterwards displaying his accustomed magnanimity by sending the young man as ambassador to England. Like so many incompetent people, Biron was excessively jealous of those who achieved success, one of whom, the Huguenot Duke of Lesdiguières, had shared with Rosny the honours of the recent campaign, being rewarded with a marshalship and a governorship, while Rosny was made a marquis.

The honeymoon over, the Queen set out for Paris, the King preceding her. Henriette was waiting for him at Fontainebleau, and they spent some days together before the Queen's arrival. The day after Marie reached Paris her husband took her to dine with the Marquis of Rosny at his official residence, the Arsenal. She was attended by all her Italian ladies, 'who, being pleased with the wine of Arbois, drank more of it than was necessary', wrote the courtly Rosny. Their liveliness annoyed the Queen but amused the King. Another incident increased her vexation. Among the princes, nobles and other persons of importance who were presented to her at Court was one of whom she had heard more than she wished to know. An old lady, the Duchess of Nemours, who disliked the duty but consented to do it at the King's urgent request, stepped forward and said : 'May I have the honour of presenting to your Majesty the Marchioness of Verneuil?' Turning to his wife Henry at once justified the introduction:

'Mademoiselle has been my mistress. She will be your most obedient and submissive servant.'

The Queen stood like a statue while the Marchioness bowed. But the courage that never forsook Henry in war and seldom upheld him with women now took possession of him. He put his hand firmly on the head of his mistress, forcing her to kneel and kiss the hem of the Queen's robe.

Henriette never forgot this humiliating scene, and whatever sort of part she may have played in the future she never became her Majesty's most obedient and submissive servant.

CHAPTER ELEVEN

Constructive

Ever since becoming King of France a grand idea had been germinating in Henry's mind. In his time, and frequently since, one great power wished to be overlord of the universe, representing in itself the general greed of humanity. The rulers of Austria, Spain, France, Germany, Russia, have all at various epochs dreamed of unlimited domination. In the sixteenth century the house of Hapsburg, with its Spanish branch, were the dreamers, and the imposition of the Catholic Church in Protestant countries was one of its objects. Henry's ambition, which grew with the internal success of his government, was to confine the Hapsburgs to Austria and Spain and restore the countries they had conquered and occupied to their native independence. He knew that there could be no peace in Europe while the Hapsburgs were at large, snapping up the territories of their neighbours and gradually increasing a power that, if not checked, would overrun the western world.

Their progress had been rapid. Starting in the thirteenth century, when a Hapsburg was king of Germany, they had added Austria, Carinthia and other countries to their dominions, and from the fifteenth century they had been Holy Roman emperors, the temporal heads of Christendom. Charles V, inheriting vast provinces, had added to them, and by the close of the sixteenth century the Hapsburg family controlled Austria, Germany, Spain, Naples, Sicily, Bohemia, Hungary, Burgundy, Flanders, Sardinia, the Balearic islands

and all the Low Countries, not to mention huge tracts of the
New World. They showed no signs of being content, and
Henry's 'Great Design' was to form a confederation of princes
who preferred freedom for their states to the almost certain
destiny of being swallowed up by the Austrian monster.
Henry foresaw a league of nations devoted to keeping the
peace of the civilized world by checking the predatory habits
of the Hapsburgs and ensuring the independence of the smaller
states.

By a strange coincidence, or perhaps not so strange when
we consider that they were the two most remarkable rulers
of their age, Elizabeth of England had hit on the same idea,
and the two exchanged their similar views in 1598. But
Elizabeth was chiefly concerned with breaking her immediate enemy Spain, while Henry's outlook was more
continental and he saw the Hapsburg menace centred in
Austria. Henry's conversion to the Roman religion seemed
to put him on the wrong side in the eyes of the English Queen,
but the Edict of Nantes showed that politics played a more
important part with him than religion, his toleration proving
that he would take no side in the conflicts of theology. The
two monarchs were thus in agreement on the main issue;
and when Henry was at Calais in 1601 for a general super-
vision of his northern frontier, Elizabeth travelled to Dover
in the hope that he would cross the straits for an interview.
But the Spaniards were closely observing him, and since
the Treaty of Vervins he wished to keep on friendly terms with
them, which made a visit to England inexpedient. He suggested
that Rosny should go instead, but as the strictest secrecy
was essential the Marquis would have to travel incognito with
very few attendants and let it be known that his journey was
for health or some other personal reason.

In late life Rosny wrote an account of the visit, the truth of
which has been questioned on the ground that there is no
corroborative evidence for it. But as the greatest care was

taken to conduct the expedition in extreme privacy, there would naturally be no official reference to it in French or English records. Rosny was recognized at Dover and taken to see the Queen, who asked 'if her good brother the King's affairs were now in a better state than in 1598, and if he were in a condition to begin, in good earnest, the great design which she had proposed to him?' Rosny replied that all the powers interested in the design must agree to combine before the enterprise could be undertaken. The Queen wanted Henry to join her in expelling the Spaniards from the Netherlands, but Rosny explained that Henry must for the time being keep to his treaty with Spain. Nevertheless he made plain to Elizabeth that the views she shared with the French King would be a pact between them, to be resolved in action when the right moment came.

This secret journey was followed two years afterwards by Rosny's officially recorded state visit to Elizabeth's successor, James I, his object being to arrange an alliance between France and England at the expense of Spain. To give importance to his embassage Henry wished to make him a duke, but the ambassador felt that he would rather not receive the title until the castle in his new domain of Sully was built. At present the foundations were being laid and he did not wish to be known as Duke of Sully before his estate was ready for the honour. Unable to promote him the King paid him so many compliments of such an extravagant nature that Rosny suffered a spasm of modesty when recalling them: 'I dare not mention what his Majesty further said in regard to that reputation of honour and fidelity which, he said, I had acquired among foreigners.'

On the eve of Rosny's departure for England in the spring of 1603 his master fell ill and sent a report that he was probably dying. Rosny at once set out for Fontainebleau and found the King in bed with the Queen by his side holding one of his hands. Having welcomed the visitor, Henry gave his wife some good advice on the subject of his chief minister: 'I know, indeed, that his temper is somewhat austere, that he is often too downright for such a spirit as yours', but if ever she took other counsels than Rosny's they would prove destructive to the state and prove ruinous to herself and their children. Valid words, which might have proved true if a man of genius, Cardinal Richelieu, had not arisen to carry on Henry's policy, though he lacked the humanity, common sense and idealism of Rosny's master. An improvement in Henry's physical condition, which had been caused by stricture, coincided with the arrival of Rosny, who entreated the King to moderate the energy he put into hunting, and recalled that: 'I did not myself return to Paris till I had seen the King make water; he would have it so, and he did it twice with such facility that I was perfectly satisfied that all danger was over.'

In the middle of June 1603 Rosny and his considerable retinue embarked at Calais in two English ships which had been placed at his disposal. The French vessel in which he had intended to cross the straits was commanded by an admiral and accompanied the others as escort. An awkward incident occurred when they reached Dover. The French admiral gave the ambassador a farewell salute by hoisting the French ensign, lowering it and raising it again, and was about to sail home with the ensign at the fore when the English admiral brought him up with a shot. Rosny with some difficulty explained that the flying ensign was merely a mark of respect to himself, but the Englishman replied with an oath that he would not permit any flag but that of England to be unfurled in the straits. At Rosny's request the Frenchman struck his flag while declaring with naval warmth that his revenge would come.

Although well received at the port the arrangements for their comfort were sadly defective. Invited to see Dover Castle, all the party except Rosny had to deliver up their swords and pay ransom money before leaving. No lodgings had been booked for his retinue, most of whom had to sleep on board the vessels that had brought them. No vehicles had been provided for their journey to London, and though Rosny and his secretaries travelled in the carriages of the resident French ambassador the rest of the party had to hire or buy at preposterous prices any aged horse or ancient carriage they could procure. At Canterbury they had a hospitable reception, but from Flemish and Walloon refugees, not from the English. Rosny was impressed by a service in the Cathedral, and by the edifice itself. At Rochester the English displayed their anti-French sentiments by rubbing out the marks placed on the lodgings engaged for the visitors, most of whom had to sleep in their vehicles. From Gravesend the chief gentlemen of the suite made the rest of the journey in the King's barges, and the salute from the guns at the Tower of London pleased the master of the French artillery, who, after some days at the French Embassy, was lodged at Arundel House, which had not been ready for him at first.

Another unpleasant incident occurred shortly after his arrival. The French were especially unpopular at the time because the followers of Marshal Biron, during his mission to Queen Elizabeth, had misbehaved themselves, brawling, fighting duels and insulting English citizens. Rosny warned his own followers that any breach of the peace would be punished with the utmost rigour and impressed upon them the necessity of good manners under whatever provocation. But to expect a high-spirited French youth of those days to behave like a gentleman in unsympathetic surroundings was the same as to anticipate similar conduct from a high-spirited English youth; and in the course of a quarrel between the adolescents of the two nations their swords were flourished and an Englishman was killed. Rosny, furious, called a council, which condemned the French duellist to death. The youngster was related to the Count of Beaumont, French ambassador at the English Court, who strongly protested against the sentence. Rosny ordered him out of the room and sent a message to the Lord Mayor, asking him to make the necessary arrangements for the execution. The Lord Mayor begged him to be less severe. He answered that what he had done was his plain duty to his own master and the English people; but he left the matter to the Lord Mayor, who could punish the lad in a manner suitable to English justice. Apparently the Count of Beaumont bribed the Lord Mayor to release the culprit, who left England.

Taking one thing with another Rosny did not form a favourable opinion of the English people.

It is certain[he wrote]that the English hate us, and this hatred is so general and inveterate that one would almost be tempted to number it among their natural dispositions. It is undoubtedly an effect of their arrogance and pride, for no nation in Europe is more haughty and insolent, nor more conceited of its superior excellence. Were they to be believed, understanding and common sense are to be found only among them; they are obstinately wedded to all their own opinions, and despise those of every other nation; and to hear others, or suspect themselves, is what never enters into their thoughts . . . Their self-love renders them slaves to all their capricious humours.

Rosny had intended that he and his retinue should appear at the English Court in black as a mark of respect to the memory of Queen Elizabeth, but to his amazement he was informed that such an appearance would be an affront to the Court, and at the last moment their garbs of woe were changed for garments of joy. He heard that James I spoke of his great predecessor with contempt, and that it was bad taste to mention the name of the late Queen. Forewarned by this knowledge, and somewhat perplexed, Rosny set off to visit James with a hundred and twenty gentlemen, the *élite* of his *cortège*. The King's guards escorted them to the river, and they were welcomed at Greenwich by the Earl of Northumberland,

175

passing through a multitude of people on their way to the palace.

'An elegant collation' was served, after which Rosny and his companions were shown into the throne-room. James, on catching sight of him, rose and advanced to meet him. The master of ceremonies whispered that this was at variance with Court etiquette, but his Majesty was not put out, saying aloud that he was aware of it but that as he had a special esteem and regard for the Marquis of Rosny his action must not be regarded as a precedent. Rosny's main concern was to open the question of the 'Great Design' on which his master and the late Queen had been agreed, but he prudently awaited a promising moment and answered the monarch's enquiries about the state of Henry's health and his love of the chase, wherein James claimed rivalry. A few remarks on religion were followed by the King's query: 'Do you, when speaking of the Pope, give him the title of "his Holiness"?' Rosny replied that he did so in conformity with the established usage of the French Court. But, objected James, such a title was offensive to God, to whom alone holiness should be attributed. It was not more sinful, answered Rosny, than the custom of ascribing to kings and princes the qualities they did not possess. James changed the subject and soon afterwards retired to rest.

The entire French suite were invited to dine at Greenwich a few days later. To the disgust of Rosny, who with the Count of Beaumont dined privately with the King, the dishes were served by kneeling attendants, an undignified and inconvenient ritual. James drank the toasts of the French King and Queen in bumpers of wine undiluted with water, and surprised Rosny by drinking 'to the double union of the children of the two royal houses', speaking the words in a confidential tone. Nothing could have answered Rosny's purpose better and he asked for a private audience. James granted it, and on two or three occasions they discussed an alliance between England and France against Spain. Rosny thought little of the King's political sagacity, and ultimately described him in a famous phrase, 'the wisest fool in Christendom', but managed to steer him on a course favourable to the alliance and to obtain his promise to sign a treaty approved by Henry.

Having exacted from James an oath 'by the Holy Eucharist' that the matter should remain a strict secret between them, Rosny then disclosed some details of Henry's grand scheme for breaking the power of the house of Austria by driving the Spaniards out of Flanders and forming a coalition of the German and Scandinavian princes. France and England were to make no additions to their own territories, but were to be content with the security achieved by the fall of the Hapsburgs. Germany would be restored to its ancient liberty in the election of its rulers and the nomination of the Roman Emperors. The United Provinces as well as Switzerland were to be republics, and all Christendom was to consist of a number of nations whose powers were roughly equal. The plan appealed to James, though Rosny perceived that his laziness gave little hope of active participation; and it did not escape the Frenchman's notice that the chief English minister, Robert Cecil, disliked the treaty of alliance against Spain. However the mission had been on the whole successful, and after the presentation of valuable gifts to the English monarch and his ministers, not forgetting their wives and daughters, Rosny and his train of followers sailed for France. The mission very nearly ended disastrously because a storm in the channel almost caused their boat to founder. They were at the mercy of the elements for a day and a half, reaching Boulogne in such an agitated condition that they practically fell ashore.

The treaty of alliance was drawn up, signed by Henry and James, and some seven thousand Scottish troops were despatched by the latter to Flanders for the defence of Ostend. As time went on Henry's 'Great Design' was developed. His first object was to make France safe and prosperous, which could only be attained if Europe were in a similar state; but soon he came to see all Europe as one great family, living in amity, without the need of armies and fortifications, freed from the bloody catastrophes hitherto so frequent. He had no desire to augment his own dominions. The essential aim was to divest the tyrannical house of Austria of its possessions in Germany, Italy and the Low Countries, and to confine the Hapsburgs to Austria and Spain, both of which should be given equality of status with the other countries and indemnification for their European deprivations. Outside Europe the Hapsburgs could keep such possessions as the Mediterranean islands, the islands off Africa, the lands they held in America and Asia. But they should no longer appropriate the imperial crown, and the Emperor of Rome, the chief magistrate of the whole Christian republic, should be elected by all the princes, never twice successively from the same family.

Rosny at first thought the plan chimerical, because of France's poverty and misery after the civil wars; but when the country began to prosper he became infected with Henry's enthusiasm and worked hard to perfect the necessary organization. Eventually, as Henry and himself came to see it, the concert of Europe would consist of six hereditary monarchies: France, Spain, England or Britain, Denmark, Sweden and Lombardy; five elective monarchies: the Roman Empire, the Papacy, Poland, Hungary and Bohemia; and four republics: the Venetian, the Swiss, the Belgic, and the Italian dukedoms. The Pope would be made a secular prince, governing Naples, Apulia, Calabria and their dependencies, and would bear rank with the other European monarchs. The delegates of each power, a senate of sixty-six persons, were to be chosen every three years to form a general council of Europe which would represent the Christian Republic or association of peaceful nations. Henry hoped that the Austrian house would decide not to fight, and every argument and entreaty would be used before resorting to force; but he knew that the negotiations would have to be backed by power because those who have conquered territory by arms do not readily surrender it to reason. If Austria decided to fight, Henry thought the campaign would last three years. Each of the allied nations would have to contribute horse, foot and artillery to the army of liberation, which would number over 150,000 men and 30,000 horses, Rosny being responsible for its provisioning. He was also responsible for an immense filing system, whereby the King could find at a moment's notice anything he wished to know about the state of the finances, the army, the navy, the artillery, the coinage, the mines, the police, of commerce and agriculture, of each aspect of government, civil, ecclesiastical, political and domestic. Every detail, from the possession of a large estate to the payment of a junior clerk, was contained in this massive collection of documents, and the King had only to ask a question about a fort or a title or a hospital or a maid of honour to get an answer within a few minutes. It was an astonishing and unprecedented compilation, and only Rosny's application, industry and keen eye for detail could have created such a record.

But all this, the 'Great Design' and the filing system, were fully developed in the last years of Henry's reign, and to make the first possible, the second needful, the country had to be transformed. The King and his remarkable minister set about the transformation. Having won security for the people by his military ability, Henry's next object was to achieve their prosperity by his organizing skill, and the first things to be done were to practise economy and lessen taxation. Economy, like charity, should begin at home, and Henry reduced all the expenses of his household, service, food and dress; his own meals and clothes had always been simple. He cut down the size of the army, and disallowed the bodyguards of governors and other functionaries. He forbade the carrying of firearms, with which people had been frightened into subjection by ex-soldiers and the ubiquitous brigands created by the civil wars. But before order could be restored it was essential that the peasantry should be freed from the tyranny of over-taxation and that the means of communication should be renovated or reformed.

Rosny went into the matter with his usual thoroughness. He discovered that the people were being burdened by the monstrous impositions of governors, military officers, civil magistrates and revenue administrators; what should have been paid by those in high places who claimed exemption was paid by those who had no influence. As we have seen, the state was being plundered by the few at the expense of the many. Bribery and corruption were rife, middlemen were enriched, and the taxes were farmed out by one lot of men who for a cash consideration delegated their authority to another lot, and so on, all the farmers and their agents filling their pockets as they passed their duties on to their successors. When this was fully revealed, Henry acquitted the people of all the arrears due from them and caused a strict examination to be made of the whole system. The plunderers did their best to escape with their booty by appeals to the law and other methods of obstruction, but Henry put an end to their tricks by passing a statute that in questions of finance an order once given could not be rescinded.

When the finances were in fair working order Henry and his minister turned their attention to the roads and rivers. After the civil wars the highways were overrun with briars and thorns and it was difficult to pick out the tracks. In a very short time the roads were repaired and greatly improved, causeways and bridges were built in places previously im-passable, the fens were drained, the streams made navigable, and canals were cut for easy communication between river and river. Though later monarchs got the benefit of their completion, Henry commenced the great canal joining the Loire and the Seine, and designed another to link the great waterways of the south. Public buildings were erected, new roads were opened, elms and other trees being planted along their borders, and better sanitation was introduced into the cities, Paris in particular, of which Henry was governor, being regularly cleansed.

Rosny disapproved of some attempts by the King to increase the commerce of France. A book on agriculture by a Huguenot named De Serres was dedicated to Henry, who read it, conversed with the author, and learnt some excellent new methods of tilling and cultivating the land. It also inspired him to plant avenues of mulberry trees all over France and to construct places for the rearing of silk-worms. Rosny was against this innovation, saying that 'time and experience will convince you that France is not fitted for these gewgaws'. But the King was right, both time and experience proving the opposite. Again, when Henry sanctioned the first company under Champlain to trade with Canada in 1603, Rosny declared that 'there was no kind of riches to be expected from all those countries of the New World which are beyond the fortieth degree of latitude'. But once more the monarch saw further than his minister. Indeed his foresight was exceptional, for the first company to be formed for trading with the East Indies was established in his reign. Rosny's chief objection to the introduction of indoor industries to a nation that had thrived on rural pursuits was his 'fear that a sedentary life in the close impure atmosphere of a manufactory would soon damp the spirits of the French and unfit them for that life of movement, of fatigue, of activity in the open air, that made the agricultural people a nursery of good soldiers'. But he need not have worried. The arts of peace are more fruitful than the crafts of war, and it was directly due to Henry that sheds were erected for two expert designers with the result that the Gobelin tapestries issued from what had originally been a dyeworks.

But on most questions Henry and Rosny saw eye to eye, and one of their firmest intentions was 'to correct the innumerable abuses of the bar, to abridge lawsuits, and to destroy the contemptible art of chicanery'. They tried hard, but in the process discovered that judges were as corrupt as the members of any other profession, as easily influenced by money or immoral pressure as those upon whom they passed judgment. Doubtless the King came to the conclusion that when law and its practitioners could be made to represent human nature at its best, the end of the world would be in sight. We may note in passing that the two optimists proposed a statute prohibiting parents from giving one of their children an unfair proportion of their property, thus anticipating the *Code Napoléon*.

Another of their well-considered projects concerned the army, and in a few years the armed forces were in a high degree of efficiency, well clothed, well paid and well cared for, with pensions if disabled and hospital treatment when wounded. Up to that time horses had been bought for the cavalry from England or Germany or elsewhere, but now breeding-studs were started in France. The artillery under Rosny became the admiration of Europe and French forts were put in a condition to withstand any guns of similar calibre that could be brought against them. The arts, too, received Henry's attention. Writers, architects, painters, musicians, designers, were encouraged and helped. When the manufacturers of rich fabrics, of carpets, linen and brocades, sustained loss at the beginning of their ventures, capital was provided to keep them going; and the same with masons, large sums being advanced for building; but the King's advice to Rosny was shrewd: 'Let them not lose, but let them not get too rich.'

Some of Rosny's methods of raising revenue were open to criticism, and the King criticized them, but Cardinal Richelieu defended and adopted them in the years ahead. Rosny however wanted to collect as much money as he could for the 'Great Design' and store it away in the coffers of the Bastille, of which he became governor in 1601. On the whole his methods were justified, for by 1605 the country had been transformed.

Perfection in human affairs being impossible, the hopes of Henry and his minister that they could create a model society such as the world had never seen were not to be fulfilled, but by 1605 the King had bought his kingdom. The debts he had contracted with foreign princes for military assistance and with his nobles for their submission had been paid off, the peasantry no longer groaned under the oppression of revenue tyrants and could sow and reap in security, the poorest tradesmen rejoiced in their profits, the nobles were busy cultivating their estates instead of despoiling the land of their enemies or wasting their time at Court, the embezzlement of financiers had been suppressed, the kingdom was tranquil, the King's authority supreme, the country affluent, and Rosny could claim that 'this happiness, which derived its source from the benevolent disposition of Henry, reflected in its turn upon him, and gave him back part of the benefits he bestowed'. But when Rosny went on to assert that Henry now enjoyed 'the calm pleasures of a private life', he overstated the case. The King was much too easy-going to be always at ease; his lax habits caused much trouble in the home circle; and though his Court was free of the criminal intrigues and murderous episodes that had horrified onlookers in the time of the later Valois monarchs, his own sexual frailties were studiously copied by his courtiers, to the detriment of domestic concord. 'The French were ever fond of novelties,' said Henry, 'and eagerly admit every change.' But his frequent change of mistresses did not add to his popularity with his fickle subjects, and Rosny was not the only person who regretted his careless disposition.

Rosny's work was his hobby. He usually rose at four o'clock in the morning, winter and summer, and apart from brief airings laboured all day, going to bed at ten. He was abstemious in everything, though few people today would use his word 'moderate' in describing his dinner of ten covers. He had no respect for persons of the highest rank and would

refuse concessions to royal princes or even to the Queen if he
thought the King's interest was at stake. As a consequence he
made many enemies, and suffered for his austerity when, after
his master's death, the Queen took the management of affairs
out of his hands. Henry had a pleasant open-handed manner,
exasperating to his minister of finance, of giving presents to
people he liked or wished to conciliate; and one day he granted
a petition of the Count of Soissons, who asked for fifteen pence
on every bale of exported goods, which, said he, would bring
in no more than thirty thousand livres a year. The Count had
given his cousin the King much trouble in early days, but what
dried up the spring of other people's sympathy opened up the
well of Henry's, and the favour was granted. When Rosny
got to hear of it he went into the matter and found that the
tax would yield three hundred thousand crowns, also that such
a toll might ruin the trade of hemp and linen in Brittany,
Normany and Picardy. He further discovered that the
Marchioness of Verneuil had helped to persuade the King to
make the grant and would greatly benefit thereby.

Rosny was on the point of visiting the King with the object
of influencing him against a number of such extortions, which
would impoverish the common people, when the Marchioness
called, probably having heard of what was in the wind. She
asked what paper he had in his hand. He told her that it was a
list of people who were to benefit in one way or another by
royal edict, adding that she herself would be a beneficiary if
the King passed the edicts favouring the exactions, of which he
personally disapproved. She said that if Rosny carried his
point with the King many people would be offended, and asked
'On whom, pray, would you have the King confer favours if
not on those who are mentioned in that paper, his cousins,
friends and mistress?' He replied:

What you say, madame, would be reasonable enough if his
Majesty took all the money out of his own purse; but to make a

new levy upon the merchants, artists, labourers and countrymen, it will never do. It is by them that the King and all of us are supported, and it is enough that they provide for a master, without having so many cousins, friends and mistresses to maintain.

The Marchioness, enraged, reported what had happened to Soissons, who told the King that Rosny had injured his honour. The King wanted to know whether he had been directly affronted by Rosny or another person had related the insult. Soissons blustered at first but soon admitted that the affront had been reported to him. 'Who reported it?' demanded Henry. Soissons declared that he had taken an oath not to divulge the name of the person who had told him. 'So, then, cousin,' said the King, 'you excuse yourself from answering my question on account of an oath you have taken to the contrary; and I likewise will take an oath to believe no more of your complaint than Monsieur de Rosny himself shall acknowledge to me; for I have as good an opinion of his veracity as you can possibly have of those who tell you these fine tales.'

Henry then strongly advised Rosny to go about guarded because Soissons was furious enough to attempt his life. Later Henry heard that the Marchioness of Verneuil's report had aroused the anger of Soissons. 'She is so full of malice and has such a ready invention,' said the King, 'that to the least word of Monsieur de Rosny's she would add a hundred, nay a thousand.'

He had cause to say so.

CHAPTER TWELVE

Between Two Fires

It was plain to everyone at Court that the Queen's two favour-
ites, Concino Concini and Leonora Galigaï, would exercise
considerable influence over her; and Henry's mistress, the
Marchioness of Verneuil, perceived that her own future would
be less liable to fluctuation if she became friendly with the pair.
Concini was a good-looking, vicious and subtle schemer,
Galigaï was ugly, hysterical and ruthlessly ambitious.
Together they made a powerful combination, and Henriette
determined to take advantage of it. She became friendly with
Galigaï, who wanted to be Mistress of the Robes, an office
the King did not wish her to hold. An alliance between the two
would benefit both; Henriette could persuade the King to
withdraw his opposition to Galigaï, while the latter could
induce the Queen to show some favour to her husband's
mistress. It was a pretty plot, and it succeeded. At first the
King took a violent dislike to the two Italian adventurers and
wanted to bundle them back to Florence. But he could not
overcome the Queen's resistance, and soon he heard that
Concini and Galigaï wished to be married, the first obviously
for ambitious motives, the second patently because she felt
flattered. For a while it seemed that the Queen might become
friendly with Henriette, which pleased Henry so much that
he felt unwilling to thwart her wishes, a situation accurately
gauged by the wire-pullers. He soon gave way. Concini and

Galigaï were married, Henry giving the lady a generous present; Galigaï became Mistress of the Robes; Concini confidently expected to be a Gentleman of the Chamber; the future residence of both in France was assured; and Henry thought that, his wife pacified, his mistress would be well received at Court.[1]

But having obtained the security and promotion of her favourites the Queen's attitude to the Marchioness of Verneuil became markedly hostile, and their relationship was not improved when Henry installed his mistress within the precincts of the Louvre. Their rivalry was intensified when the Queen gave birth to a son (afterwards Louis XIII) on 27 September 1601. Shortly before the event Henry wrote to comfort his wife: 'Don't be afraid. I shall be one of your midwives.' Not to be outdone Henriette produced a boy exactly a month later, the latter being legitimized by the King to the annoyance of the Queen, whose temperature would have risen dangerously if she had read her husband's letter to Henriette about the Dauphin, written at Fontainebleau:

My dear Heart
     My wife is going on well and my son also, praise God. He has grown and filled out so much that he has become half as big again during the five days I did not see him. For my part I have slept remarkably well and am free from all pain save that of being absent from you, which though a grief to me is moderated by the hope of soon seeing you again. Good-morrow, *mes chères*

[1] After Henry's death Concini became the chief favourite of the Queen, who loaded him with riches and honours and created him Marquis of Ancre and Marshal of France. Hated by the nobility, he was murdered at the Louvre by order of Louis XIII, his wife Leonora being publicly burnt as a sorceress. Asked at her trial by what means she had bewitched the Queen Regent, she said: 'By the charm of a strong mind over a weak one', adding that her sole witchcraft had been her wit: 'Is it at all to be wondered at that I governed the Queen, who had none?'

amours, always love your *menon*, who kisses your hands and lips a
million times.

Henry's delight over his children, both natural and legitimate, was not always shared by their mothers, who could not
help remembering that deliveries were expected elsewhere.
The birth of the Dauphin transported him. He embraced
everybody, and when the nurses said that the noise of gratu-
lation would disturb the Queen he cried: 'This child belongs
to all the world, and everybody must see him and rejoice.' He
took the baby in his arms, blessed him, asked Heaven to do the
same, and prayed that he would never draw the sword except
for the glory of God and the good of his subjects, which
implied that God was a Frenchman. Feeling that the capital
should enjoy the pleasure of seeing the heir to the throne, he
ordered that the cradled baby should be placed on a litter and
conducted through Paris with nurses and soldiers in attendance.
Rosny celebrated the occasion by firing off all the cannon in the
arsenal.

But the versatile King was afflicted in a similar manner over
the son of his mistress. According to a trustworthy chronicler,
he 'kissed the child and dandled him, calling him his son, and
saying that he was a finer child than that of the Queen, his wife,
which he declared resembled the Medicis, being dark and
stout as they were . . .' He certainly left no doubt in the mind
of Henriette that, whatever he may have felt about the children,
he preferred her to the Queen, for he wrote soon after the birth
of their boy: '*Mes chères amours*, love me always and rest
assured that you will always be the only one to possess my
love. With those true words I kiss and re-kiss you a million
times, and the little man as well.'

A fresh cause of vexation was given the Queen when Henry
insisted that all his children should be brought up together,
Gabrielle's, Henriette's and her own. Saint-Germain was
regarded by him as more salubrious than Fontainebleau, and

the royal nursery was established there. On this point he remained adamant, and the nursery, with regular additions, continued at the same spot for the rest of his reign. As the babes were all legitimized, none could crow over the rest on reaching years of articulation, but it is possible that the Queen's children learnt to feel a little superior to the others owing to the greater deference paid them by the nurses. On such points the chronicler is silent, and we must fall back on our knowledge of juvenile contentions.

A year after the birth of the Dauphin a girl was born to the Queen, and two months later a girl was born to the Marchioness, the sequence becoming almost a ritual. The Queen, deeply disappointed because she had not produced another boy, received consolation from the King, who told her that if she had not been of the same sex as her daughter she would never have been Queen of France, and that in any case the misfortune might be repaired. Rosny was deputed to do everything in his power to please and amuse the Queen and keep her quiet—'also, if possible, in a good temper'. At all times the King longed for a peaceful domestic life, and though he could not do the one thing that would have achieved it he never ceased to strive his utmost to placate his wife. Once, when she was in a good mood, he said to her: 'How charmed am I to see you in this humour, my dear! I beseech you let us always live together in this manner.' Rosny tells us that Henry was much concerned over his wife's health and happiness, and that 'he never omitted giving her every instance of respect and tenderness that was able to make her forget the uneasiness she received from his amours'. But that was precisely the trouble. She thought that his kindness was a blind to cover his infidelity; which was but partly true, kindliness being the essence of his nature. But her own nature was the opposite of his, and in her eyes his virtues were extinguished by his vices. She was jealous, stubborn, bad-tempered, and, as her friend Galigaï gave witness, stupid. She thrived on emotional scenes, and made life a hell for her husband or anyone who took his part. Sometimes she even threatened him physically, her arms being strong, her nails sharp. The thing that drove her to distraction was his passion for Henriette, whose sarcastic remarks about herself were duly reported by her spies.

Henry's loyalty to both was severely tested by the names they called each other. A strong man in war and diplomacy, he was a shuttlecock between two women. Henriette used her sexual power to torment him, and they constantly quarrelled. She pretended to forget the facility with which she had yielded to his desires and she could not resist mentioning the letter he had written her with a promise of marriage, claiming as a consequence that her son was the rightful heir to the throne. The Queen's eavesdroppers were everywhere and in time she got to hear of that letter, nagging Henry so persistently that he promised to obtain possession of it, although obviously it was no longer valid. He ordered the Marchioness to return it, but she refused in offensive language and a storm of rage, threatening to break off all intimacy with him. She told him that his age made him jealous and suspicious, and she spoke of his wife in such contemptuous terms that he was on the point of striking her, but left suddenly in order to calm down. He put his wishes in writing, but her reply failed to ease the situation and he tried again:

> I perceive from your letter that neither your eyes nor your understanding are extremely clear, since you have taken what I wrote to you in quite a different sense to what I intended. An end must be put to these pertnesses, if you propose to keep the entire possession of my love; for neither as a King nor a Gascon can I submit to them. Besides, those who love sincerely as I do expect to be flattered, not scolded.

Again he complained: 'You have promised me to behave with more prudence, but you must be sensible the style of your other letter could not but give me offence.'

Thus he was between two fires, exposed to the fury of two women, and though he longed for concord his needs produced discord. There were periods when his wife 'deprived him of the privileges of a husband' and his mistress deprived him of the pleasures of a courtesan. Rosny advised him to adopt a decided tone with women, saying 'I wish it' or 'Such is my desire', but Henry found such an attitude impossible. Rosny could not understand his master's weakness. When any difficulty or argument arose between the Marquis and Marchioness of Rosny it was quickly settled, for we read in his memoirs: 'I imposed silence on my wife.' Henry could not impose silence on any woman, and his only escape from the shrew and the vixen was to run away. But he found it difficult to run away from Henriette, who enslaved him at one moment and enraged him at another; and though he sometimes left her with the firm intention of staying away, his wife's bitterness and gloom soon drove him back to the liveliness of his mistress. 'I find nothing of all this at home,' he told Rosny:

I receive neither society, amusement, nor content from my wife. Her conversation is unpleasing, her temper harsh; she never accommodates herself to my humour, nor shares in any of my cares. When I enter her apartment, and offer to approach her with tenderness, or begin to talk familiarly with her, she receives me with so cold and forbidding an air that I quit her in disgust and am obliged to seek consolation elsewhere.

He begged Rosny to prevail on the Queen to alter her behaviour and adapt herself more to his humour. Though aware that mediators usually win the resentment of both parties in a dispute, though he hated the task and thought himself constitutionally unsuited to it, Rosny became a sort of liaison officer between the King and Queen and between Henry and Henriette. He warned the King that his Majesty alone could mend matters at home by banishing his mistress and satisfying his wife. Henry replied that, if he did so, it would not have the desired effect, because the Queen would plague him for the rest of his life on account of his past. Already she displayed a violent hatred for all his natural children, even though some of them were born before she came to France, which showed that she was governed by passion and resentment. The only thing, then, was for Rosny to persuade her to be more reasonable without letting her suspect that he was acting at her husband's request.

Knowing in advance the futility of his mission, Rosny saw the Queen, who worked herself into a temper, called the Marchioness every opprobrious epithet that came into her head, and accused her husband of being blinded by lust. Rosny waited patiently until she had talked herself out, and then diplomatically urged her to write a mollifying letter to the King, which he dictated. Henry wrote a tender reply, and all went well between them until her spies reported that he was still visiting the Marchioness, with whom he joked about his wife's credulity. Again Henry was subjected to 'the hourly shot of angry eyes', and again Rosny was called in to mediate.

And so it went on. At times the Queen appeared to be gracious and well-disposed, and all was running smoothly when the machinations of the Marchioness or the Queen's secret informers precipitated another crisis. Henry himself was tossed on a sea of emotions, and Rosny could never trust him to show strength of mind in dealing with either female. A tempest of wrath from the Queen drove him into the arms of Henriette, who could aggravate him so much that he sought refuge at home, and he passed his time between them in a fever. Henriette was probably unfaithful to him as well, and jealousy was added to his grievances. On hearing a report of her infidelity, he asked Rosny for advice, and was told that he had better hear what the Marchioness had to say for herself before condemning her. 'Oh heavens! hear her!' cried Henry: 'She has such power of expression that, if I listen to her, she will persuade me that I am to blame and that she is injured. Yet I will speak to her and show her the proofs of her perfidy.' He did so, and she fulfilled his prophecy.

In the matter of fidelity Henry was vulnerable. He had become enamoured of Jacqueline de Bueil, and after her marriage in October 1604 to a man who would not insist on a husband's privileges she was created Countess of Moret and the King's mistress. But she was a brainless doll and Henry searched for comfort elsewhere, finding it with Charlotte des Essarts, soon made Countess of Romorantin. Both women had children by the King, and the latter caused him some trouble because she expected to exercise the same sway over him as his other mistresses had done, her failure resulting in scenes. But Henry had enough of these elsewhere to keep him occupied, and with Rosny's help she was bribed away to some country retreat.

The existence of other mistresses did not affect the King's passion for Henriette, who maintained her power over him by indulging in periods of chastity and galling him still further with the pretence that her asceticism was enforced by religion. She explained that she had been living with him in a state of mortal sin and that her soul's safety depended on fasts, penances and other religious practices. This was particularly vexing to a man whose physical desires were more insistent than calls to a spiritual life and whose participation in the frailties of his partner made him feel responsible for her spasms of holiness. Disregarding her yearnings for sanctity, he treated the affair on a basis of give-and-take:

If your words were followed by effects I should not be so dissatisfied with you as I am. Your letters speak solely of affection, but your behaviour towards me is nothing but ingratitude. For five years and more you have persisted in that style of life which everybody finds strange. Judge what it must be to me, whom it touches so closely. It is useful to you that people should think I love you, and shameful to me that they should see I suffer because you do not love me. That is why you write to me and I reply to you by silence. If you will treat me as you ought to do, I shall be more than ever yours; if not, keep this letter as the last you will ever receive from me, who kisses your hands a million times.

The arrival of Holy Week in April 1604 seems to have brought celestial cogitations, and on Good Friday he informed Rosny:

Since Madame de Verneuil is resolved on what you write me, I also am resolved on what I told you on Monday. I shall inform her of my intentions, and show that I have more command over myself than is said, and I do not think that this news will trouble her thoughts, which I would not do during these good days.

We may remark here that Rosny, who found his master entirely honest and trustworthy in all other matters, noticed that in affairs of the heart he was mendacious, his jealousy and rage making him wholly unreliable.

Henriette was alarmed when Henry began to take a strong line. She became less religious and they were soon reconciled. He had given her a house at Fontainebleau and took the risk of asking her to settle there while he was in residence at the palace. The moment the Queen heard this she made a scene and the usual family rumpus followed. But a storm of a different kind was now gathering, which very nearly obliterated Henriette.

Her half-brother the Count of Auvergne was a born plotter and spent his life intriguing as another might spend it hunting or gambling. He resembled the man who had plotted four times against the King and, having been forgiven for the fourth time, earned the monarch's comment: 'He has no sooner got a pardon in one pocket than he has a scheme for a plot ready in the other.' It happened that Auvergne was involved in the transference of important state papers to the Spanish ambassador. The man who actually effected the delivery was drowned in the Marne while fleeing from justice, but Auvergne fell under suspicion, and in order to sidetrack this he went to the King with a story about his mistress, saying that he had discovered an affair between Henriette and the Duke of Bellegarde. As Henry had suffered in the past from Bellegarde's success with women, he insisted that Auvergne should charge his half-sister in person. She of course denied it hotly. He named his informant, who on being produced called him a liar. A duel would have resulted if the King had not forbidden it. Auvergne left Paris hurriedly.

About this time James I of England wrote to Henry warning him to keep an eye on a man named Morgan, who was in the pay of Spain and earning his money by espionage in France. The apprehension of Morgan disclosed a number of compromising letters, some of which had been written by Henriette's father, Entragues. Naturally Henry asked his mistress for an explanation, but she said that they were probably letters of introduction to her cousin the Duke of Lennox, English ambassador to the Court of France. Not so, Henry replied, since her name was mentioned in them. He then sent for her father, who after much fencing admitted that he had been in communication with Spain over matters concerning his daughter. Again Henry asked his mistress to explain, and again she denied all knowledge of it. He begged her to persuade her father to make a clean breast of it; and when next they met Entragues went so far as to confess that he had been concerned over his daughter's future in the event of Henry's death to ensure which he had sounded various people with the object of providing a safe asylum for her in Spain or elsewhere. He also said that the Spanish envoy had offered him 200,000 crowns for the promise of marriage which Henry had written to his daughter, but that as a loyal man he had instantly refused the bribe. This implied that a great deal more was in the wind than a safe retreat for the Marchioness of Verneuil, and Henry decided to act with vigour the moment he heard that Entragues had immured himself in the fastness of Marcoussis.

There was in fact a very serious conspiracy on foot, involving Entragues, his daughter Henriette, his stepson Auvergne, the Duke of Bouillon (erstwhile Viscount of Turenne), and several more nobles both Catholic and Protestant. Ambition and desire for power were, as always, at the root of these treasonable plots. The would-be traitors disliked Henry because he was unlike themselves; the Catholics thought him too indulgent to the Protestants, who thought him too favourable to the Catholics; all of them hated Rosny and his revenue reforms which prevented them from fleecing the poor; most of them were displeased with the good order of the realm because they reaped profit from disorder; above all they were no longer independent rulers, Henry having made up his mind from the first that government must reside in the Crown, since feudalism in effect meant not only lack of national unity but disobedience to the central authority, possible insurrection, no generally recognized system of laws, and localized tyranny that could not be checked. Briefly the intention of the disaffected nobles was to restore their own rulerships in their various territories, in short to revive feudalism. They had no wish to see a France consolidated and prosperous; they were solely concerned with their own positions as absolute rulers in their districts. Even as it was, the governors of Provence, Limousin, Poitou, Champagne, Picardy and other regions, appointed by the King as his lieutenants, were free within limits, but they were answerable to the monarch for their stewardships and liable to be dismissed if they transgressed. The discontented nobles were relatively few, but they hoped in time to induce others to join them in the dismemberment of France, and the fact that if the country were broken up into a number of small principalities, as in Germany at that time, it would become the prey of Spain, did not cause them anxiety.

Indeed it was with the help of Spain that they hoped to accomplish their designs. Henry's promise of marriage to Henriette was the bait, and though that document was quite invalid the ministers of Philip III believed that by its judicious use a war of succession might be started in France, its object being to place Henriette's son, the legitimized offspring of Henry, on the throne. Entragues, his daughter and family were promised a secure refuge in Spain, large pensions, and the Spanish King's support in claiming the French throne for a boy whose birth did not fulfil the bargain in the King's written pledge.

The sudden discovery of their intrigues with Spain upset their plans, which required more time to mature, and all they could now do was to sit tight and hope for the best. But the King was not in a mood to leave them in peace, and he ordered the provost-marshal to arrest Entragues. The castle of Marcoussis was too strong for an open assault, so the provost-marshal gained an entry by artifice. Entragues was in bed, but faced with a party of archers he had to leave it. His attempt to bribe the officer failed, and he was taken to the Conciergerie in Paris. The King then instructed the provost to search the castle. Many documents were found, including letters of a treasonable character written by Auvergne and the Spanish King's signed promise that on the death of Henry IV he would acknowledge the Marchioness of Verneuil's son as legitimate heir to the French throne. Several of the lesser conspirators were at once arrested; Auvergne escaped and sought refuge in an ancient fort, from which he was allured by a stratagem and captured; while Entragues, in an attempt to save his life, offered to return that written promise which had caused so much anxiety to the King and Queen and might have helped to plunge France into another civil war. Henry accepted the offer, Entragues described where it was hidden, and the paper emerged from beneath some cotton stuffed into a bottle which was concealed in a castle wall.

At first Henry would not believe that his mistress had taken part in the conspiracy, and he asked her to St-Germain where her children were gambolling with those of Marie and Gabrielle. But when things began to look black against her, and she wished to plead for her father, Henry would not see her, ordering her back to Verneuil. In the search of her castle that had been made by the King's order during her absence, nothing much of a political nature had been found, but there were some lover-like letters from a certain noble which caused Henry anguish, and it was at this moment that he tried to transfer his feelings for Henriette to the girl who soon became the Countess of Moret; but she was unable to absorb them and left the residue to another girl, afterwards Countess of Romorantin.

With her father at the Conciergerie and her half-brother in the Bastille, the Marchioness of Verneuil was now under house-arrest in the Faubourg St-Germain, where a messenger from the King informed her that if she would make a full confession of everything she had done and of which she had knowledge she might receive a pardon, which would also be granted to those she named. She replied: 'Death does not frighten me. On the contrary I shall welcome it. If the King takes my life it will at all events be said that he had put his wife to death, for I was Queen before the Italian was.' The messenger pressed for an answer to the King's proposal. She refused at first to say a word, but perhaps the memory of Auvergne's effort to traduce her eventually loosened her tongue: 'I desire but three things, justice for myself, clemency for my father, and a rope for my brother.'

Entragues, Auvergne and Henriette were interrogated by the president of the Paris parliament before their trial. The first tried to get out of the difficulty by repeating his story that he was arranging a refuge for his daughter in case of need, the second put all the blame for what had happened on his half-sister, and the third maintained her pose of scornful aloofness. They were duly tried by parliament, which convicted Entragues and Auvergne of treason, deprived them of their ranks and honours, and condemned them to be beheaded on the Place de Grève. Henriette was found guilty of an intention to take her children out of the kingdom without the King's permission; but the court stated that her case should be investigated further, until which she was to remain in custody at the abbey of Beaumont, near Tours. The King at once called a meeting of his council, which commuted the death sentences to perpetual imprisonment and permitted Henriette to live at Verneuil. Later the council declared her innocent and prohibited further enquiries into her behaviour, their final decision having no doubt been influenced by a passionate letter she wrote to the King. It was probably due to her that her father received his freedom, though for a while his movements at Marcoussis were closely watched. Auvergne's wife begged his pardon of the King, who said: 'I feel for your sorrow and your tears, but if I were to grant your request it would be the same as declaring that my wife is a woman of evil life, my son a bastard, and my kingdom fit prey for anybody.' Auvergne remained in the Bastille for some years, and it is clear from a letter the King wrote to Henriette that he had no faith in the loyal protestations of Entragues:

My dear Heart,
    I have received three letters from you, to which I will make but one reply. I consent to your making a journey to Beaugency, and also to your seeing your father, whose guards I have had removed. But remain with him only one day, for the contagion from him is dangerous. I deem it good that you should go to St-Germain to see our children. I will send you La Guesle, for I also wish that you should see their father, who loves and cherishes you too much . . . Love me, my little one, for I swear

to thee that all the rest of the world is nothing to me in comparison
with thee, whom I kiss and kiss again a million times.

For a year or two Henry tried to solace himself with the
company of the two ladies of whom we have spoken; but his
correspondence with Henriette in the autumn of 1606 shows
that they were on the old intimate terms, quarrelling as usual
and making it up as before. Once she upbraided him, saying:
'I pray you never come to see me again. You have never
brought me anything but misfortune.' He rejoined: 'Reflect a
little, madam, I do not deserve this treatment.' They continued to meet, though each complained that the other was
unfaithful. Whenever she wanted him to grant her a favour
she forgot his infidelity and wrote as a trustful lover, knowing
quite well that his heart could easily be moved by warmth of
feeling. On one such occasion he responded in this manner:
'My Heart, my joy is extreme at the thought of seeing you
on Saturday. Make up your mind to cherish me well when I
arrive.'

Their relationship continued up to the end of 1608, and
he had to brave the Queen's temper whenever she heard that
he had visited Henriette. Apparently Marie did not much
object to his affairs with the Countesses of Moret and
Romorantin, even though they bore him children, but she
regarded the mere existence of Henriette as an outrage,
possibly because she could not endure the insulting descrip-
tions by that lady of herself which reached her ears, such as
'the banker's fat daughter'. Henry disliked these quips at the
expense of his wife, but could not resist the sprightly conversation and seductive charm of Henriette, his sentimental
affection for whom came out in a letter of April 1608 during
a hunting expedition which took him near Bois-Malesherbes,
where they had first met:

A hare led me to the rocks before Malesherbes, where I
experienced 'how sweet the memory is of pleasures past'. I

wished I had held you in my arms as I once saw you there. Recall it while you read this letter. I feel sure that the memory of the past will cause you to scorn everything of the present. In any case you would do so did you follow the paths along which I so often passed in going to see you. *Mes chères amours*, if I sleep my dreams are of you, if I lie awake my thoughts are the same.

She made further demands on him early in 1609, when she wished to be received once more at Court, to have the guardianship of her children, and to be given the city of Metz as a safe retreat. But Henry was by then in the grip of a new passion, and sent polite replies.

CHAPTER THIRTEEN

Conspiratorial

The endurance of personal hardship, which creates callousness or resentment in most people, deepened Henry's humanity. From the horrors of protracted civil war, the cruelties of religious bigotry and the constant danger of assassination, he emerged with a charity, sympathy and geniality unmatched among the great leaders of men. All his life he did his best by gentleness and kindness to gain the affection and loyalty of treacherous men, and when they continued to be disloyal he forgave them, still hoping to win what their natures could not give. His friend Rosny was more realistic, affirming that 'From men all things may be expected; they are not to be kept firm in their duty, integrity and the laws of society by fidelity and virtue, but by their hopes and wishes.' Henry's curious position as a Catholic King whose crown had been won for him by the Protestants provided an excuse for the actions of men with restless ambitions. The Protestants could not forgive him for being a Catholic hero, and the Catholics could not forgive him for having once been a Protestant hero. He had won famous battles in both characters, with the result that neither side was pleased, and aspiring peers were therefore able to exploit popular dissatisfaction in their own interests. With the exception of the Entragues-Auvergne cabal, the most serious conspiracies Henry had to face after becoming King in more than name were those of Biron and

Bouillon, the first a Catholic, the second a Protestant, each using his faith to excuse his love of power, to appease his vanity, and to mitigate his sense of inferiority.

Biron's father, the old marshal, had been among those Catholic nobles who had immediately supported Henry on the death of his predecessor, supported him on payment of a good round sum; and though the Marshal's behaviour at the siege of Rouen had aroused suspicion that the job could have been conducted with greater vigour, he had been faithful to his obligations and had been killed in the King's service. His son, a courageous soldier, earned Henry's good opinion, and in time his affection. The young man did well at the siege of Amiens before the King's arrival there, but soon began to show signs of envy at the other's success. Henry ascribed this petulance to youth, and gave him a good command in the campaign against Savoy. As we know, Biron started conspiring with Charles Emanuel, guessed that his intrigues would reach Henry's ears, made a confession, displayed contrition, and received forgiveness. By now he had become a marshal, a duke and governor of Burgundy. A further honour awaited him. Henry sent him as Ambassador Extraordinary to Queen Elizabeth, who must have heard of his duplicity because she lectured him on the wickedness of rebellion and held up the fate of the Earl of Essex as an example of what happened to disturbers of the peace. Biron was then sent to Switzerland for the purpose of renewing an alliance with the cantons. On returning to France he could not keep out of mischief. Conspiracy was in his bones; he loved secrecy and trickery, the excitement of a gamble; for him two birds in the bush were worth more than one in the hand; there was something romantic and dangerous about whispers behind locked doors and missives so confidential that they must be eaten if in jeopardy; the peril was thrilling, the promise sensational.

As usual Spain was the instigator of the conspiracy in 1602.

Biron was promised the dukedom of Burgundy, which would be an independent state, large sums of money, and the Duke of Savoy's daughter as wife. He managed to secure the Duke of Bouillon and others as fellow-conspirators, their main object being, as later with Entragues, the dismemberment of France to the greater glory of Spain. Negotiations took place between Fuentes, the Spanish governor of Milan, and La Fin, who was in the confidence of Biron. But Fuentes distrusted La Fin and after discussing the matter with the Duke of Savoy decided to get rid of him. La Fin disliked the prospect of being murdered and wasted no time in leaving Italy. Partly from policy, partly out of anger, he made up his mind to acquaint the King of the whole conspiracy. In order to obtain convincing proofs of Biron's part in the business, he repaired to Burgundy, leaving his nephew to break the news to Henry. He knew that the whole plan of the plot, drawn up in Biron's hand, was in that nobleman's house; so he told the Marshal that the possession of such a document was extremely dangerous and strongly advised him to have it copied and then destroyed, after which he could repudiate it if necessary. Biron saw the point, gave La Fin the document, and told him to copy it there and then. La Fin did so, but instead of committing the original manuscript to the flames he slipped it into his pocket, crumpled up a sheet he had brought with him for the purpose, and threw that into the fire, thereby proving himself a worthy conspirator. The dealer in treachery should not be surprised when his minions turn traitor; but owing to his twisted nature he cannot see straight; and Biron's egotism did not allow him to suspect that he could be hoodwinked so easily.

Having secured the plan without much trouble, La Fin had little difficulty in persuading Biron to write him a letter directing him to destroy all the papers in his possession. This further evidence, together with the damning document in the Marshal's own hand, were sufficient for La Fin's purpose, and he made haste to Fontainebleau, where he unfolded the scheme to the King with all the written proofs.

At first Henry could not believe it, though no one who had known the later Valois kings had less cause for confidence than he. But there was nothing in his own nature to explain the treachery of others; he had heaped honours on Biron, of whom he was very fond; and he found it almost impossible to believe that a brave French soldier should betray his country to her chief enemy, knowing that a Spanish army would enter France and that the small sovereignties then to be created would be fiefs of the Spanish Crown. It took some time for the knowledge to sink in, and Henry visited Poitou to settle some trouble there before taking any measures.

Returning to Fontainebleau he sent a message to Biron desiring his presence at Court. Biron excused himself from attendance, upon which Henry sent word that if he did not come he would receive a visit from the King, and at the same time he was assured of Henry's friendly intentions. Biron obeyed and was affectionately received by the King, who said: 'You have done well to come, otherwise I should have set out to seek you.' They walked together in the gardens, while Henry calmly spoke of the rumours that had reached him concerning treasonable designs that implicated the Marshal, who promptly and positively denied his complicity, La Fin having privily assured him that the King knew nothing of his plan. Henry pursued the matter in some such words as these: 'Biron, you know how highly I have esteemed you, how I have admired your intrepidity as a soldier, your ability as a general. I now promise to pardon fully those acts of high treason you have been led into against me, if you will acknowledge them and promise to avoid such acts for the future.' Instead of appreciating the King's extraordinary indulgence, Biron stood on his dignity: 'I have nothing to acknowledge, nor do I understand why a man of honour should be pressed to accuse himself of crimes he has not committed.'

Later the same day Henry tried once more to make Biron confess his guilt. Failing in the endeavour, the King asked the Count of Soissons to do his utmost to make Biron acknowledge what he had done, but the Marshal made an insolent rejoinder. Henry knew that if the case went out of his hands there could be but one result, and the next morning he made a last attempt to move the man, promising total oblivion of his misdeeds; but Biron's emphatic denials were discourteous, his air of bravado putting any further approach out of the question. That evening he was arrested, together with the Count of Auvergne, who was a party to this plot as well as the later one already described. They were sent to the Bastille, and were tried by the parliament of Paris. Having protested his innocence, Biron was faced with the document containing a full plan of the conspiracy in his own handwriting, as well as a number of his letters to La Fin, all of which he thought had been burnt. The evidence was shattering and for him stupefying. He sent an appeal to the King in which he referred to the wounds he had received and the battles he had fought, soliciting pardon chiefly on account of his mother, 'the aged widow of the hero killed while sustaining the royal cause', who should not be condemned to see her son die on the scaffold. His relatives as well as his mother begged the King to take a lenient view of his faults; but now that the whole conspiracy had been published to the world Henry could not grant their request, saying that 'the Marshal had contemned the royal clemency when open to him, and for the good of my children and my people I cannot now prevent justice from taking its course'.

In the last stages of the trial Biron became hysterical. He accused La Fin of being responsible for his ruin: 'It was his reports, his insinuations, his perfidious counsels, his demoniacal arts, that exasperated me against the King and threw me into the arms of Spain and Savoy. It was he who, to draw me deeper into his plots, showed me a waxen figure which had spoken and announced the King's death.' Having made an eloquent and impassioned speech in his defence, he completely lost control of himself when the verdict of guilty was given, vociferously interrupted the Chancellor while the sentence of death was being pronounced, taxed the King with ingratitude because his father had placed the crown on Henry's head, and for nearly an hour held up the proceedings of the court. He was declared guilty of high treason and sentenced to lose his head in the Place de Grève. By the King's order the place of execution was changed to the court of the Bastille.

At five o'clock in the afternoon of 31 July 1602, he was led to the scaffold where, according to those historians who have never been threatened with decapitation, he displayed a pusillanimity unworthy of a brave soldier. He cursed, he resisted, he threatened the executioner, who at last 'was obliged to conceal his knife and seize the Marshal unawares,' said a contemporary. Auvergne and the rest of Biron's accomplices were forgiven, and lived to conspire another day. La Fin, with a pardon for all offences in his pocket and a guard of armed men, went on his travels, not wishing to meet any of Biron's friends or relations. In the hope that their memories were short, he returned to Paris in 1606 with the object of begging the King's favour for a son committed to the Conciergerie. But their memories were not quite as short as that, and riding one day past the bridge of Notre Dame he was unhorsed by a party of men and despatched with a volley of pistol shots.

The stalwart Protestant soldier, Turenne, now Duke of Bouillon by the King's favour, had taken a prudent part in the Biron conspiracy, and for two or three years had tried to make his co-religionists dissatisfied with Henry's Catholicism, his main purpose being to unite the provinces south of the Loire into a federal republic with a strong Protestant ascendancy.

Needless to say Spain encouraged such a move, solely in the hope of disuniting France, and negotiated secretly with Bouillon, whose intrigues were revealed during Biron's trial. But though he could be accused of sedition, evidence of high treason was lacking, and Henry resolved to pacify the Duke by having a friendly talk with him. Bouillon, who should have known the King better, feared that Biron's fate might be his own and refused to attend the Court. Henry changed the request into an order; whereupon the Duke left for Germany, where he stayed for some months with his brother-in-law the Elector Palatine, pretended to be a victim of Catholic persecution, and carried on his plots with disaffected Protestants elsewhere in the belief that he would be chosen as their leader.

To be represented as the persecutor of the Protestants evoked Henry's irritation, particularly as he knew that he could not remove all their objections to the Edict of Nantes, which failed to give the two religions complete equality: for example, the Catholics could conduct their services everywhere, the Protestants theirs only in certain places, simply because many cities were so predominantly Catholic that the introduction of Huguenot worship would have led to bloodshed. Also the Calvinists could not be permitted absolute freedom of speech because they abused it. For instance they wished to insert in their articles of confession that the Pope was Antichrist. This could not be allowed in a Catholic country. The Protestants had further cause for grievance when Henry allowed the Jesuits to return to France, an act that was opposed by the Paris parliament and registered by order of the King. His insistence enraged the Huguenots, who now claimed their right to political action and called an assembly at Châtelhérault in 1605. Rosny attended it and found those of the reformed faith in a refractory mood, wishful to renew their oath to the Union of Evangelical Churches, whereby their lives and property were devoted to the maintenance of their rights against any power that challenged them. In effect such an oath committed them in the last resort to armed rebellion, and Rosny opposed it in the King's name. His arguments impressed them and they proceeded no further in that business, satisfied with the royal permission to keep their fortified places.

Henry stepped warily through the morass of sectarian differences. He knew that in governing a country it was more necessary to be a statesman than a theologian, and his policy was always dictated by his practical sense of what was good for France. He once confessed that, necessity being the law of the times, he would contradict himself frequently, saying to one man that he remained a Huguenot at heart, to another that he had always been a Catholic, both statements being true unless the Almighty were a partisan. When his friends urged him to reconsider his decision to recall the Society of Jesus to Paris, he first answered that it was better to have the French Jesuits on his side than on the side of Spain, but finding that his friends were unimpressed by that argument he switched over to a personal appeal, saying that the Jesuits in exile would conspire to kill him. 'Better to die at once,' he declared, 'than to live in continual fear or expectation of the poisoned cup or the assassin's knife.' Rosny was grieved to hear such an expression from so valiant a monarch. But he need not have been distressed over what was merely a convenient lie, which had the desired effect of putting an end to the argument.

Henry's main object was to keep the balance level between the two religions. He was loyal to the Protestants, knowing how much he owed to them, and when he was reminded by the Pope, through the cardinals and prelates of France, that the conditions of his absolution had not been fulfilled – namely, that the Huguenots should make restitution of whatever they had taken from the Catholics, and that the decrees of the Council of Trent should be published throughout the kingdom–he replied that he had no inclination to establish the Inquisition in France, and that the restitution, if insisted on, should work both ways. It was generally known that, in whatever concerned the service of his person and his table, he preferred Protestants to Catholics, saying that the first revealed, the second concealed, whatever hostility they felt; and he was well aware of the risk he ran in permitting the Jesuits to return. But policy guided his action.

Moreover, his confessor, Father Cotton, was a Jesuit who managed to persuade him that the Frenchmen in their Order were as loyal as any other Catholics, and only those who were French by birth were authorized to return, making an oath 'not to engage in anything prejudicial to the King's service or the peace of the kingdom – and this without any exception or mental reservation'. They were to be subject to the laws of the realm and amenable to the officers of the Crown. Agreeing to do all that was required of them, they knew that the King would free them from petty inconveniences and rigorous restraints. Father Cotton was able to help them frequently through his influence with the King, and before long they were empowered to open colleges at Bourges, Poitiers, Amiens and other cities, the inhabitants of which sometimes opposed their designs. The influence exercised by Cotton may have been due to his indulgence and sympathy. Henry's little frailties of the flesh demanded some consideration, and it was agreeable to receive absolution on easy terms and not disagreeable to undergo light penances. To make up to the Protestants for these favours to the Jesuits, he permitted the institution of a Reformed Church near Charenton. This infuriated the Jesuits and other Catholics, who did not omit to tell him that by the Edict of Nantes the Protestants were not permitted a public place of worship within ten leagues of the capital, and Charenton was within two leagues. But Henry felt that edicts were made for men, not men for edicts, and allowed their wrath to evaporate with time.

Indeed his main policy was patience. It was the nature of human beings to let off steam and to feel better for it. Henry granted them the indulgence, knowing that their storage of vapour was limited, and that when it had run out he could continue from where he had left off. His moderation, no less than his lack of resentment, vexed those of an opposite temperament, and by reflecting on their less exalted natures may have excited their latent tendencies to conspiracy and sedition; though it is well to remember that virtue and vice are indigenous in mankind and that what Shakespeare said of jealousy is true of all imperfections. Jealous souls, says one of his characters:

> are not ever jealous for the cause,
> But jealous for they are jealous; 'tis a monster
> Begot upon itself, born on itself.

Few people in the France of those days were more jealous of Henry's achievements than Turenne, his one-time ally in the Protestant cause, who had become the Duke of Bouillon by the King's influence and whose ambition was disguised by a display of indignation over Henry's generosity to the Catholics. The Duke had returned to his capital, Sedan, after failing to incite the German princes against the French King, and from there continued his plotting. Henry tried hard to pacify him, to keep him loyal, and negotiations between them lasted for some months, the monarch being most desirous to arrive at an agreement without resorting to arms. But towards the close of 1605 it became obvious that Bouillon's conspiracy was spreading, fostered by Spanish gold, and the King determined to march on Sedan with the latest artillery. Strongly advised by his council not to carry the matter to extremities, and by certain experts that Sedan was impregnable, Henry ignored the former and laughed at the latter. A fit of gout temporarily prostrated him and he thought it as well to appoint someone to take his place in case the gout continued or returned. His choice fell on the Grand-Master, Rosny, whose artillery would be the decisive factor in taking Sedan. But the commander-in-chief of a royal army must have a rank equal to his responsibility, and Rosny at last agreed to the promotion, becoming Duke of Sully in February 1606.

Following a parliamentary ceremonial attended by all the royal princes and grand seigneurs, Sully invited sixty of the principal nobles to a magnificent banquet at the Arsenal. Arriving there after the ceremony, he entered the great hall and to his amazement was greeted by the King, who had escaped unobserved from the official proceedings and now gaily greeted the host:

'Master-General, I am come to the feast without being invited. Shall I have a bad dinner?'

'It is possible you may, sire, since I did not expect to be honoured with your presence.'

'I assure you I shall not, for while I awaited your return I visited your kitchen, where I have seen the finest fish imaginable and *ragoûts* to my own taste; and since you stayed so long, I have taken the edge off my hunger with some oysters and drunk some of your famous wine of Arbois, which I think is the best I ever tasted.'

Henry's high spirits put everyone into good humour. He jested with all and sundry, laughed continually, and feasted as if he had never heard of gout.

Once more, through their common friend the Princess of Orange, he tried to reach an amicable understanding with the Duke of Bouillon, who flatly declined to acknowledge his errors or to ask the King's forgiveness, always freely bestowed. There was nothing for it but to humble the man, and in April 1606 the King left Fontainebleau to take Sedan with an army of 15,000 men and fifty of Sully's largest siege-guns. Personally Henry enjoyed war, partly because he liked physical exercise and partly because it took his mind off domestic problems; but he was imaginative enough to hate bloodshed, destruction and suffering. Feeling convinced that his show of arms would settle the matter without combat, he enjoyed the expedition, and we learn from Sully that his spirits were exhilarated from the moment he took horse. The years seemed to fall from him; he was back at his old profession; his face brightened with pleasure; his heart expanded with joy. Unlike those early days when his military movements were so rapid that his enemies rubbed their eyes, this march on Sedan was like a promenade, leisurely and spectacular. On the way Henry pleased himself with hunting, telling Sully one day that he had failed to capture a stag but had taken two wolves, which he felt augured well for the enterprise.

Bouillon did not wait to see what damage Sully's guns could do to his fortress, but surrendered it without firing a shot. Every other conqueror in history would have made him pay dear for his sedition, not to mention the trouble he had caused to make him submit; but Henry was unlike every other conqueror in history, embraced the Duke cordially, restored his offices and dignities, and requested his presence at Court. For one month Sedan was placed under control of a Protestant officer, after which it was handed back to Bouillon. This was carrying confidence and generosity too far, in the opinion of Sully and others, to whom the King explained: 'I would rather that the Duke should be in his own principality than a wanderer in the German Courts.'

Like most open-hearted disinterested men, Henry retained certain childlike qualities, one of them being a love of display. He wanted to give the Parisians a treat by making a triumphal entry. Sully, rather annoyed that his wonderful artillery had not been given a chance to exhibit its power, thought little of the notion, and replied to the King's messenger who overtook him on the way to Paris:

Eh! Monsieur de La Varenne! What is the King thinking of? Have we given a single blow with either sword or pike, or fired a shot from cannon or arquebus, that we should play the victorious, when in fact we are the vanquished, having bought with credulity what the King should have owed to his courage? Tell him that everyone says so, and that entering the capital in triumph will expose us to mockery and derision.

On hearing this Henry lost his temper, but he calmed down and sent a second message saying that the idea of a triumphal entry was not unreasonable. Sully persisted in his view that it was silly. This second refusal to make the necessary arrangements made Henry really angry, and he shouted: 'This abominable man! With his arrogance and obstinacy, he thwarts me in everything; but, by heaven, he shall obey me!' A third messenger was sent off commanding Sully to do as he was told without further discussion. Sully peevishly resolved to give the King all he wanted and something more, and the royal army was saluted with terrific explosions from all fifty cannon that had done no service at Sedan. The Parisians were startled by the uproar, louder than anything they had ever heard. Henry saw the joke, laughed heartily, and after a tumultuous reception he slapped Sully on the shoulder with the words: 'Grand-Master, you have proved yourself worthy of the office you hold; I must embrace you.'

The two men were so different in mental outlook and physical disposition that occasional rows were inevitable, but one incident reported by Sully as serious was more likely to have arisen from the King's sense of humour and his love of testing character. Sully's gravity, austerity and integrity were not liked in a Court where gaiety, indulgence and mendacity were the disorders of the day. His religion, too, was against him, and he occasioned much animosity, his enemies never losing an opportunity of pointing out his defects to the King, insinuating that the minister's diligent endeavours were for his own profit and glory, not for his master, nor for the good of the state. Once at Fontainebleau, probably to try or tease the Grand-Master, Henry professed to believe his traducers and put on an air of coldness and restraint when discussing affairs with Sully, who was accustomed to an easy familiarity from his monarch. Conscious, sometimes too conscious, of his rectitude, the minister appeared to notice nothing and waited patiently for the King to disburden himself. This constrained atmosphere prevailed until Henry's impulsive nature dissipated it by asking Sully, at the conclusion of a more than usually formal interview, where he was going. 'To Paris,' was the reply. 'The business we have been discussing, as your Majesty knows, necessitates my immediate return.'

'But have you nothing to say to me before you leave?'

'Nothing, sire. I have already said all that occurs to me on the subject you spoke of.'

'Then I have much to say to you.' Turning to his valet, who was about to pull hunting boots on the royal legs, he said: 'Take these away and tell them not to bring out the horses, for I see that the weather is unfavourable for the hunt today.' As the day was particularly fine, the valet mentioned the fact. 'I say it is not,' proclaimed his Majesty. 'Do as I have ordered you.'

The courtiers who had accused Sully of feathering his own nest now had the mortification of hearing, first that their senses had deceived them about the weather, and next that the King was closely closeted with his minister. They knew that Henry would tell him everything they had said, adding picturesque details of his own invention; and when next day the King made it plain that his friendship with Sully was for life, all those who would have liked to see him beheaded, or at least degraded, overwhelmed him with their attentions.

Sometimes, on the subject of the royal love-affairs, Sully seriously upset the King, whose passionate nature rebelled against the puritanical frowns of his mentor. Once at Fontaine-bleau Sully took him to task for his amours, saying that they were 'so little suited to his age and dignity' and calling them 'so many baneful wounds to his glory, which would probably end in something more fatal.' This exasperated Henry, who used violent language and stormed out of the room, being heard by his courtiers to exclaim: 'It is impossible to bear with this man any longer; he is eternally contradicting me and approves of nothing I propose; but, by heaven, I will make him obey me; he shall not appear in my presence these fifteen days.'

But Henry could not keep it up. 'Our little resentments ought never to last more than a day,' he once said to Sully; and the following morning at seven o'clock he appeared at the Arsenal, would not allow himself to be announced, walked to the Grand-Master's private apartment, and tapped at the door. Sully maintained his usual demeanour of stern pre-occupation, and when Henry asked what he was doing answered that he was writing letters and preparing work for his secretaries. 'And how long have you been thus employed?' 'Ever since three o'clock.' To Sully's surprise, since the subject had caused an altercation the previous day, Henry asked his advice over a love-affair. Sully replied coldly that he had no advice to give, since Henry was displeased whenever their sentiments did not coincide. 'Oh, oh!' said Henry, giving Sully a little tap on the cheek, a habit of his in playful mood:

> You are aloof with me because you are angry at what happened yesterday. However, I am so no longer with you. Come, embrace me, and live with me in the same freedom as usual, for I love you not the less for it. On the contrary, from the moment when you cease to contend with me on such occasions as I am convinced you cannot approve my conduct, I shall believe you no longer love me.

Sully was perhaps the only man Henry could completely trust. The whole Court was seething with intrigue, made more sinister by the Queen's Italian favourites Concini and Galigaï, the first of whom became Marie's lover. Sully knew himself to be the most unpopular man in those surroundings, knew too that he would be victimized by secret accusations if the King died from some mysterious cause, to guard against which he told an acquaintance: 'I have taken an oath never to recommend either a physician or a cook to the King.' Every action of his was condemned on principle by his enemies, and frequently he had to exonerate himself in the eyes of his master.

'Your temper is a little too precipitate,' Henry wrote after one of these self-justifications,

> and I perceive by your letter that you believe all that has been said to you. However, report is an absolute liar. Moderate your resentment, and be not so easily prevailed upon to believe all the stories that are brought to you. By indifference you will revenge yourself on those who envy and hate you for the affection I bear you. This is the first time that I have taken a pen into my hand since this last fit of gout. My resentment against these slanderers has surmounted my pain.

His repeated counsel was: 'Since I take your advice in all my affairs, do you also take mine in everything that relates to you, as that of the most faithful friend you have in the world and the best master that ever lived.'

But there was one piece of advice that Sully could not take. From the moment he became a Catholic the King was as loyal to his new religion as he had been to his old one. Two cardinals were made Popes through his influence, backed by the expenditure of considerable sums of money, and he constantly presented buildings, land and cash to the Church. He felt that for the good of the state and the harmony of the Court it would be serviceable if his chief minister were to become a Roman Catholic, and not long after the Sedan affair he resolved that Sully should be promoted Constable of

217

France, governor of Normandy, Grand-Master of the King's household, that Sully's eldest son should marry one of the King's daughters, receiving a large dowry plus two governorships, and that in short Sully and his family were to be placed permanently on velvet if only they would abandon the faith in which they had been brought up. 'I entreat you not to refuse me this satisfaction,' said the King; 'it is for the good of my service and for the full and assured establishment of your house.' Sully was duly impressed but dared not answer for his son who was old enough to decide for himself. For his own part he could not sell his conscience and would never change his religion except from internal conviction: 'Were I to do otherwise, I should give your Majesty good reason for suspecting the sincerity of a heart I could not guard faithfully for God.'

'Why should I suspect you for doing what I have already done myself, and which you advised me to do when I put the question to you?' demanded the King. 'Think well of it, and gratify me by falling in with my wish. I give you a month to reflect on it.'

Sully spent the month in reflective retirement, while cardinals, bishops, and even the Pope, did all in their power to persuade him that salvation as well as opulence would result from his joining their communion. But 'the man of the arsenal', as his enemies called him, remained firm, and when Henry made a final appeal his answer left no hope of a conversion. Although he seemed to be occupied with worldly affairs and mundane grandeur, he said, and although questions of faith did not appear to occupy his thoughts, he was nevertheless so much attached to his religion that he placed it before his family, his country, his fortune, and even his King, to whose service his life had been devoted. There was nothing more to be said, and Henry dropped the subject without showing any resentment over the implication that what was good enough for the King was not good enough for his minister. Besides, Henry knew that his own conversion had been recommended by his friend for the sake of the nation, a reason that had no cogency in Sully's case.

Also, deep in his heart, Henry did not believe that redemption was a Catholic prerogative. When his sister Catherine, Duchess of Bar, died in 1604 he refused to see anyone for over a week, saying: 'It is only when alone with God that I can find consolation.' He ordered the whole Court, including the Queen's household and the foreign ambassadors, to go into mourning; and when the papal nuncio excused himself from doing so on the ground that the Princess had lived and died a Calvinist, Henry said: 'I will not insist on his wearing mourning but I shall decline to receive him until the period of mourning is over.' Thereupon the nuncio donned the necessary garments and asked for an audience, at which he informed the King that the Pope feared for his sister's salvation, since she had died outside the pale of the Church. Henry did not share the fears of his Holiness, and gave the nuncio the benefit of his thoughts:

> To think worthily of God, one must believe it possible that, as the last breath is drawn, some ray of light illumines the mind, and renders the sinner, whoever he may be, in a fit state to enter Heaven. I have no doubt of my sister's salvation, and I will not allow it to be doubted in my presence.

Believing in the divine mercy, Henry never ceased to show human mercy. He had suffered much from the tricky humours and disloyal actions of his first wife, Margaret of Valois; but when she tired of her life and loves at Usson and asked permission to live again in Paris, he granted it. Indeed, she could have returned some years before if she had wished to be received at Court. But the beds in the south were soft, and she did not reappear in public until the winter of 1605–6, when her arrival in the capital coincided with a general derangement of nature. There were earthquakes, floods, storms, epidemics, mad dogs, murders, a total eclipse of the sun, tidal waves, and the whole repertory of disturbances with which the earth occasionally agitates its inhabitants, making them believe in the wrath of God or the fun of Satan, according to individual temperament. Had Margaret been a Protestant, these eruptions would have been explicable. As she was not, the only people to reap a harvest were the astrologers, who prophesied doom and desolation for the entire country. Margaret had kept on friendly corresponding terms with Henry's various mistresses, and as she had lost her beauty the Queen had nothing against her. Sully advised her to keep clear of Court squabbles, and the King constrained her to take care of her health and not to turn night into day as in the past. She founded a sort of literary *salon* and became popular with men of letters.

A man's vanity is chiefly in evidence where his relations with women are concerned, and nothing exhibits Henry's forgiving nature so clearly as his treatment of men and women whose behaviour made him look foolish and whose indifference to his feelings hurt him. Like other men he was capable of murderous thoughts in the heat of passion, but unlike other men he felt no resentment when his mind was clear. At one time his nephew, the Prince of Joinville, was strongly suspected of having been intimate with Henriette, Marchioness of Verneuil, but Henry preferred to believe that the young man's letters to her were forged, and when the Prince admitted that he had merely been playing a game to win Henriette's favour he received this note from the King:

My Nephew

You do right to confess your fault, which could not have been greater, bearing in mind myself and her whom it concerned. Since you regret that you offended me and beg me to forgive you, I will do so on condition that you behave better in the future. In proof of that, get ready to go to Hungary with M. le Duc de Mercoeur when he returns there; and when he is ready to start on that journey I am willing that you should come to me, so as to be near me for three or four days, in order that before your departure I may make it known to everybody as well as yourself that it is my nature to love my relations when they are upright and well-behaved.

At a later date Henry heard that Henriette had carried friendship too far with the Duke of Guise, who had 'tasted her sweet body'. An outburst of rage was inevitable, but philosophy came to Henry's aid and he said: 'We have taken so much away from these Lorraines that we might as well leave them bread and bitches.' Rumours of her infidelity constantly reached him, the Court being a hot-bed of scandal, but he was lenient to liars: 'If one replied to slander by cutting out all the tongues which speak evil, many would be stricken dumb and one would have difficulty in finding servants.' The priests and pamphleteers who had filled the mob with false-hoods about 'the Béarnais' during his long struggle against the League failed to arouse his animosity: 'You must no longer reproach them with that. The League was the evil of the time. They believed they acted rightly and like many others were deceived.' Men who are incensed by lies against them-selves do not as a rule admit a corresponding weakness; but when the Count of Soissons declared that his honour had been insulted by an accusation of duplicity, adding that his word ought to be sufficient as he was not accustomed to lying, Henry looked surprised: 'In that case, my dear cousin, you are unlike the rest of the family, for at times we all tell the most appalling lies. Your elder brother the Cardinal was notoriously proficient at the game.'

In his last years Henry was well aware that his mistress Henriette constantly deceived him. He made no attempt to deceive her, since his affairs were known to everybody in and about the Court. It is probable that she had tired of him; and although his early passion for her had subsided, her con-versation still attracted him, and his last letters show that his affection survived his disillusionment. 'I am very well, thank God, and love you much better than you do me,' he wrote in April 1608, 'for my love is not restrained and qualified as yours is.' In the summer of that year her behaviour provoked him and he tried to signify indifference:

> You have succeeded so badly in lording it over me that you ought to have become wise. You threaten that you will go to Verneuil. Do as you please! If you do not love me, I can very well dispense with seeing you. If you say you love me, it is a very bad proof of it to leave when I arrive. By this action I shall know what you are. I shall be in Paris on Thursday, as ill-satisfied with you as ever, unless you change your style.

Another attempt to delude him brought this:

> I have never robbed you of anything, but you have deprived me of everything you could. This is a reason against which there is no answer. Do not torture your mind to discover one, for it is better to remain silent than to utter a bad excuse. For me, I love you dearer than I do myself. I swear this to you, my love; but do you think to feed me with stones after having given me bread? Consider my age, my rank, my mind and my affection, and you will do what you do not. Good-day, my all. A million kisses.

Henry's first wife and last mistress ended their days in similar fashion. Margaret and Henriette ate too much, became fat, and both, having given free rein to their carnal appetites, turned to religion and philanthropy. Impotence frequently produces piety, and good works are promoted by wrinkles.

CHAPTER FOURTEEN

The Stroke of Fate

Within ten years France had been transformed by the wisdom of Henry, the efficiency of Sully. As an absolute ruler Henry could do what he liked, and as he happened to be that rarest of mortal objects, a great man whose virtue equalled his ability, what he liked was always for the benefit of his people. For once in a way an autocracy was justified because the autocrat was benevolent. With his gaiety, valour, wit, sanity, industry, common sense and sensuality, he typified what was best in his countrymen, adding to these characteristics some qualities peculiar to himself: toleration, serenity, loyalty, fortitude, an acutely sensitive humanity and a complete lack of vengefulness and malice. He was in fact a thoroughly civilized human being, and the only monarch in history who can claim to share most of his attributes was his grandson, Charles II of England, whose mother was the daughter of Henry and his Queen. It is true that Charles never had the opportunity of displaying his grandfather's bravery and leadership in war, and that no one ever accused him of being too diligent; nor was he ever in a position to remake a nation; but with his fewer opportunities he displayed the charity, gaiety, mental alertness and gentleness of Henry, together with the subtlety and guile of his Medici blood as a substitute for the other's frankness and vigour. He also inherited the Frenchman's addiction to women, though he never abandoned himself to their seduction so whole-heartedly as his ancestor.

Henry's pliancy in this respect sometimes made him very unhappy. Reconciliations with his wife seldom lasted for more than two days, and Sully, who loathed acting as mediator, was constantly being called upon to make peace with the Queen on one hand, with Henriette on the other. Marie gave much money to her favourites, lost a great deal more at gambling, and once pawned some Crown jewels, which Sully had to retrieve. Henry too gambled incessantly, and every night Sully handed him a purse filled with gold in the hope that it would see him through; but it seldom did, and his losses were paid in rings and chains, pearls and diamonds. Sometimes Sully expostulated, reminding the King of the necessity for strict economy if the 'Great Design' were to be accomplished. Henry would answer that his early hardships had enforced economy with such ruthlessness that he was now making up for it: 'Surely I may at last take my ease and enjoy some of life's pleasures.' Another of life's joys was hunting, which he loved and indulged to excess. At the Louvre one day in 1606 his sense of well-being, due to his pastime, was communicated to Sully:

I have not found myself so light and so easy these three months as today. I mounted my horse without help; I have had great pleasure in the chase this morning; my hawks have flown and my greyhounds have run so well that the former have taken a great number of young partridges and the latter three large hares; one of the best of my hawks, which I thought lost, has been found and brought back to me. I have a very good appetite, have had some excellent melons, and they have served up some quails, the fattest and tenderest I have ever eaten.

He then related the good news he had received from various countries and referred to the excellent company he was now enjoying. His friends at table had been praising him for his great qualities, but 'I did not suffer all they said to pass without contradiction,' he told Sully, and he had admitted many faults. As for their congratulations on his good fortune, he had said to them that if they had been with him from the time his father died they would have known that some of their compliments might have been spared, since his miserable moments had far surpassed his happy ones. But he was trying to forget the calamitous aspects of his life, and though in the midst of his early struggles he could satisfy himself with a crust of bread for supper he now took an interest in the culinary department. After a morning's hawking he brought in some partridges, handed them to Coquet, the master of his household, and said: 'Take care to keep for me those birds that are least bitten by the hawks; there are three very fat ones which I took from them myself and are scarcely touched.'

Now and then his keenness for the chase harmed him. One day at Fontainebleau in 1608 he spent some time hunting a stag and caught a cold in the head. While it lasted, recorded Sully, he 'wet eight or ten handkerchiefs in a day: he had at the same time a defluxion in his ears and throat, which was very troublesome to him; and afterwards, preparing himself by purges to drink the waters of Spa, he was seized with a looseness, from which he suffered violent pains for two days, and which left a weakness upon him for a considerable time'. He never allowed his pastimes to interfere with his work, and once remarked: 'Some say I am a hunter, others that I make love; but I wake when they sleep.' Not a heavy eater, he believed that those who over-indulged themselves at table and slept too long were incapable of generous impulses. 'If I love the table and good cheer, it is because they enliven the spirit,' he asserted.

His spirit was nearly always lively and his comments had a corresponding pungency. For example he tried to influence the nobles to improve their estates instead of idling away their time at Court, and he described those who spent much money on clothes as wearing 'their mills and their tall forests of timber on their backs'. He made sumptuary laws, one of

which prevented the unnecessary embellishment of dress with
gold and silver, though in characteristic vein he excused two
classes of people from obedience to it: *'Filles de joie* and pick-
pockets, in whom we take so little interest that we will not
honour them by ordering their conduct.' He disliked any form
of snobbery or pretentiousness; and when a rich merchant
with whom he had been friendly bought a patent of nobility,
his manner towards the man became rather frigid. Asked for
an explanation, he said: 'Formerly I considered you the first
among my merchants. Now you are merely the last among my
gentlemen.' The same thing happened with his valet Varenne,
who had made a large fortune in a quiet way, often as
messenger between the King and his mistresses. Seeing an
elderly officer in attendance on his valet's son, Henry asked
his name. 'He is only a gentleman I have given to my son,'
said Varenne casually. 'You mean you have given your son
to this gentleman,' returned Henry. On the other hand he
always took the part of anyone who was doing his job well in
whatever walk of life, provided the fellow did not put on airs,
and Henry might be described as a democrat two centuries
before the Revolution. A troupe of strolling players performed a farce before their Majesties, some of the quips
therein being of an extremely outspoken nature, for which
the performers were imprisoned by a pompous Court official.
The moment Henry heard of this he ordered their release,
saying: 'They made me cry with laughter; I couldn't be
angry with them.' Pomposity always amused him. A particularly solemn councillor moved him to say: 'There goes
Pontcarré without his red robe, but he hasn't forgotten to
bring his red nose.'

Although he seldom failed in sympathy with his soldiers,
he could deliver a home-thrust on occasion. A captain whose
salary was overdue addressed him in the laconic manner
Henry affected: 'Sire, three words: money or discharge.'
'Captain, four: neither one nor t'other,' was the reply. But

some days later the officer received a larger sum than he expected. Henry had much less sympathy with priests and civil servants than with peasants and soldiers. The pressure of business sometimes prevented him from attending Mass, and he excused himself to the prelates who took him to task: 'When I am labouring for the public I think I am forsaking God for God's sake.' Not the least of his business troubles was the raising of money, but he drew the line at certain methods. One proposal was to tax fountain-water to pay for the entertainment of foreign ambassadors, who were thirsty. Henry vetoed it as burdensome to his people, adding: 'Only Jesus Christ could turn water into wine.'

He had no illusions about himself or his popularity. A courtier remarked on the wonderful ovation he was receiving from the mob and seemed to think that it exhibited their affection for him, but Henry disagreed: 'They are a people like any other. If my greatest enemy stood in my place and they saw him pass, they would do as much for him and would shout even more loudly.' He knew that human beings were as easily led by the nose as any other animals, and it partly distressed, partly amused him to watch their antics. Some of his nobles felt that he did not take life seriously enough; but this simply meant that he never mistook a trickle for a cataract and what other people thought momentous he thought frivolous. He could laugh at himself as readily as at others and make fun out of his own discomforts. He and the Queen were crossing the Seine at Neuilly when the boat capsized and both monarchs were compelled to drink more water than they found agreeable; but as the soaking cured Henry of a violent toothache he always recommended it as a remedy.

The Queen never appreciated her husband's sense of humour, and apart from her anger over his gallantries among her sex they were temperamentally opposed. With concord in the state, discord reigned in the domestic circle, and the man who could manage a country failed to control a wife. She did not even admire his ability as a ruler, since nearly all his successes aroused her hostility. Her nature responded to intrigue, his to candour, though Sully perceived that where women were involved his instinctive sincerity became warped by apprehension of emotional scenes or jarring conflicts, for he had all the weakness of a good-natured sensual man. To escape from the atmosphere of suspicion that pervaded the Louvre, he asked Sully to let him have rooms at the Arsenal, which he could use whenever nauseated by the Court. With the help of Concini and Galigaï, the Queen knew all about her husband's private affairs and allowed her knowledge to pervert her judgment of his public life. Yet even she must have recognized that he had become the chief political figure in Europe when in 1607 both Rome and Venice accepted his mediation in the dispute between the Pope and the Venetian Republic. For years the two powers had indulged in fierce contentions, and the Pope had threatened that if the spiritual authority were ignored the temporal sword would be employed. Attempts were made to assassinate the most rebellious member of the Venetian Council of Ten, but they had the effect of making him more intractable, and a deadlock had been reached when Henry's help was invoked by both parties. Somehow he managed to make the Pope yield on the chief points at issue and a treaty was patched up.

But this was a small affair compared with the next quarrel in which Henry was asked to intervene. Here he was not disinterested, since he had befriended the Dutch and warred with Spain. Both nations had practically fought one another to a standstill, though the Dutch had recently humiliated the Spaniards by gaining possession of Gibraltar in April 1607. Negotiations for a truce were started and Henry's representative quickly became the chief influence at the conference. In the French King's view it was vitally necessary that Spain should recognize Dutch independence, and he gave point to his determination by sending reinforcements to the Netherlands when it seemed that the discussions would break down. Philip III of Spain did his best to win Henry over by sending Don Pedro of Toledo as a special envoy to the French Court. A grandee of Spain and a relation of the French Queen, he was given a spectacular reception, and during his residence at Fontainebleau he found that the Queen was entirely pro-Spanish, while her husband, though very hospitable, was pro-Dutch.

The question of a marriage between the Spanish King's second son and Henry's daughter was raised, which would result in the governorship of the Netherlands passing to a Spaniard. No such alliance, said Henry, had been proposed to him, 'and as to consenting to abandon my allies I would prefer to have my head cut off.' Their talks were not harmonious, and when Don Pedro spoke of the greatness, riches and power of Spain he received no encouragement from Henry: 'Spain is like the statue of Nebuchadnezzar, composed of various metals but having feet of clay.' At one of their sessions Don Pedro was unwise enough to say that his master could support the factious subjects of the French King as easily as the latter could sustain the rebels of the Netherlands. 'Let him beware of attempting it,' replied Henry, 'for I shall be in the saddle before his foot is in the stirrup.'

Henry knew that his Queen was intriguing against him and this did not help to calm him. 'Monsieur l'Ambassadeur,' he exclaimed, 'you are a Spaniard, I am a Gascon; let us no more excite or aggravate each other.' But they were doomed to disagreement even on the subject of religion. One day Henry was conducting Don Pedro over the palace at Fontainebleau and asked what he thought of the alterations and improvements that were being made. The Spaniard had not been impressed by the chapel and replied: 'I find no one so badly lodged as God, sire.' Henry swiftly retorted:

We Frenchmen lodge God in our hearts, not between four walls like you Spaniards. Indeed, if you lodged him in your hearts as we do, he would still be lodged in stones. But my chapel is not yet finished. I don't intend to leave it in its present condition. There are few gentlemen in my kingdom who lack chapels in their houses and I shall not want one of them.

Don Pedro outstayed his welcome at the French Court. He could report to his master that a magnificent new bridge over the Seine, the Pont Neuf, had been opened, that new buildings were going up all over the place, that the country seemed to be flourishing, and that the Bastille contained enough money and artillery to prevent anyone from taking liberties with France; but his mission had failed. Spain was compelled in April 1609 to sign a twelve-years truce with the United Provinces and to acknowledge their independence; while Henry had become the chief arbiter of Europe.

He had also achieved his wish to be acknowledged as father of his people. When in 1608 the river Loire overflowed its banks, causing widespread damage and ruining many of the families in those districts, Henry ordered instant relief to all in distress, saying, 'God has given me subjects that I may preserve them as my children.' This was not a momentary gesture called forth by a crisis: the feeling behind it was habitual with him, finding expression in all sorts of ways, from the care he took for the well-being of his soldiers, pensioning the old ones and building places where the wounded and decrepit could be looked after, to the emancipation of the poorer classes from the arbitrary exactions of taxation. The dreadful mortality due to lack of sanitation had been reduced, hospitals erected and endowed, rivers made navigable, land irrigated, industries encouraged, posts reorganized, commerce freed, agriculture revived; Frenchmen could travel safely about their country on level roads, and the peasant could put a chicken in his pot on Sundays. Within ten years Henry had lifted France from nadir to zenith, and the generation that had witnessed the horrors of religious dissension knew to whom they were indebted for the change from war to peace, from poverty to affluence, from peril to security, from chaos to order, from impotence to power.

Henry was not content with material progress. He helped writers financially and talked freely with them. He knew Montaigne well, Malherbe wrote poems for him, and he complimented Aubigné by saying that a word of discontent from him was worth another man's gratitude. His own table expenses were cut down in order to pay the professors of the Royal College. Many writers, scholars and artists enjoyed his patronage, and if Cervantes had been lucky enough to be born in France instead of Spain he would not have known the poverty and distress of his later years, for in 1608 the first part of *Don Quixote* was read aloud to Henry during an attack of gout and became a favourite book. He loved *Amadis of Gaul*, also D'Urfé's romance *Astrée*, which soothed him during an illness, when his friends Bassompierre or Bellegarde or Gramont sat by his bedside and recounted the story of platonic loves, the rustic and remote charm of which appealed to him in a convalescent state. There were times when he felt the attraction of innocence more strongly than the impulsion of sex, times when he would rather romp with his children than 'tumble on the bed of Ptolemy'. He loved all his children, both legitimate and natural, with an equal affection, his lack of discrimination making their mothers fretful. He would not allow them to call him 'Monsieur', insisting that they should call him 'Papa'. His desire to establish and maintain comradely relationships was innate, an aspect of his benevolent nature, to illustrate which we may note that the woman who as Marchioness of Guercheville had rejected his amorous advances was by his insistence made Mistress of the Queen's Robes, and that Corisande's son by her husband the Count of Gramont was appointed Viceroy of Navarre by the

King, who attached the young man to his person. So strong was his wish for general harmony that he continued on occasion to share his wife's bed, though it cannot have been a comfortable one for either of them. We have proof of this in his reference to the severe winter of 1608, which was so cold, he said, that his beard froze in bed with the Queen beside him.

Unfortunately, Henry's friendships, so equable, so agreeable, were not matched by his love-affairs, which were often stormy and always passionate. The last of them occurred at a period of life when most men of his prolonged sexual activity would have been thinking of planting cabbages or entering a monastery. But he was a rarity in love as in war; and when he caught sight of Charlotte of Montmorency, daughter of the Constable of France, during a rehearsal of a ballet supervised by the Queen at the Louvre in January 1609, he experienced the feeling, known to younger men who have lost their heads in some such manner, that he had never been in love before, added to the exasperation of one who knew that his powers were failing and could not endure the thought that such an emotion would never recur.

Charlotte was four months short of her fifteenth birthday; Henry was fifty-six, old enough to be her *grand-père* but not too old to be the victim of a *grande passion*. Careless of ridicule, he made up his mind that she must be his mistress, though he covered up his intention by professing that at his age and with his infirmities (an attack of gout just then bore him out) he merely wished for her care and companionship. As usual he thought it advisable that she should be supplied with an obliging husband; but there was an obstacle in the way. It had been arranged that his young companion François of Bassompierre should marry her, and François happened to be in love with her. The obstacle had to be removed. Henry, in bed with gout, sent for Bassompierre and informed him that he was to marry Mademoiselle d'Aumale and that the Duchy of Aumale would be revived for his sake. The young man remonstrated, saying that he was already betrothed to Charlotte of Montmorency. The King then opened his heart, or part of it:

I will speak to thee as a friend. I am not only in love, but madly, desperately in love, with Mademoiselle de Montmorency. If thou shouldst marry her, I should hate thee. Should she love me, thou wouldst hate me. It will be best to prevent the possibility of this becoming the cause of a breach of our friendship, for I love thee with great affection and by inclination. I am resolved to marry her to my nephew, the Prince of Condé, and to have her in my family. She shall be the comfort and entertainment of my old age, which is coming on. I will give my nephew, who loves hunting a thousand times better than he loves the ladies, a hundred thousand livres a year to amuse himself with. I shall desire no other favour of her but her affection, without pretending to anything further.

Bassompierre complied, the King wept, and the sportsman Condé married Charlotte in May. According to all accounts she was a captivating and extremely beautiful girl, as well developed physically as a girl of nineteen nowadays. To Henry's chagrin, his nephew did not play the game according to the rules. When Condé noticed that the King could not take his eyes off Charlotte, he withdrew from the Court with his wife. He had to return in the autumn of 1609 for the *accouchement* of the Queen, who gave birth to a girl, Henrietta Maria, afterwards married to Charles I of England. Henry seized the occasion to upbraid Condé for taking his wife from Court; but the man who did not love ladies had determined to prevent his wife from loving other gentlemen, hinted that the King was being despotic and accused him of injustice. Henry lost his temper: 'Injustice! I never did but one unjust act in my life, and that was when I recognized you as a legitimate Condé. If you wish I will point out your father in Paris.' In those days, and even in later times it is said, women sometimes mistook their lovers for their husbands in bed, and it was commonly believed that the present Prince owed his existence to a confusion of the kind. Anyhow, Henry's observation upset him, and he resolved to leave France.

It is impossible to say whether Charlotte returned the King's love, the accounts being conflicting. '*Jésus, qu'il est fou!*' she is reported to have cried when he attempted to see her in disguise, a childish repetition of his earlier pranks. Beyond doubt she was flattered by his attentions. He called her 'Dulcinée', the name of Don Quixote's lady-love, and she sent him a portrait of herself. Clearly she disliked being removed from Court by her husband, and the prospect of being immured with him in some foreign castle did not attract her.

On hearing that the pair had decamped and were on their way to Flanders, Henry was distraught. He despatched officers to arrest them and to call upon the authorities to hand them over if they had already crossed the frontier. By the time the King's emissaries caught up with them the frontier had been passed, and all depended on whether the Spanish Archduke would oblige Henry or refuse his request. As the Spaniards felt mortified over the recent truce, the Archduke took a minor revenge and declined to surrender the runaways. Frustrated, the King sought the advice of Sully, who said that he would like to sleep on it as his judgment was not clear at the moment.

'No?' replied Henry. 'This is not true. I know you too well. Tell me your thoughts immediately.'

'It is impossible, sire, and if you persist in pressing me so earnestly I repeat that I shall say nothing to the purpose. I beg you to excuse me until tomorrow.'

'Indeed I will not. You must speak now. Therefore tell me what I should do.'

'Nothing at all, sire.'

'How! Nothing! This is no advice.'

'Pardon me, sire, it is the best that you can follow. There are maladies that require time rather than remedies, and I believe this to be of such a nature.'

'Your declaration is unseasonable. I must have reasons. Are these yours?'

'I have no good ones, sire, if these are contrary to your inclinations. In my opinion the affair does not admit of much doubt as to what should be done. It is necessary to wait for further particulars before anything is undertaken, that you may fix upon the best expedients. And till then I think it ought to be talked of as little as possible; nor should it appear of any consequence to you, or capable of giving you the least uneasiness.'

Condé and his wife were lodged in the palace at Brussels, whence letters from Charlotte to Henry indicated that she deplored her imprisonment and wished to see her 'gallant knight' again. An attempt was made by a French noble to kidnap her, apparently with her consent, but it failed. At length Henry managed to persuade Charlotte's father to start divorce proceedings, and a letter written by the latter to Condé implied that Charlotte approved. But a few days later something happened to make them unnecessary.

'It is often a mere trifle that produces effects which are always attributed to the most serious causes,' wrote Sully. But it is equally true that a serious cause sometimes needs a trifle to set it in motion, a spark to explode the gunpowder. In March 1609 the death of a petty prince, the Duke of Jülich-Cleves-Berg, gave Henry the excuse he needed for curbing the predatory ambitions of the house of Hapsburg in Austria and Spain and founding his 'Christian Republic' or fraternal association of independent peoples, the precursor of the League of Nations or United Nations in the present century. Throughout the early years of the seventeenth century Henry had used all his skill as a diplomat to secure the cohesion of the Protestant German princes and the support of the Dutch and English in his 'Great Design' for a confederation of European states to destroy the Hapsburg powers and achieve a permanent peace; while Sully had been employed in collecting the necessary money and creating the implements of war. By the end of 1608 France was ready for the undertaking, and the formation of the Evangelical Union suggested that the other powers were ready to follow Henry's lead, though James I of England, weak and timid, friendly now with Spain, now with France, could not be relied on.

The Duke of Jülich-Cleves-Berg died without issue, and as the dukedom lay on both banks of the Rhine near the frontier of Holland its possession was vital to the houses of Hapsburg and Bourbon. Henry was willing that two Protestant principalities, Brandenburg and Neuburg, should govern it in common, and he made it known that if their occupation were disputed he would support them with arms, for he could not allow a threat to the Netherlands and politically he remained opposed to an unyielding Catholic predominance. But the Hapsburgs held different views and in July 1609 the Archduke Leopold, a fervent Catholic acting on instructions from the Emperor of Rome, took the fortress of Jülich, the commandant of which was a paid agent of Spain. Their designs being thus disclosed, Henry decided to act. The autumn and winter of 1609 were spent in feverish preparation. The Dutch sent regiments to their frontier and every effort was made to unite the minor states that feared the scourge of Europe. Even the Pope, anxious at first to see a new duchy gained for the Catholics, was soon persuaded that the Hapsburgs were employing religion as cover for their political projects, and promised neutrality. Besides, he was not averse to the new temporal power he would receive in the event of Henry's success. The King's general plan was to invade northern Italy in conjunction with the Duke of Savoy, to obtain control of Navarre in the south, and to occupy Jülich-Cleves, the monarch himself leading an army of 30,000 men through Luxemburg. It is interesting to note that the chief commands were all entrusted to Protestants.

In the midst of his warlike preparations Henry was engaged in correspondence with Charlotte and had employed the poet François of Malherbe to write love-lyrics to her or laments over their tragic separation. The Queen and her leman Concini were meanwhile busily corresponding with the Spanish Court, so that the King's enemies knew exactly what was happening. Sully got to hear of it and told Henry, who had now become a fatalist, saying 'This intrigue can only be founded on the expectation of my early death.' But he was in excellent condition and seemed to his companions to have regained his youth. Affected by much Spanish propaganda and by the fact that Henry's love-affairs always drove him to extremes of utterance and behaviour, several historians have entertained the opinion that the object of the war about to commence was not to win a lasting peace but to gain possession of Charlotte, an idea industriously broadcast by those who hated Henry. It is a shallow estimate, revealing a superficial knowledge of human nature. Henry never allowed his passion to deflect his policy, though even his intimates were some-times under the impression that he did. What had happened in this case was that the sudden burgeoning of his passion for Charlotte had rejuvenated him; he had been endowed with a fresh lease of life; the vital spark in him had been rekindled; and a long-fixed idea that had remained quiescent during the years of social progress and domestic broils was suddenly converted into action. Charlotte of Montmorency was not the aim of his operation but she had caused the impulse behind it. He knew perfectly well that in time she could be divorced and become his mistress, and there was no need to commence a European war in order to obtain a bed-companion a few weeks earlier. His whole career is witness to the folly of a belief propagated by those who have disapproved of his private life or envied his public achievements or disliked his Protestantism or distrusted his Catholicism. One of his sayings ran: 'Great men are always the last to advise a war and the first to execute it.' The present crisis had been precipitated by the action of the Hapsburgs in occupying the fortress of Jülich, and their objects being revealed Henry acted with his usual celerity.

For the internal government of the country during his absence at the war Henry appointed his wife as Regent with a council of fifteen advisers. But a single vote in a council did not satisfy the Queen, who now insisted on a coronation, such a ceremony having been long delayed either from indifference or for economy. Henry tried to argue her out of her purpose, but could not budge her. Apart from the expense he felt a twinge of superstition. 'Oh, my friend, this coronation does not please me,' he confided in Sully: 'I don't know the meaning of it but my heart tells me some fatal accident will occur.' He jumped up, exclaiming: '*Pardieu!* I shall die in this city; they will murder me here; I see plainly that they have made my death their only hope. Oh, this cursed coronation! It will be the cause of my death.'

He was eager to join the army at Châlons-sur-Marne, but was compelled to remain in Paris for the Queen's coronation at St-Denis on 13 May 1610 and her public entry into the capital three days later. The grand ceremonial took place and Henry's usual gaiety was apparent to the nobles who surrounded him; but at the Louvre that night he seemed full of gloomy forebodings. '*Pardieu!*' he cried, striking his head, 'there is something here which gravely troubles me. I don't know what is the matter.' He could not sleep and looked so careworn on the morning of 14 May that his companions begged him not to go out. His natural son, the Duke of Vendôme, warned him that La Brosse the astrologer had predicted great peril for him that day, but he laughed it off: 'La Brosse is an old fox, who wishes to have your money, and you a young fool to believe him. Our days are counted before God.'

Having attended to much business that morning, he went to the church of the Feuillants to hear Mass; then walked restlessly in the garden of the Tuileries with the Duke of Guise and Bassompierre, the last of whom tried to cheer him up by speaking of the great prosperity he had achieved. 'My friend, all this must be quitted,' he said. Guise spoke of the affectionate loyalty that Henry had inspired in himself. 'You people don't know me yet,' observed the King, 'but I shall die one of these days, and when you have lost me you will know how to value me and how different I am from other men.'

At dinner he talked with his usual animation, and afterwards played with two of his infant sons. Still uneasy, he ordered his coach with the intention of driving to the Arsenal for a talk with Sully. The captain of his guard asked permission to accompany him, but the King had no fears: 'Go along! For more than fifty years I have guarded myself without the captain of my guards, and I shall continue to do so without help.' But he must have had some premonition of danger because he kept asking the Queen, 'Shall I go, my love, or shan't I?' and repeatedly kissed her good-bye.

Several nobles were with him, two or three in the coach, others on horseback. The leather curtains of the vehicle were drawn back, so that the King could see the preparations being made for the Queen's public entry. Leaving the Rue St Honoré for the narrow Rue de la Ferronnerie, the coach was momentarily held up by two carts. Taking advantage of the halt, a religious maniac, François Ravaillac, jumped up on a wheel and stabbed the King, who cried 'I am wounded!' The assassin quickly stabbed again, this time reaching the heart. Henry, with a deep sigh, said weakly 'It's nothing,' and expired.

Under dreadful torture Ravaillac confessed his belief, prompted by his pastors, that Henry was about to make war on the Pope, and gave as a further reason for his act that the monarch had not brought back the Protestants to the true faith, the Catholic, Apostolic and Roman Church. And so at last, inevitably, the spirit of fanaticism had triumphed over the spirit of toleration.

A groan of sorrow for the stricken King welled up from the nation he had so greatly benefited. But the emotion of pity usually derives from a sensation of self-pity, and, as their past and future history proved, his subjects had every reason to feel it. *Henri Quatre* remains the only ruler of France who lives in the love of her people.

BIBLIOGRAPHICAL NOTE

Although the memoirs of Brantôme, Nevers, Bassompierre and other Catholics, those of Péréfixe, Aubigné, Duplessis-Mornay and other Protestants, and the histories of L'Estoile, Matthieu and de Thou, tell us much of interest concerning Henry IV and his times, the fullest and most intimate portrait of him is to be found in the Memoirs of his chief minister, the Duke of Sully, an English translation of which, in four volumes, appeared in 1856.

Several works by British authors have been written, among them:

The Life of Henry the Fourth by G. P. R. James, 3 vols., 1847.

The Last of the Valois by Catherine Charlotte, Lady Jackson, 2 vols., 1888.

The First of the Bourbons by Catherine Charlotte, Lady Jackson, 2 vols., 1890.

Henry of Navarre by H. D. Sedgwick, 1930.

Henry of Navarre by George Slocombe, 1931.

Henry of Navarre by Quentin Hurst, 1937.

For historical background we have:

The Cambridge Modern History, vol. 3, 1904:

Chapter 1. *The Wars of Religion in France* by A. J. Butler, M.A.

Chapter 20. *Henry IV of France* by Stanley Leathes, M.A.

Henry's wives and mistresses are fully described in:

The Favourites of Henry of Navarre by Le Petit Homme Rouge, 1910.

Index

Index

B
Henry
Pearson
Henry of Navarre, the King
  who dared